The UNSEEN ESSENTIAL

a story for our troubled times... PART ONE

JAMES P. GILLS, M.D.

CREATION HOUSE

THE UNSEEN ESSENTIAL by James P. Gills, M.D.
Published by Creation House
A Charisma Media Company
600 Rinehart Road
Lake Mary, Florida 32746
www.charismamedia.com

Unless otherwise noted, Scripture quotations are from the Holy Bible, New International Version. Copyright © 1973, 1978, 1984, International Bible Society. Used by permission.

Scripture quotations marked AMP are from the Amplified Bible. Old Testament copyright 1965, 1987 by the Zondervan Corporation. The Amplified New Testament copyright © 1954, 1958, 1987 by the Lockman Foundation. Used by permission.

Scripture quotations marked KJV are from the King James Version of the Bible.

Scripture quotations marked NKJV are from the New King James Version of the Bible. Copyright © 1979, 1980, 1982 by Thomas Nelson, Inc., publishers. Used by permission.

Cover design by Terry Clifton

Library of Congress Control Number: 2005924884
International Standard Book Number: 978-1-59185-810-2
E-book ISBN: 978-1-59979-513-3

17 18 19 20 21 — 11 10 9 8 7
Printed in the United States of America

To my beautiful wife, Heather...
whose love and insight
have enabled me to share the unseen essential
with others.
I love you.
JPG

CONTENTS

PROLOGUE

ADULTHOOD IS CREEPING up on our cinnamon-colored Vizsla puppy. His former ultra-wrinkled look, not unlike that of a walrus, has been replaced by the sleek, streamlined build of a greyhound. "Luke…hey Luke! C'mon over here, buddy. You're sure gettin' big, aren't ya, boy?"

At the sound of my voice, he tries to screech to an immediate halt. The slick hardwood floor leaves much to be desired in four-legged maneuverability. Still sliding in the opposite direction, he casts a helpless glance at me. With his best effort, and toenails tapping clicketyclack, he attempts a sharp turn. What a comical sight he is—all four legs flying every which way!

In mid-laugh, my arms fill up with Hungarian hound. As I lay back in an overstuffed chair in the living room, Luke plops his whole body lengthwise on mine. His front legs bear-hug my neck, while his huge, warm tongue laps me with boundless enthusiasm. I do enjoy Luke. He is such fun. He makes me feel like a kid again. Professional demands lose their importance as we romp together.

Come to think of it, dogs have always been valuable "members" of our family. Memories drift through my mind and settle in on a day over twenty years ago. Kismet and Quill, our pet black Labradors, accompanied me in their usual fashion as I hiked through the woods near our

1

home in Florida. Questions about life plagued me.

I wondered aloud, "Where is the church headed?" Then the truth hit. "Rather, where am I going spiritually?" Something vital—essential to my very existence—was lacking in my walk with God. But what?

Those questions ushered in a major turning point in my life. From that day I began searching in a deeper, more fervent way for the key to my relationship with an invisible God. Today, my quest is far from over. The goal is clearer now, though. I am much closer to the Lord than I was then. Has it been easy? On the contrary. My spiritual struggle has been my ultimate challenge. With the Lord's help, I have learned to stop struggling. Mind you, that is not to be confused with complacency.

All my "class notes" from a daily Christian walk (via the Scriptures, other Christians, and personal experiences) burgeoned into a manuscript I decided to name, *The Unseen Essential*. HeartLight, my editorial team, contemplated and speculated and deliberated. And prayed. And prayed. "How can we bring to life what the Lord has shown you over the years?" they asked. "Maybe through a fictional story this time—the spiritual journey of a man who learns to live by 'the unseen essential.'"

Those of you who know me, know I have always been the adventuresome type. I agreed to let them give it a try. Over the weeks, I watched my notes assume an exciting new dimension. "Michael," the central figure, is a composite character. He evolved in part from the imagination and experiences of HeartLight, from people they have known, and from me, Jim Gills—all of us on our own spiritual walk.

Well, my friend, I am settled into a comfortable chair. I have a chilled glass of fruit juice within handy reach and the finished manuscript on my lap. Luke, reassured of my love for him, is falling asleep at my feet. Why don't you pour yourself something healthy to drink and read along with me? Perhaps Michael's journey will become yours. Better yet, maybe his story will capture your heart.

—JIM GILLS, 1990
TARPON SPRINGS, FLORIDA

ONE

SUMMIT

Handsome, olive-skinned Michael Nastasis sat at the head table reflecting on his achievements for the last twelve months. The year had been a great one, the best of his outstanding career. He glanced at the empty chair beside him. Where could his wife be? Stephanie should have been sitting next to him long ago. He peered at his watch, then at the empty chair again. He took a deep breath and wished she would...

His thoughts were interrupted when he heard his boss mention his name. Dale Ambrose was coming to his point. "Dr. Nastasis, in recognition of your outstanding contribution..."

Michael slipped back into deep thought, casting unfocused eyes across the floor beneath the raised platform and the head table that gave him that ultra-important feeling. He nervously nibbled at the inside of his lower lip and ran his hand through his styled hair, graying considerably for his age of thirty-seven. It nearly was his moment. The audience had waited patiently, and most were finishing dessert. Finally, Michael brought himself back to the bright lights and gazed at Dale's poised profile. The man spoke with eloquent confidence from behind the lectern. He was a natural.

Though the ice in Michael's tea had melted, the amber liquid cooled his cottony throat. His strong hand on the glass displayed a gleaming, diamond-studded gold wedding ring. A Rolex watch graced his wrist. Again, Stephanie invaded his thoughts as he wished she shared his ambition for success, along with his zest for the good life.

Ambrose's voice resounded, snapping him back again, "And for your single-minded pursuit of unsurpassed excellence in the field of aeronautical engineering," Dale continued, "we would like to present you with this esteemed token of our appreciation." As he held up a large plaque, several members of the audience gasped at its beauty. "The coveted *President's Golden Eagle Award*," he announced. It was stunning.

Michael was flushed as he savored the sweet sound of those words. They were a long time in coming, but this was his hour. He had been preparing for a moment like this all his life. Now, at the brink of true success, he felt payday had arrived at last. He would reap after the manner of the rich and famous.

Again, Dale's words kept his mind from drifting into too much of what the future held, yet he realized that nothing was impossible for him. He was set. He stretched his arm across the back of the chair next to him—the chair his wife should have occupied. He glanced at the door, hoping Stephanie would show up just as the presentation was made. How he wanted her to share this dynamic moment! In readiness, he leaned forward. "And now, ladies and gentlemen, without further ado, I present to you our guest of honor this evening, Dr. Michael Nastasis." Dale motioned to him. "Michael, would you come, please, and accept this token of our appreciation?"

Relishing every delicious moment amid the sudden thunder of applause as the people stood throughout the banquet hall, he pushed his chair back, slowly rose, and eased his way to the lectern. With measured calm, punctuated by the flash of reporters' cameras, he reached Dale's side.

Michael extended his left hand to receive the plaque and stiffened slightly under Dale's arm around his shoulders. At the same time, as inconspicuously as possible, he tried to erase every lingering trace of nervous perspiration from his right hand, wiping it on his pant leg in preparation for the big handshake. A clammy hand would never do for his boss. Dale, the lean, clean-cut CEO of Eagle Aeronautics, never allowed himself to appear ruffled in public. Michael wondered how Dale kept so cool all the time, whereas he felt all too conscious of the eyes following his every move.

Face to face with Dale now, and in his own private world despite the audience, Michael listened. "In addition to this beautiful plaque and the award check for $10,000, Michael, we thought you and Stephanie would enjoy a trip to the Bahamas. You've been working so hard these past months, the board felt you two might need some time to get reacquainted. Enjoy yourselves." He strengthened his squeeze on Michael's shoulders. "For the next few weeks, don't even think about this company. And as your boss, consider that an order!" Dale chuckled, finished his comments, and relinquished the award, tickets, and the lectern to Michael.

For a long moment, Michael admired the plaque before he turned and held it up for the audience. He nodded to Dale as his boss was seated at the head table. Then Michael faced the crowd, scanning it for prominent people. He cleared his throat. "Thank you kindly, everyone." Once again he surveyed the ebony plaque at arm's length, admiring its 14K gold eagle, then turned it to the audience and smiled proudly. Another camera flash highlighted the moment. He leaned forward to the microphone and hesitated, distracted for a moment as Stephanie's finely sculptured face flashed across his mind. "This is much more than I expected. I'm at a loss for what to say." He glanced toward the door. Shaking his head, his smile tense, he added, "I've worked hard, and this moment has been a long time coming. But I can say it has all been worth it. Once again, thank you." He held the tickets up in his right hand and waved. "Steph and I certainly will have a good vacation. Forgive us if we don't think of this place until we get back." Several women in the audience twittered.

Michael turned in time to greet Dale, who appeared at his side with his arm outstretched. He slipped the tickets into his jacket pocket and they clasped hands again. Another camera flashed. Then, with the weighty plaque in his left hand, check in his right, Michael returned to his place of honor. He mopped the perspiration from his brow with the cloth napkin and folded it carefully.

The rest of the evening passed without incident. Much too quickly, it was over. Surrounded by a few last minute well-wishers, he collected the gifts and glanced one last time across the auditorium. The crowd had thinned to a few scattered stragglers. Soon, all but the memory would be gone. Disturbed by the neatness of his wife's still unused place setting, he excused himself from those few guests who lingered. The clean dishes looked inappropriate amid the disarray of after-dinner clutter. He wondered, *Why wouldn't she show up for the most important night of my life?*

On his way from the banquet room, he saw Dale and Kathryn. They waved and waited for him to catch up. A smile spread thin his lips, uncovering even, pearl-white teeth. "Kathryn, you look fabulous, as always. It was a pleasure sitting with you and Dale at the head table."

Kathryn was a stately, auburn-haired woman with a tailored look of sophistication. Her green eyes twinkled, hinting of the little girl deep inside, but nothing escaped her notice. She stretched a slender hand toward him and spoke in a manner reflecting years of cultural polish. "Congratulations, Michael. Stephanie should be proud of you. I'm so sorry she couldn't be with us this evening." Her voice took on a thoughtful tone. "I do hope nothing is wrong. She'll love the trip, though. It's the same one Dale and I took last year. Remember how we raved about it?"

Michael nodded.

"Please...tell her I missed her and hope to see her soon."

"I will, Kathryn. Thank you."

Together, they entered the main atrium. As they made their way toward the lobby, a man rose from a nearby bench and walked up behind Michael. He coughed softly. "Excuse me, sir. You...are you Dr. Michael Nastasis?"

Michael turned in response. Light filtering down from the ceiling spotlights caught the flash of a deputy sheriff's badge pinned to the inside of an open wallet. Deep furrows wrinkled his brow. "Yes, I am. What can I do for you?" A glare reflected off the shiny shield. Through some trick of the light, the badge expanded to fill his entire field of vision.

The officer retorted, "I have some papers here for you to sign."

"Papers? What kind of papers?" He wondered, *What on earth needs to be hand delivered by a deputy sheriff?*

The deputy hesitated. He glanced toward Dale and Kathryn and back to Michael. "Would you mind coming with me a minute, Dr. Nastasis?" Michael shrugged.

As the officer headed for an uncrowded corner, Dale leaned forward. "Hey pal, is everything okay? Do you want us to wait?" He took a step closer, and offered in a conspiratorial whisper, "If it's money you need..."

"No, no...but thanks, Dale. In the mall parking lot the other day, some kids were slashing tires. I came out of Lord and Taylor and surprised them. They all ran before I could make out their features, though. The papers probably have something to do with that. You and Kathryn run along. Don't wait for me. I'll be fine."

"All right. If you're sure there's nothing we can do, we'll be on our way. Enjoy your vacation."

"Yes, Michael," Kathryn added. "You two are overdue for some time alone. Make the best of it."

"We are overdue, aren't we? Stephanie's a great woman when it comes to that. She understands." Waving good-bye, and sounding more confident than he felt, Michael turned and strode to where the officer stood waiting. He straightened his silk necktie and said offhandedly, "Okay, officer. I can assure you I couldn't identify either of those kids. But let's have a look at the papers anyway." He set the plaque on the bench, took the papers, and began to read:

IN THE CIRCUIT COURT, SIXTH JUDICIAL CIRCUIT
IN AND FOR CONNOR COUNTY
CIVIL DIVISION

C.C.S.O.

FUGITIVE DIVISION

Case No. 90-33137

Stephanie M. Nastasis, Petitioner
and
Michael J. Nastasis, Respondent

With each word he lost more color. Ironically, his hands stopped shaking, but his insides turned to jelly. Slowly, gripped by sudden fear, he unfolded the document to read further. Engrossed by the words unraveling before him, he failed to notice the lone reporter standing in the shadows near the foyer. The camera flash went virtually unnoticed. All his attention and strength were focused on what he held in his hands:

EX PARTE TEMPORARY INJUNCTION

THIS CAUSE came on to be heard upon Petitioner's application for an Order seeking Temporary Injunction pursuant to state Statute 373.1, and the court having before it the Petition for Injunction for Protection attached hereto, it is hereby

ORDERED AND ADJUDGED that:

_JH_ Respondent is hereby restrained from committing acts of domestic violence, to wit; assault, battery, or sexual battery against Petitioner, and is restrained from harassing said Petitioner directly or indirectly.

_JH_ Petitioner is hereby awarded temporary exclusive use and possession of the dwelling that the parties share.

_JH_ Respondent is hereby excluded from the dwelling that the parties share or from the residence of Petitioner except by further Order of this Court.

_JH_ Petitioner is hereby granted temporary custody of the children of the parties.

He flipped the page and scanned the words rapidly. One line glared at him in defiance amid the blur of text: "Divorce will be filed." Those seven letters, D-I-V-O-R-C-E, made his head spin. The document was signed by a Judge Hardigon and sealed by the Clerk of Court. That was it. He could not read another word. He felt sick to his stomach. Dazed, like a drunk weaving on his front porch struggling to fit his now-too-big key into the suddenly shifting keyhole, he groped for the nearby bench.

But where was the plaque? Like a drowning man reaching for a hastily-thrown lifeline, Michael snatched up the coveted award. He stood there, looking first at his left hand, then his right. Success in one…failure in the other.

"Divorce. Restrained from sexual battery…on my wife?" The words escaped through lips that scarcely moved. "This is the most ridiculous thing I've ever heard. There…must be some kind of mistake."

The deputy stepped up behind him. "I can assure you, Doctor, it's no mistake. If you'll read, sir, your wife, the petitioner, has requested a court order that you, the respondent, be restrained from going near the dwelling you both share."

"What? It's my house, too. I paid for it. And my children, what about them? You can't keep me from seeing Stephen and Michelle."

"On the contrary, Doctor, we can, as long as they're at home. But everything is explained in the papers, so read them carefully. Your son and daughter will remain with their mother until the matter is decided by the courts." The deputy's mouth tightened; his shoulders squared. "And, I must warn you. Should you be found on the premises or attempt to contact your wife in any way, you could be arrested."

Michael's mouth dropped open. He was confused and angry. "You've got to be kidding. Where can I go? What'll I do for clothes? All I have is what I'm wearing."

"Where you go, and what you do, is up to you, just as long as it doesn't involve that house or any of those living there." He tapped his finger authoritatively on the restraining order in Michael's hand.

"Well, officer, I've got to pick up some clothes and personal items, at least," he snapped. "You can't expect a guy to survive without anything to wear to work, can you? I'll have a friend go with me when Stephanie isn't home..." His voice trailed off.

"I'm sorry, Dr. Nastasis, but that won't be possible. Judge's orders." The officer softened slightly. "I tell you what. If you're ready now, I'll give you a ride to your house to get whatever you'll need for tonight. Then, if you have to go back tomorrow to get anything else, I'll go with you one more time. But that's it."

Michael's shoulders slumped and his arms hung heavy at his sides. He finally understood what was happening. The plaque, still clutched in his right hand, felt like a ten-pound weight as he strained to gesture with it. "You mean to tell me, I have to be escorted like some sort of common criminal...to my own house?" he snorted.

"That's right. Judges don't issue restraining orders without good cause." The officer glanced at his watch. "It's almost nine o'clock. The sooner we get going, the sooner this will be over." He made a feeble effort to ease the tension. "I can bring you back here to your car after we get your things."

From inside the squad car as it parked in his driveway, Michael stared at *The Nastasis Family* sign attached to the lamppost. It was gently swinging in the evening breeze. The porch light and gaslight illuminated the entire yard. Before the door lay the welcome mat. The sidewalk was still immaculate, as if it had just been swept. The lawn, though ready for its weekly trim, had a carefully manicured look. Together, they bore silent witness to his meticulous nature and the hours spent in grooming.

On the surface, everything around the Nastasis' home appeared normal. What a far cry the truth! He was not sitting in the driver's seat of the family car. The person sitting next to him was not his wife. With his right hand on the door latch, he took a deep breath and said, "I guess I'm ready. I still don't know why it was necessary to escort me. For that matter, none of this makes sense."

"Dr. Nastasis, I know this is a shock to you, but it's standard procedure any time a restraining order is issued. It's for your protection as much as anyone else's." The officer opened his door. "Come on. Let's get this over with."

The car door slammed. Michael followed the deputy. He had no choice.

He stood by as the officer grabbed the polished brass eagle knocker and gave a couple of raps. The pleasant, crisp tap it made on the outside was deceptive. He knew from experience how irritatingly loud the crack could be inside the house. How he wished he had gotten around to padding it like he had planned. All he could do now was stand and wait. Meanwhile, he studied the lower left corner of the knocker plate where a screw was missing.

The two men heard someone moving around inside, just before the dead bolt slid back. Michael exhaled a breath he did not know he had been holding and thought, *Ridiculous. I'm nervous about getting into my own house. And seeing my own wife.* Then he had no more time to think. The door swung open.

Stephanie stood defiantly in the doorway. Her eyes were hard, yet red and puffy as if she had been crying. She was wearing a pale blue blouse with a burgundy print silk bow at the throat and navy linen skirt. The outfit gave her a businesslike appearance that Michael had once found such an attractive combination. Now, it intimidated him. The golden luster of her streaked blond hair shone in the amber porch light. She was as beautiful as ever.

All his preparation—the carefully thought-out speech on the drive over—failed him. The words lodged in his throat. He simply stared, open-mouthed, at the woman who no longer wanted to be his wife.

The deputy broke the strained silence. "Excuse us, Mrs. Nastasis. We're here to get some of your husband's belongings." Michael stood mutely at his side.

This is my wife, he thought. *My wife, and I didn't even get a chance to say a word. How dare this guy take over like I'm some kind of idiot or something. And it's my house!* He blurted, "Stephanie, what is the meaning of this nonsense? You can't be serious! I mean, what...what have I done?"

Stephanie closed her eyes and took a deep breath. "Come in, please officer." She hesitated. "Both of you may come in." Michael closed the door and stood waiting. "Officer," she said, "I'll talk with him for a moment, if you don't mind." He nodded his assent. She turned to her bewildered husband, glared at him, and took another deep breath before speaking.

"Michael, it's not just what you've done, but what you haven't done. It's...it's everything. I can't stand being alone anymore. I want a husband, not just a provider. I'm tired. Tired of being married to an egotistical, hot-tempered, success machine. You're so capable at everything, you don't need us at all." Her voice rose. "Besides, nothing we do is good enough, anyway. I know I can never please you. The children can never earn your approval, either. Michelle's only eleven and Stephen's barely six, yet you expect them to perform like grown adults. You always manage to find something to criticize about everything they do. Constant putdowns. You certainly don't care about any of us." Her voice grew louder yet. "All you care about is your stupid job. You're married to Eagle Aeronautics, not to me. Well, you can have the job now, because I've had it! Maybe Kathryn Ambrose can live with Dale's workaholism, but not me. I won't take it any more. Do you hear me?"

Stephanie's tirade had gained such vehemence that her words drove Michael back, until his heel touched the door. This woman verbally attacking him bore no semblance to the sweet, cultured girl he married. Not in all their twelve years of marriage had she ever stood toe-to-toe with him like this. And in front of a total stranger? *What's gotten into her?*

"Steph, we need to talk this out," Michael whined, hating the sound of his own voice.

"You should have thought of talking a long time ago. It's too late now," she blasted back. "Whenever I needed you, you were always gone!"

"That's not true, Stephanie..."

"Oh, yes it is! Even when you were home, you were never really here. I always had to share you with that job. Your mind was there...on some new project or something. I'm sorry, Michael, but it's over. I can't take it anymore."

"All right, all right. At least tell me why you needed a restraining order, for Pete's sake. How could you do this to me? First, you humiliate me by not showing up for the awards banquet—the most important moment of my life! Then you have a divorce notice and a restraining order slapped on me." His voice was incredulous. "You couldn't possibly think I'd hurt you or the kids."

She smirked, turned to stare at the far wall, and taking another deep breath, whirled around to face him. "What about all those things you said during our last fight? Every time I tried to say anything, you got mad. And it kept getting worse, until you did threaten me, Michael." She jabbed her index finger into his chest to punctuate each of her last words as she ended breathlessly, "You did!"

"But I didn't mean it, Steph. I was just upset. I've been under a lot of strain at work."

"Oh, you meant it all right, just as much as I mean this. And don't call me 'Steph' anymore, thank you."

With that, she turned her back on him and addressed the deputy who stood nervously, shifting his weight from one foot to another. "Officer, would you be so kind as to make sure he doesn't take any more than he's supposed to? We'll let the judge decide who gets what later."

"Yes, ma'am. He'll just be taking his personal items now."

She cast an icy glare at Michael before continuing. "Thank you. I think it's best that I go in the kitchen until you get through here. If he needs to come back tomorrow, would you please call ahead of time and let me know? I'd prefer to be gone then."

"I'm sorry, Mrs. Nastasis. I'm not allowed to take sides in domestic squabbles. Your husband may call you in my presence to advise you of the time, and I'll escort him over."

Stephanie, her chin trembling, blinked her eyes. "Oh, I see." After a moment, she turned back to her husband. "Michael, please be quiet when you go upstairs. Michelle and Stephen just got to sleep."

Mention of the kids revived a somewhat deflated Michael. "Don't be silly. You can't expect me to leave without even saying good-bye to them," he challenged.

"Yes, Michael, I can...and I do. Now keep your voice down," she hissed through clenched teeth. The strain was beginning to show. Nearly exhausted, Stephanie appealed to the officer. "It took so long for them to fall asleep. The last thing they need now is to see their father looming over them like some sort of midnight spectre or something."

Glad at last to have something to do, the officer stepped toward Michael. "Remember, those were restraining orders you signed. You do know what that means. If the Mrs. doesn't want you to see the children here at the house, then it's settled. Until the court says otherwise, that's the way it is."

Michael's shoulders slumped. His head drooped forward, but only for a moment. Then it snapped back. He lifted his hands, palms up, appealing to the officer. "Don't I have any say at all?" Like a granite stone, the officer simply stood, saying nothing. Michael turned to Stephanie. "Well, don't I?" Silence was the only answer he got.

He determined not to give in. Already, anger and hurt were turning into firm resolve. He would never let them know how much this hurt. *You watch,* he thought. *You won't get away with this! It won't keep me down.* He squared his shoulders and took a couple of deep breaths to stem the rising anger. A little calmer, he faced the officer. "Okay, okay, I'll get my stuff," he retorted as he walked in the direction of their bedroom.

In minutes, he had gathered what few belongings he needed. With his suitcase still open on the bed, he paused to notice a faded rectangular spot on the wall. *Well, I'll be...* Their wedding portrait, a permanent fixture above the headboard, was gone. "It sure didn't take long for that to come down. Twelve years of our life, wiped out as easily as taking a picture off the wall! And for what?" That was enough. He had to get out of the house. He snapped the suitcase closed and jerked it from the bed. "Let's go!" he bellowed to his escort as he stomped from the bedroom. Stephanie was nowhere in sight. Part of him felt relief...the rest, total disgust.

TWO

AFTERMATH

Michael rose early the next morning after an almost sleepless night. Seated at his friend's breakfast table, he wondered what had happened. Foggy with fatigue, he watched his coffee grow cold and tried to piece together the previous night's events.

He had left the house in a mad rush. Good thing the deputy was driving, he decided. No telling what might have happened in his frame of mind. Long after the officer had returned him to his car, he continued driving in circles. He remembered thinking, *This is ridiculous. I can't keep this up all night.* Then he had thought of his friend, Pat. They had been through tough times together before. There was one time at college, when Pat nearly got expelled for his prank in the laboratory. Even as Michael contemplated those things, he turned his car in the direction of Pat's place.

Just as he thought, his buddy had welcomed him with open arms and no questions. Perhaps it was the expression on Michael's face that kept him from prying. Whatever the reason for Pat's silence, he was grateful. Now, sitting at his friend's kitchen table, he still didn't feel like talking. As he idly stirred his coffee, his thoughts wandered.

What he had every reasonable expectation to believe would be the highlight of his rising career had plummeted into a nightmare in a matter of hours. Only today, facing the future, was worse. It could not be escaped so easily. Though night had passed, his life looked bleaker than ever.

Dreams have funny ways of dying. Some slip quickly and quietly into oblivion. Others resemble sand castles built too near the incoming tide. Little by little, the ceaseless routine of daily living eats away at them until even the memory of a lost hope is all but gone. Worse yet are the ones brutally snuffed out of existence. One minute they are alive and shining brightly...the next, gone without a trace. Such were Michael's dreams. He felt like an ant carelessly squashed under foot. His vision of success, his hopes for a happy life—ball games with his son, shopping sprees he had promised his daughter—gone.

And what a night he had! He tossed and turned, but answers eluded him. Wondering why, staring wide-eyed at the ceiling, caused the ache in his chest to become unbearable. Thoughts of what could have been, but now never would be, brought on the tears. He fought them. With teeth clenched and eyes squinted, he struggled to stem their escape. No way, he resolved, would he give in to such an unmanly response as crying. That was for women...or mama's boys!

But then, rolling onto his side and cradling his head on his left arm, the will to resist had deserted him. Sometime between 2:05 and 2:15 a.m., the face of the clock on the nightstand began to blur. Its ghostly green hands glowed in the dark, but the numbers shimmered out of focus. They swam through eyes filled to the bursting point with tears. Once started, they would not be denied, no matter how hard he fought.

Wracking sobs tore through him. He curled up with his arms folded across his chest. Clutching his sides, he could not choke back the sobs. He was grateful no one could see him. Silent tears streaked his face and ran in rivulets to soak the unfamiliar pillow. Finally, he fell asleep for a short time.

Thinking on it now did little to improve the picture. Divorce still stared him squarely in the face. Michelle and Stephen—his own flesh and blood—were still beyond his grasp. And later that morning he would have to pick up the rest of his belongings at the house. He was not looking forward to that, but there was no way he could avoid it.

He gulped the last of his cold coffee and grimaced at its bitter taste. His eyes fell upon a magazine casually tossed on the countertop. On the cover was a picture of a campsite; tent set up in a beautiful wooded area, a campfire blazing nearby, and a man dressed in khaki pants and a flannel shirt. Beneath the photo was a caption that read, "Tired of the hustle and bustle of the city? Get away for a day. Go camping!"

Maybe that's just what I need, Michael mused. *I'm tired, and definitely need to get away for a day. I wonder if Pat goes anymore? He used to go quite a bit way back when. But what do I know about the sport? It's been ages since I was a Boy Scout...*

While Michael sat mulling over the idea, Pat walked into the kitchen. He saw the direction of his buddy's gaze. "Thinking about a camping trip, huh?"

"Nah." He had been contemplating exactly that.

Pat would not be put off so easily. "Why not? That may be just the thing you need right now. Get away for a while. From the way you looked last night, it sure wouldn't hurt."

He sighed. "Oh, I don't know, Pat. What do I know about camping? I've forgotten more than I remember, and I was never an expert to begin with."

"Don't be silly, old boy. You've always done anything you made up your mind to do." He thought for a moment. "Then, are you gonna take that trip the company gave you? You didn't say last night. I wasn't trying to eavesdrop. But...the walls are thin."

Michael's face reddened. "I'd rather not discuss it, Pat, if you don't mind. But I won't be going to the Bahamas now. I don't know what I'll do. After the banquet, everything fell apart."

"Oh. Well, even if you aren't going to the Bahamas, you still have the time off. I've got plenty of camping gear. All you have to do is throw a few things together and hit the road. What d'ya say?"

Michael looked over at the camping magazine. The campfire did intrigue him. He closed his eyes, rested his elbows on the table, and let his head settle in his hands. He rubbed his palms in his eyes, trying to erase the word—*divorce.* It was still there, bold as ever, mocking him. No one in his family had ever been divorced. Opening his red-streaked eyes and tilting his head back to look up at his friend, he heaved a sigh. "I just don't know."

Pat cleared his throat and ran his right hand through his slightly unkempt, sandy hair. Straightening up, he urged Michael, "C'mon pal, I've never seen you like this before, so down and indecisive. You're always on top of things and full of self-confidence. Snap out of it. Everything'll work out. Look. I've got a great camping manual filled with all sorts of info on how to pitch a tent, gather kindling and firewood, build a camp-fire…even how to break camp without doing any harm to the environment. What more could you ask for?"

Michael thought over those words. "Maybe you're right. Moping around here isn't doing me much good. The idea does have a certain appeal, and I do need some time alone to sort things out."

Pat breathed a sigh of relief. "It's settled, then. I'll put some gear together while you get your stuff from the house. And Michael, I really am sorry about whatever's happened between you and Stephanie. I didn't say much last night. It wasn't because I don't care. You just didn't look up to a quizzing at the time. Besides, I didn't know what to say, but I'd do anything for you two."

The "you two" snapped Michael out of his daydream. He jerked back in his chair and slammed his balled-up fist down on the kitchen table. Coffee cups rattled in their saucers. Pat's eyes widened in surprise. "It's not the 'two' of us anymore!" Michael spat back. The muscles in his jaw tensed as he struggled to suppress the rising tide of bitterness threatening to carry him away.

Pat waited to see what Michael would do from there. When nothing seemed forthcoming, he walked around to his friend's side. He put his hand on his shoulder and gave it a hearty squeeze. At the same time, he reached with his left hand and slid a chair over so he could sit down. Then he gave Michael's shoulder another squeeze. "Hey, look at me. That's not the Michael Nastasis I know talking like that. The guy I admire was never a quitter. Sure, I know you're hurting. But you've been jilted before. And you're angry. Since when did that ever stop you? No, sir! It's not over, yet. Not by a long shot. That is, unless you quit."

The pep talk caught Michael off guard. He looked deep into Pat's eyes to see if his friend was making fun of him. He found only genuine concern and not a hint of sarcasm. Finally, he looked down at the few coffee grounds left in his empty cup. "This is different, Pat. I've lost everything. There's nothing left to fight for."

There are times when an encouraging word works wonders. And sometimes it's best to keep quiet—anything else only makes matters worse. Pat opted for the latter. Without a word he got up, grabbed the coffee pot, and silently refilled their cups. Sitting back down, he picked up the camping magazine. He thumbed through the pages, but he was not looking at them. His attention was on Michael.

The uncomfortable silence mounted. Michael continued staring into his cup. Occasionally, he took a sip of coffee. Pat looked at his watch. It was nearly eight o'clock. Soon he would have to go to work, but he did not want to just leave his friend sitting there. And he had something else on his mind.

Michael, if he had looked up, would have noticed the set expression on his buddy's face—his features, the crease of his brow, the way he squared his jaws—spoke of his heightened concentration as if he was trying to recall something just beyond his grasp. But Michael did not look up. He was lost in his own thoughts. *Pat's right. I'm not a quitter!* That was one point Michael could proudly declare. When others would grow weary and fall by the wayside, he was the one who kept going. He always finished what he started, regardless of the cost.

Over the years Michael had learned one lesson. Count on no one. He was a staunch believer in that timeworn expression, "If you want something done right, do it yourself." Where had it gotten him? He was a success, wasn't he? But success was supposed to feel good. That was what he had always been taught. Why, then, with the coveted prize already his, did he have such a bitter taste in his mouth?

It's her fault! Of all times to drop this on me. Barred from my own house. She's got no right. Yet, that was exactly what she had done. And for now, he could not do a thing about it.

Pat interrupted his thoughts. "Michael, what was the name of that guy you met a few months back…the one who was so sick? Was it Ralph? Ralph something or other? You know who I mean?"

"Ralph," Michael replied with a puzzled look on his face. "Oh, yeah, Ralph. What does he have to do with anything?"

"Well, forgive me for saying so, but if anyone had nothin' left to fight for, it was him. Not you! You've got it made compared to him. What kept him going? Come on, you knew him."

"Sure, Pat, I'll give it some thought on the way to the house. I better get moving. Thanks for pulling together the stuff I'll need for the camping trip." He deliberated over the word *camping*, and even smiled weakly. "That'll be a big help."

"You got it, pal. I'll put it right here on the front porch before I leave, and here's an extra key. You can drop your things off, pick up the gear, and be out in the woods in nothing flat. You have my phone number, so call if you need me."

"Okay. I guess I am sort of looking forward to a change of scenery for a while. See ya." Michael headed out to the car to go find a pay phone. Taking a chance on Pat's finding out about the restraining order and police escort was more than his wounded ego could handle.

———

Finished at the house, and now almost to the interstate, he thought, *Well, at least that part's over. I'm glad Stephanie wasn't home. That made things a lot easier. The officer was pretty decent, too.* He still had a lump in his throat, but gradually it diminished. He relaxed. From the on-ramp, he eased into the steady flow of interstate traffic. Settled in for the ride, he allowed his thoughts to drift back to Ralph. Pat was right. He was an unusual guy, for sure. Michael had never given ex-cons much consideration...and certainly no admiration. But Ralph was different. Different even from most ordinary people he had met in his life.

Michael remembered how, after meeting Ralph, he could hardly concentrate. His work seemed so empty and shallow, which unnerved him somewhat. And there was that day, months later, when Ralph looked at him through pain-filled eyes.

"Jesus loves you, Dr. Michael," Ralph had assured him with a big, strong bearhug that caused him to stiffen self-consciously. They were not the hugging type in his family. Such open displays of affection made him quite uncomfortable.

What was it about the guy that was so unique? he wondered now. He could not put his finger on it. *Ralph was always serene, so peaceful. And he loved everybody he met. Thing is, most of them loved him, too. An ex-con. Imagine that! The joy inside him literally bubbled over when he talked about God...which was most of the time. In spite of the pain from the disease that ravaged his body, his joy was contagious,* Michael thought.

When Michael was around him, he felt wrapped in a warm, cozy blanket of gentle kindness. He almost wanted to curl up for a nap—Michael Nastasis: world-famous aeronautical engineer. And talk about patience! Ralph remained as unruffled as an early morning mountain lake over circumstances that would have sent Michael into an angry tirade. (His Sunday morning religion often flew out the window by early Monday.) Not Ralph's. He seemed unflappable.

His stocky little Latin American buddy, dying of a rare muscle disease and lung cancer, had the courage of a lion. He faced life head-on, alright. Twelve years in prison. Then, to be released to endure a debilitating fatal illness? Ironic.

Michael remembered when Ralph got the mandatory notice to go back before one northern state's parole board. "In person," they wanted him, so they could grant him a pardon for charges there. The state had convicted the wrong guy. (That was long after he had suddenly been yanked out of a southern state prison to go to trial up north on those charges.) He was not bitter, either.

Michael did not see any possible way for Ralph to make the thousand-mile trip in his condition, parole board or not. He was losing his sight, as well as recovering from recent eye surgery on one eye. His legs and ankles were so swollen he could hardly get shoes on, much less travel. Did that stop him? No way! He wanted to make sure he had that pardon hearing before he died…or before he married—whichever came first.

That was the real clincher. A woman by the name of Marsha was willing to marry him. They had met while he was still in prison. After a bewildering but lengthy "pen pal courtship," intended only as friends, they decided to get married. Ralph showed continued visible signs of serious illness. He had worked a few years before in the prison wastewater treatment plant without protective gloves. Some blamed that for the illness that had turned his face purplish-black. At any rate, an accurate diagnosis was never made while he was in prison.

By the time he was a free man again, he was no prize catch of a husband, in Michael's opinion. With his face swollen like a balloon, breathing difficulties, cracked skin, and a mouth full of sores, he was miserable. His throat muscles slowly stopped working, such that he could barely swallow. And he suffered extreme fatigue all the time.

Then came the fateful day. The happy couple learned that he had only a few months to live. Not the ideal portrait of a soon-to-be groom.

Marsha held true to her devotion to Ralph. She exuded his same tranquility as she made preparations for their long-awaited wedding day. They kept believing that, in whatever way was best, Ralph would be "healed." Their naiveté stirred Michael's pity.

He wondered aloud, "Or was it envy more than pity I felt toward Ralph and Marsha?" He shook his head.

The familiar interstate landscape whizzed by Michael's windshield—fences, an infinite variety of billboards hawking every conceivable ware, huge kelly green and white signs denoting what city and town would be around the bend from the next exit. There were little milepost markers, and medium-sized, vertical rectangular, black and white speed limit signs—speed limit signs! His reverie broken, he glanced down at the speedometer. It stared back at him with a definite, almost proud, ninety-five mph.

"Whew!" he whistled. "Good thing the highway patrol isn't out in force today. I'd have been a sitting duck." He let up on the accelerator until the needle settled in on the posted sixty-five mph and then engaged the cruise control. That way he would be safe if his thoughts carried him away again.

You know, it's funny, he muttered. *Anyone looking at me would think I had it made. International renown. Investments. A nice house. Respectable religion.*

His left turn signal clicked on, almost of its own accord as he eased out to pass a slow-moving truck. He mentally coached himself, *Flip the right turn signal. Glide back into the lane and leave plenty of room.* Normally, careful driving was a part of his ordered and mostly moral lifestyle. He winced, thinking of his recent slip to ninety-five miles per hour.

Bright red blinking lights on the tailgate of the car ahead interrupted Michael's mental meanderings. *Wide load* was written across the banner in bold black letters. He was so preoccupied that he had failed to notice the prefabricated home, its bulk sliced in half like a giant sandwich, looming directly in front of him. "Man, I've got to pay more attention to my driving," he exclaimed aloud. "How could I miss something as big as that?"

Try as he might to control his thoughts, he could not keep them focused on anything for too long. The recent strain was taking its toll. No sooner would he settle down to some attentive driving than his gaze would be drawn to one of the passing cars or the scenery flying by his window. Then, more memories would crowd their way back to his consciousness.

What a study in contrasts—his life and Ralph's. Even their wives. He had everything, yet could not hold his wife and family together. Ralph had nothing, not even the dim hope of a happy life. Yet, not even impending death could tear his wife away. Why? What would a perfectly healthy woman with a full life ahead of her want with a dying man? An ex-convict at that.

A second time, Michael was jolted from his reverie, this time by the fuel indicator. So much for his customary practice of never letting the tank dip below the one-quarter mark. It registered a blatant empty. *Hope it's not too far to the next exit. That's all I need, to run out of gas miles from civilization,* Michael thought.

Luck was with him, or so it seemed. Exit number seven, hidden from sight by the bend in the road, appeared as if by magic. Michael, an acknowledged nuisance to service station attendants, breathed a sigh of relief. He was not one of those self-service drivers. Whenever he pulled up for gas, he wanted the works, which is why most of the stations he visited on a regular basis hated to see him come. *Hah! That's what they get paid for, isn't it? Let 'em earn their keep,* he mused as he eased onto the exit ramp.

A familiar sign appeared not too far off in the distance. He had a credit card for that brand. He slowed his speed long enough to swing gracefully into the lot, around the self-service pump, and to a stop in front of the pump marked, *Full Service, Premium Unleaded.* He rolled down the electric window, turned the key off, and waited for the attendant to make his way over.

None too soon, a potbellied man in greasy overalls ambled over from the mechanic's bay. He was wiping grease from his hands with a dirty rag. "What can I do for ya, Mac?" he asked cheerfully enough.

Michael reached for his wallet. He opened it, selected the appropriate credit card, and handed it to him. "Fill it up, please, with premium unleaded. By the way, what's the octane rating of your premium?"

The attendant grunted something barely intelligible.

"*Typical,*" Michael thought. Then he retorted, "That will be fine," a sharp edge crept into his voice, "and check all the fluid levels and tire pressure...and wash the windshield."

The attendant glared at him across the pump. Disapproval was written across his brow. His gaze held Michael's a moment longer before scanning the full length of the luxury car. As he finished inspecting it, his eyes darted to the back seat, to Michael, and then back again. With his face screwed up in consternation, along with a shake of his head that did wonders for his partially disheveled hairstyle, the attendant bent under the hood of the car.

"Oil's fine. Wiper fluid's a bit low, but okay. Coolant level's fine." He dropped the hood with a bang. "Looks good up at this end, buddy. You got a fine machine here. Just a second and I'll check those tires."

While he fitted action to words, Michael looked around. Aside from the noise of the passing cars on the interstate, it was quiet. A warm breeze was blowing. Birds chirped. It felt peaceful. He leaned his head back on the headrest and closed his eyes.

Tires are okay, too, distracted him. "Looks like you're all set, 'cept for the money." As the attendant stood at the window, his face once again wrinkled in confusion over what lay in the back seat.

Whatever is he looking at? Michael wondered. Hunching up and around, he peered over his shoulder. *So that's it,* he thought. There lay the carefully folded tent Pat had loaned him. On its plastic wrapper was a picture of the tent as it would appear fully assembled and properly set up. His well-worn army duffle bag, stuffed with all his camping gear, lay next to it. Both items stood in stark contrast to his sleek luxury car and casual designer clothes.

The station attendant returned his card and gas receipt for him to sign. He accepted it and watched as the other's eyes flicked again toward the back. He scrawled his signature across the bottom, lifted his card off, and returned the original to the attendant.

"Say, Mister, I don't mean to be nosy, but is that your tent all folded up there?" He flashed an almost toothless grin at Michael. "You sure don't look like the outdoor type to me."

"Well, to be honest, it's not mine. A friend loaned it to me for a while. I'm...I'm just getting away for a few days. You know, get out in the country away from it all and sort things out."

Maybe it was the tremor that crept into Michael's last words. Perhaps it was the way his eyes grew misty. Then again, it might have been something else entirely. Whatever the cause, the attendant warmed toward Michael. He placed his left hand, still with the dirty rag, on the pump, his right hand on the car and leaned towards the open window. "Yeah, I understand times when you just wanna get away. My oldest boy was killed last year. A farmin' accident. Wishin' didn't do us much good, though. We're poor folks, the wife and I. Had to keep workin' to feed her and the other young'uns. Hospital bills from the baby keep pilin' up. And they sho don't put no food on the table."

He paused. "So, here I am."

Michael listened politely, a pang of guilt tugging at the corner of his conscience.

"Don't you pay me no never mind, Mister," continued the attendant. "You don't need t'hear my troubles. And whatever it is your lookin' for on your trip, I hope ya find it. I mean that, with all my heart." He extended his ruddy, grease-stained hand through the open window.

Michael grasped his hand and gave it a hearty shake. "Thank you, sir," he responded to the act of friendship. He struggled within himself because of his earlier harsh words. Guilt was not a familiar feeling to him. Neither was remorse. "I'm sorry about your son," he offered, in an effort to soothe his conscience. "That must have been difficult for you all."

The attendant's eyes grew moist with tears. He looked straight into Michael's eyes and held his gaze for an awkward moment. "Yes, sir," he whispered hoarsely, "it was." One second passed. Then another. Neither seemed willing to break eye contact, sensing in it something of the other's pain.

With a nod, the attendant glanced away and straightened up. "By the way, you ain't gotta call me 'sir.' I'm just plain ole Jed. Says so right here," he indicated, pointing to the partially obscured nametag over his greasy, left shirt pocket.

"All right, Jed it is. My name is Doctor...I mean, Michael. Just plain Michael. Good-bye, Jed. The best of everything to you and the family."

"Good luck to you, too," Jed called. "So long."

Michael glanced in the rearview mirror as he drove off. Jed was still standing on the pump island, hat in hand, waving good-bye.

For reasons Michael did not understand, he turned right instead of left toward the interstate.

THREE

SURPRISES

THE ROADSIDE SCENERY that greeted him left much to be desired. Dismal, at best. A few scrawny cows, lazily chewing their cud, lifted their heads to check him out as he drove by. He saw abandoned, rusty metal sheds and farming equipment, broken-down fences, litter—nothing in view explained why he felt drawn in that direction.

Farther on down the road was the beginning of what looked like woods. *That might be nice,* he thought. *A quiet drive.* Within seconds, he passed under the shadows of the trees. Their long branches like many giants' gnarled fingers interlaced above the roadway, creating a living tunnel. Michael slowed to give his eyes time to grow accustomed to the dimmer light.

All too soon, it was over. Michael blinked, his eyes blinded by the brilliant sunlight. The sudden appearance of a little hill on the other side of the trees startled him. At the bottom of the rise, the country road forked. Driving in the city had not prepared him for this. Not sure which way to go, Michael pulled off the road just before the fork and coasted to a stop in a shady area.

He sat quietly, making no attempt to choose. So much had happened. Even one more choice seemed overwhelming.

The minutes slid silently by. Then, out of the stillness, a distant, yet familiar chord began vibrating deep within his breast, *"Two roads diverged in a yellow wood..."* Hmm, he thought, *Robert Frost, The* Road Not Taken—*that used to be my favorite poem.* He slipped his left hand down the outside of the seat and released the recliner lever, then leaned back, folded his hands behind his head, and closed his eyes. "There, that's better," he sighed.

He had memorized the famous stanzas of *The Road Not Taken* for a middle school literary contest. His recital had earned him a blue ribbon, a certificate, and five dollars in prize money. One judge in particular stood out in his memory. Dabbing her still moist eyes with a lace-trimmed, powder blue handkerchief, she handed him her comment sheet. He could still hear her, clear as a bell, even after all those years:

> "Michael, I felt as if I were Robert Frost himself, deliberating in front of two wooded paths. You made it come alive. I've never heard it done better. Thank you, son, for a superior job."

He had floated from the auditorium that afternoon.

How ironic! In the middle of this mess, to think that, twenty-five years later, I'm actually sitting in front of a forked road, he thought.

He shook his head, opened his eyes, and sat up to take another look. It was still there, almost exactly as he had pictured it the afternoon he recited Robert Frost's poem. Uncanny. He wondered if he would be able to remember all the lines. Settling himself back into the seat, he let the words he had labored over for so many hours fill his thoughts. Gradually, the whole poem came back to him.

More reminiscing about the contest, one of the highlights of his youth, caused a lump to form in his throat. He felt the stark contrast between past and present and swallowed hard. Painful thoughts once again clamored for attention. The uniformed officer. Dale and Kathryn's puzzled looks. Legal papers. Kicked out of his own home...escorted by a deputy sheriff, no less! Humiliating was not the word for it. And the house. He paid for it with his own sweat and blood. *If it wasn't for me, Stephanie never would have had the place.* He clenched his teeth at the thought and reached up to grab the custom steering wheel with both hands. It felt good to have something solid to hang onto. He squeezed hard until his knuckles stood stark white in his blood-engorged hands. How dare she kick me out!

Michael sat bolt upright and raised his seat back. It was time to decide. No use making myself more miserable than I am already. *She will not get away with this, but what should I do right now? I can't sit here all day mooning over my childhood.* Leaning forward, Michael peered as far as he could down each of the two roads. He looked to the left first, squinting against the sunlight, and then back to the right. *Guess I'll try the left one. It looks about as interesting as the other,* he decided.

His choice made, he turned the key in the ignition and started the car. The engine coughed once and then caught. Michael shifted into *Drive,* turned left, and drove slowly down the dirt road. Streams of late afternoon sunlight filtered through the trees as he followed long, slow curves and rolling hills. The car ran smoothly, sounding on the quiet country road like the purr of a great cat, coiled and waiting to spring into action.

A short way down the road, something along the right captured his attention. He slowed to get a closer look. Weeds, long overdue for cutting, all but obscured an old weather-beaten sign. Hand painted on it were the words, *Camping... Turn Here.* An arrow pointed left to another dirt road. He made the turn.

Thinking to himself that this might be just what he was looking for and might even turn out to be fun, some of his earlier misgivings faded. *After all,* he encouraged himself, *it was fun in Scouts. And I've got Pat's manual.*

Soon, an old wood frame house, sadly in need of some fresh paint, appeared on his right. It sat back off the road a ways. Above one door, posted crookedly and misspelled, was a *Camping Registeration* sign.

It did not look like much of a campground. He was about to turn around when a young boy, about nine or ten, came running barefoot out to meet him. Shocks of unruly red hair framed his freckled face. He wore overalls, faded and patched, over a dingy t-shirt torn in several places.

"G'mornin', Mister, D'ya wanna camp? It's only eight dollars a night, an' Ma really needs the money. She's been tryin' to keep the lan' since Pa died. It's real purty over there by the river...clean enough to see the bottom. Stocked with lotsa fish, too. You kin catch as many as you want and pick the wild blueberries. Sometimes you even see deer 'n fox in the woods. We ain't seen no bears, tho." He stopped, out of breath from his homespun sales pitch. "An' my name's Sandy, short for Sanderson. What's yers? Ya sure don't much look like the campin' type." Finished, he shoved his hands into his pockets and waited for a reply.

Michael stared at Sandy in astonishment. The corners of his mouth curled ever so slightly as he tried to take it all in. He felt conspicuous in his expensive car and clothes. The beginnings of his smile disappeared. He was at a loss for words. The place seemed a bit too earthy, but how could he disappoint a young boy trying so hard to help his mother? Maybe roughing it would do him good—get back to nature for a couple of days. He spoke, "Oh, Sandy, it's nice to meet you. My name's Michael, and yes, I came to camp. Here...here's twenty dollars for two nights, plus a little tip in advance for you and your mother. Now, tell me which way to go and I'll be on my way."

"Oh, Mister...uh...Mr. Michael. Thanks!" A low whistle escaped as he studied the crisp twenty-dollar bill in his hand. He looked up and pointed. "Just keep goin' on down this road a piece. It'll wind back into the woods all the way t'the river. There's a country store back the other way, if yer fixin' t'git any food 'n stuff. You got a tent an' sleepin' bag? I'll hep ya put up yer tent, an' show ya how t'build a fire, if ya want." He nodded his head once. "I'm good at it," he added. "Pa taught me."

"Well, thanks for the offer, but I'll manage fine. And yes, I do have a tent. Sleeping bag and cookstove, too. I've been camping before, even though it's been a while. If I need you, I'll come on back. How's that?"

'Yep, you got it. Just don't pitch yer tent too close to the river bank, Mr. Michael. Cover yer campfire with dirt before ya leave and keep any food outside yer tent at night." He paused to fill his young lungs, then continued, "Are ya sure ya don't need any hep? Lotsa folks come through here, an' I seen me a city slicker or two before," he squinted at Michael, "an' you sure look like one."

Michael doubted the "lotsa folks." From appearances, he may have been the only one to ever come this way. "I'll be fine, Sandy, honest. I came to get away for a few days. You know, relax and unwind. Thanks again, though." With that, he put the car in *Reverse* and eased out of the grassy driveway.

Back out on the road again, he continued following its winding curves until he could see the river Sandy mentioned. The woods were fairly thick, and there were not many cleared areas that looked like campsites. Not a single tent in sight, either. *Lotsa folks, huh? I thought so.* But then he thought of being completely alone—no phones, no interruptions. "This might not be so bad after all," he declared to the surrounding countryside. "Who needs Stephanie anyway?"

He parked near a weather-beaten picnic table and unloaded his camping gear from the back seat. He chuckled when he remembered Jed. *Now, let's see. First, the tent,* he thought. *Better get it set up before dark.* At least that much came back to him. His eyes scanned the immediate area and found what looked to be a nice spot—fairly flat, sheltered from the wind, and situated at the bottom of a little hill. Not too far from the river, either.

After carrying his gear closer, he took out the instructions, unpacked the nylon tent, and spread it out on the ground. The aluminum poles fit together nice and snug, even the curved supporting ones. He was all thumbs, though, when it came to inserting the poles through the loops on the top of the tent. It stood, slightly lopsided and somewhat unstable for a moment, before collapsing in on itself. He moaned in frustration, but he refused to ask for Sandy's help. No, he would not be outdone by a kid. Again and again, he tried. Finally, on his fourth attempt, the tent—full of wrinkles and a bit off kilter, not at all like the picture on the directions—stayed up. It was not perfect, but it would do for the night. Satisfied, he dragged his gear inside.

Next came the waterproof pad. He laid it over the plastic tent floor. On top of that, he unrolled the down-filled, mummy-style sleeping bag. Fluffing it up with a couple of hearty shakes and healthy slaps, he spread it out and stepped back to survey his handiwork. *Not bad. Now to get into something more comfortable.*

Changing clothes made him realize how exhausted he was. Just lifting his arms into his sweatshirt was an effort. His eyelids drooped in rebellion against staying open for another minute. Stress had really taken its toll. All of his energy was gone. He crawled into the sleeping bag and wriggled around. He had forgotten how much he used to enjoy those long days out in the woods...and how great it felt at the day's end to snuggle deep inside his sleeping bag, reveling in the cool smoothness against his skin. He used to breathe softly and slowly on the part nearest his face. Then, after it had reached the right temperature, he would hold it next to his cheek and drift off to sleep. Yes, he had forgotten. It was good to be camping again. He snuggled deeper into the cloud-like softness. *This is just what I need to get back on track. I'm glad Pat suggested...* He heaved a huge sigh and was sound asleep. For nearly two hours, he did not budge.

Michael awoke with a start. His first conscious thought was, *Where am I?* He looked at his watch in the semi-darkness. Seven-thirty. *Morning or evening?* he wondered. He was completely disoriented, but the tent walls and mummy sleeping bag soon triggered his memory. His senses returned slowly, like the sun breaking through the early morning fog. It was only his brain that was hazy. *Oh yeah, that's right, camping… to get away for a while… and be alone,* he remembered drowsily. Thoughts of sleep and rest vanished, however, with the sound of someone outside calling, "Michael, Mr. Michael. Watcha doin'? Are ya sleepin'? It ain't even dark yet."

"Man, it's that kid again," he groaned. "What's he doing here?" he complained as he struggled to free himself from the confines of the sleeping bag. He sat up and leaned over to unzip the door flap so he could see through the screen.

There, looking down at him with a concerned expression, stood Sandy. Michael halfheartedly tried to hide his displeasure, but it was obvious anyway. "Hello, Sandy. I was taking a nap, trying to catch up on some sleep. What do you want?"

"Nothin', Mr. Michael. I jes wanted t'be sure you wuz okay over here by yerself. I told Ma I wuz worried cuz you's so citified. She gave me permission t'come an' check on ya." He stopped and craned his neck around to peer down the hill. "Got yer tent pitched pretty good, I see. Onliest trouble is, yer gonna git wet where ya got it now…if'n it rains, that is. And it's s'posed t'tonight. Yer too low in this valley, ya see, cuz the water will run down from up high and go right under yer tent. Yer too close t'the river, too."

Michael grunted as he rubbed sleep from his eyes. He unzipped the screen door and stepped outside to inspect his site. The red-headed kid was rather likable. It was hard to stay frustrated with him. "Sandy, you're right, much as I hate to admit it. I see what you mean about being in a low spot. Feel like helping me move my tent to a more suitable place?"

"Yes, sir!" Sandy agreed, eager to help. "First we gotta scout around fer a high, flat place. That's what Pa always said. Little farther from the river, case it rises quick, but not too far, cuz that's yer water supply. C'mon." Sandy grabbed Michael's shirtsleeve and led him off, away from the river. Several hundred yards away, he stopped and pointed. "See that hill right there...kinda flat on top with clay dirt and no tall grass? That's a good spot. Ya won't git no chiggers 'n ticks. They like t'hide in tall grass. It's flat so ya won't git a sore back from no lumps pokin' through. B'sides, you'll git a better breeze up there."

Sandy blossomed in his role as wilderness expert. "Look at that big boulder. Whooee! It'll give ya shelter from a strong wind that might come up. Now look up high." Michael lifted his head and peered into the sky. Sandy giggled. "No, Mr. Michael, not that high. Yer just checkin' fer a tree that might have dead branches hangin' over yer tent. Wouldn't wanna get bopped on the head in yer sleep, would ya?"

Michael coughed in embarrassment. "No, I certainly wouldn't, Sandy." Standing with hands on hips, he surveyed the area. "So, that's the campsite I need, is it?" he asked his young guide, who stood with his much littler hands on his own hips in imitation of Michael.

"Yep," he declared, locking his eyes on Michael's and giving him a nod that set his red hair flying.

"Let's go get my car and bring the gear over here, then." He looked down at Sandy with his most businesslike expression. "You can help me set up the tent if you still want to." The freckled, boyish face—so serious from a moment before—broke into a grin that spread from ear to ear. Together, they walked back toward Michael's site.

In no time at all, Sandy had the tent disassembled and all the gear stowed in the trunk. Michael slid behind the steering wheel and unlocked the passenger door with the remote button. The boy still stood on the outside, waiting. He stared in disbelief when Michael lowered the electric window to tell him the door was unlocked.

"How'd ya do that?" Sandy asked, as he climbed into the passenger seat. "Wow! I ain't never seen a car like this before. Look at all them buttons an' numbers an' little round windows." He rubbed his hand over the genuine leather upholstery and closed his eyes. His features took on a dreamy expression. "An' this seat is so soft. Boy, Mr. Michael, you must be one 'portant person t'drive a car like this!" He sighed and wriggled even deeper into the ample cushion. It enveloped his slender body.

They rode in silence the short distance to the new campsite. Michael pondered the irony of Sandy's observations. *I must be one of those important people, all right. Important enough to be thrown out of my own house.* He winced at the thought and glanced to his right. Seeing the young boy sitting there brought to mind his own children. He could not help wondering how they were doing and what they thought of everything. At least he would not have to disappoint this kid. *Let him think what he wants.*

Michael parked at the new site. He even allowed Sandy to press the remote trunk latch, showing him how, of course. As it clicked, Sandy squinted. Then his eyes opened wide with delight as the trunk lid slowly opened. He turned back to Michael before breaking the silence. "You jes stay here 'n rest. I'll git yer tent set up in a jiffy." With that, he hopped out of the car and got to work.

Michael watched the tent take shape. The boy was adept, alright. No wrinkles on the first try. The rest of his gear disappeared inside. Within minutes, Sandy's red head popped out. "Okay, yer ready for the night," he called. "Yer flashlight's right beside yer sleeping bag where ya kin reach it." Dusk was beginning to settle in.

"Thank you, Sandy. You're quite the camping pro," he encouraged. "Say, do you think that little country store is still open? I need to pick up a few things."

"Well, if they're not, I know the folks that runs it. They live right upstairs." He hesitated. "Kin I go with ya? If ya stop at my house, I'll ask Ma, so she don't worry. Maybe she needs somethin', too."

"That'll be fine. But when we get back, Sandy, I must get some sleep. I'm exhausted." They both climbed into his car and drove back to Sandy's house. All the while, Sandy sat and stared, fascinated at the lights on the dashboard. Michael could tell he had a thousand questions to ask, but did not. And when the car pulled up close to the front door, he slid out with only a "Be right back." Less than a minute later, he reappeared on the porch. "Bye, Ma," he called, easing the screen door shut. He bounded down the steps, two at a time, and got back into the car. "She said I could go, an' we need bread an' milk. An' Ma says I'm t'thank ya." He laid his head back on the cozy seat and sighed again.

The headlights beamed, illuminating the little dirt road. Sandy was quiet. "Is this it, son?" Michael asked, slowing down at a building on his left.

"Yep. Looks like they's still workin', too. Good!" He jumped out of the car as soon as it rolled to a stop. "Evenin', Mrs. Parks," Sandy greeted the storekeeper, as he opened the door. "I brung ya a new customer.

His name's Michael, an' he's campin' on our property." Michael entered behind Sandy and nodded a greeting to the gray-haired woman.

"Pleased to meet, you, Mister . . . ?"

"Nastasis," he replied, his eyes scanning the rows of canned and pre-packaged goods.

Mrs. Parks stared at him. "My, you do look familiar. You're from around here?"

"No, ma'am. Just visiting for a few days." He was about as used to open friendliness with strangers as he was to bear hugs from people he knew. "I need some strong insect repellent and ice, please." He strolled to the newspaper rack, picked one up, and glanced at the front page. His face turned ashen. "Oh, no!" he breathed aloud. There in full color, were two photos—one, of him smiling as he received the cherished *President's Award* from Dale and the other (he blinked in amazement), him again, being served the restraining order. Seeing the headlines, "Fame to Shame at Honor's Banquet!" he wondered, "*How? When?*" Then he remembered the camera flashes while he signed the papers. His face flushed and his temples throbbed as anger mounted inside him. *What about privacy? I'll sue them, whoever's responsible. I'll sue the pants off 'em!* he promised himself.

His mind raced as he looked to see if anyone was watching. He could not let them see those newspapers. Neither Sandy nor Mrs. Parks was paying attention. He gathered the remaining stack of papers in his arms and walked to the checkout counter. Forcing himself to appear calm and pasting a smile on his face, he laid them on the counter, photos down. "Sandy, are you about ready?" he asked hoarsely. "We've got to be going." A sharp edge tinged his voice.

The boy came running with a gallon of milk and a loaf of discounted bread in his arms. "Yes, sir." He glanced at the countertop. "How come yer buyin' so many papers? I kin show ya how t'gather kindlin' fer a fire. It's much better." He paused to look at Michael a second, his little head cocked at an angle. "Gosh, are you all right, Mr. Michael? Ya don't look too good. What's wrong?"

"Nothing. I'm just overtired. That's all."

Mrs. Parks returned with the ice and insect repellent. Knitting her eyebrows, she stared at him again. Then she totaled the items on a piece of scratch paper, took the money he held out, and gave him his change. Sandy started to unfold the twenty-dollar bill that Michael had given him earlier, but the woman shook her head. "Tell your mom this one's on us, Sandy. And give her our love."

"Yes, ma'am. Thank ya kindly."

He turned to follow Michael, who was already heading out the door to the car. "Are ya sure yer okay? Yer actin' so funny. Didn't ya like Mrs. Parks er somethin'? Maybe I took too long? I git carried away lookin' around, I guess."

"Sandy, I said I'm fine. It's nothing you did. I'm just worn out, that's all. You should be getting ready for bed, too, and not driving around with strangers."

"Yes, sir." Sandy didn't utter a peep until he slowly eased out of the car in front of his house. Michael's use of the word *stranger* was like a cold slap in the face. "Well, g'night, Mr. Michael. Hope ya sleep good tonight so ya feel better t'morrow. And thanks fer takin' me with ya." The dark almost hid the tears forming in the corners of his eyes.

"Good-bye, Sandy." Michael backed out on the worn path to the road as Sandy, silent tears trickling down his cheeks, stared after him from the steps. Only when the red taillights disappeared around the bend did he take his eyes off the road and let his head drop. Even his red hair seemed less alive, less vibrant than before. Still clutching the milk and bread, he turned, made his way up the last two steps, and stopped. He slowly set the milk down to open the door. "It's me, Ma." He cast one more long look in the direction of the campsite. Then he turned and plodded inside.

Michael drove to the campsite in a daze. He was in shock, numb all over. He stopped as close to the tent as he could and grabbed one of the foreboding bundles from the front seat. His body felt like lead as he shifted out of the car and stumbled through the dark to the tent. He ducked inside, zipped the flaps together, turned, and half fell across his sleeping bag. "OUCH!" he screamed. Something hard gouged him in the stomach. "What's that?" he yelled, as he raised himself on his hands and knees. "A flashlight! How'd that get..." Then he remembered Sandy saying something about putting it next to his sleeping bag. "Oh, that kid," he growled. He picked it up in a rage and made as if to throw it, but stopped in mid-reach. "It might come in handy," he conceded. "But the kid's got to go! Why on earth did I even let him near the tent, let alone inside? I should have known the country bumpkin would do something stupid, like lay a flashlight right where I'd jab myself half to death on it!"

He grabbed the newspaper, and with a mighty shove, flung it against the ground with all his might. Papers scattered everywhere.

He lay back on his stomach, oblivious to the mess. Tears filled his eyes. "How could you do this to me?" he cried. "Front page headlines. I'll be a laughing stock. 'Fame to Shame...'" And then he was up on his knees, pounding his fists into the ground with all his might. "Stephanie Marie Nastasis, I hate you! I...hate...you!" Again and again, he screamed out into the night.

At last, utterly spent, he managed to strip off his shirt and pants and kick off his shoes. The night air had cooled, and he shivered. He eased his aching body back into the sleeping bag and dozed peacefully in the womb-like environment. Once, he awoke with a start, but after a few minutes, the sound of gentle rain lulled him back to sleep.

———

Dawn. The forest awoke. Birds chirped, each singing its own unique melody, but he did not notice. The earth smelled fresh and clean. His nose was too congested, his head pounding too much to take in the beauty of the rain-washed earth. He opened his eyes and stared up at the yellow plastic ceiling. It glowed in the early morning sun. He looked around at the pages of newspaper strewn about the tent floor. Memories of last night's rage came flooding back. He rolled over on his side, but could not bring himself to pick up the front page and read the article. "I'll never read it!" he vowed. "The bum who wrote it won't have that satisfaction. And neither will she."

Michael was ready to pack up and leave. Where? He had no idea. Just so he could get away from everything that reminded him of failure. *Maybe,* he thought, *I'll feel better if I just get moving.* Unzipping his way out of the sleeping bag, he stood up and stretched as much as possible in the confined area and set about looking for his pants and shirt. He found them and dressed in a hurry, before he would begin to feel claustrophobic. Shoes in hand, he reached over to grab the big tent zipper and opened the door flap. He stuck his head through the opening and inhaled deeply of the fresh morning air. "Ah, that feels much better." Satisfied, he popped back into the tent long enough to slip into his shoes, then stepped outside.

Soggy clay dirt squished beneath his feet. "Oh, no...my new top-siders. That stupid kid! Telling me to pitch my tent up here so the rain could turn it into a giant mudhole. I'd rather have ticks and chiggers," he lamented, looking down at his expensive leather shoes. "Ugh!"

Breaking down the tent and stowing his gear in the trunk were chores for city-bred Michael. His head still throbbed, his throat was raw, and he felt irritable. Dark circles showed under his eyes. So much for roughing it.

The packing done, he slammed the trunk, and half-stomped around to the driver's side, yanking opened the door. He started to get in, but at the last second, he remembered the mud. His shoes were covered, and he didn't want to get the car's interior dirty. Keeping an immaculate vehicle was one thing he took great pride in. No running water nor a rag to clean them off with left him little choice. It was either drive in stocking feet or muddy the floor mats. He opted for the latter. "Well, that will remind me never to come this way again. Camping, hah!" He slammed the door, started the car, and shoved the gearshift into *Drive*.

Retracing his route so as not to get lost, Michael approached the house where Sandy lived. He decided they could keep the extra night's fee. It was worth not having to listen to any jabbering that morning, especially from a little red-headed urchin. When he neared the place, he turned his head to the right, just in case the boy was in the yard. He did not want to see him at all.

Meanwhile, Sandy, still dressed in the same patched overalls and torn t-shirt, was hanging out the wash. He heard an approaching car and looked up. Recognizing it as Michael's, he dropped the towel and clothespins and started running at top speed. Waving his arms frantically, he called as he ran, "Mr. Michael! Mr....Mi...chael..." The car never even slowed down. Sandy stood there a moment, arms hanging limp at his sides. All hope of having a new friend was dashed to the ground. He was crushed.

As he gazed into the distance, he murmured, "What's the matter with 'im? What'd I do wrong?" He did not understand, but then, there were lots of other things he did not understand either. Like his father's death. Turning around slowly, head down, he shuffled over to the wash basket. He looked like the weight of the world was planted squarely on his thin, trembling shoulders.

FOUR

SEARCHING

MICHAEL DROVE BACK to the fork in the road. Was it only yesterday he had parked there? It seemed like weeks ago. He turned his car around and stopped at the same spot. For a long time, he sat peering down one road and then the other, pondering what the future held. Life, for him, had reached a crossroads. There was no avoiding it. Time to "pull himself up by his own bootstraps," as his father used to say. Michael wondered if he ever could...or even wanted to.

The undercurrent of fear that, in times past, had driven him to pinnacles of achievement, now churned his insides until they were no more solid than water. His feelings of success had always been so tenuous— on the verge of collapse. But he never let fear get the best of him. *Run!* it urged now. *Run! You're finished. Run!* Pride clamped that door shut tight. Escape was a luxury he would not allow himself. He gathered his thoughts from their treacherous wanderings and looked one last time down the two roads. Where did the right fork lead? Maybe he could find some answers down that way. Or at least, a moment's peace. After last night, anything was worth a try.

Turning the car to the right, Michael settled himself in the seat in preparation for a long drive. To his surprise, a sign came into view around the first bend. It was old-fashioned and expertly crafted. "*Caleb's*

Country Corner Retreat. Accommodations, Antiques, Pottery—1 mile," he read aloud. That sounded more like it. More in his league. And pottery, too. He drove with mounting anticipation. A roomy, white wood shingle house appeared on his left. Prim-looking forest green shutters and window boxes full of bright red and yellow flowers caught his eye as he pulled into the cinder parking lot. Still a bit cautious, he shut the car off and got out to survey Caleb's Country Corner Retreat. A neat white picket fence surrounded the spacious, manicured lawn. He relaxed. He felt at home with the meticulous appearance. Fruit trees and elaborate flower beds dotted the unbroken green. To him, it was like an oasis in the middle of the Sahara desert.

He lifted the black, wrought-iron latch on the gate and approached the porch. A pleasant melody jingled from a set of wind chimes. Glancing at the *Open* sign in the window, he pulled the brass door handle. The tangy scent of fruit and spices greeted him as he entered the foyer. He inhaled deeply and allowed the first tentative traces of a smile to cross his lips.

Another step and he was inside the room. He glanced at the wall behind the empty desk. His mouth opened wide in disbelief. Opposite the guestbook hung a handmade, wooden plaque bearing two lines from the same Robert Frost poem. He shivered. *Incredible,* he thought. *I haven't seen or heard of it in twenty-some years. Now two days in a row. What next?*

He tore his eyes away from the wall and took in the rest of the room. *Hmm...homey. Pleasant. Neat as a pin,* he thought. He liked that. To his right was a little anteroom with the appearance of a shop of sorts. With the owner nowhere in sight, Michael's curiosity got the best of him. He stepped inside.

Lined with rows of rough-hewn shelves, displaying some of the most beautiful earthenware and stoneware pottery he had ever seen, the shop itself was an invitation to browse. No two pieces were alike. Each boasted a unique shape, with various glazes and textures. Some were large and looked to be vases or jugs. Others were small and delicate, not much bigger than the tiniest tea cup. They ranged in color from palest pink to deep midnight blue. Minutes passed with him standing there, but he hardly noticed.

Finally, a lean and muscular white-haired gentleman appeared in the doorway. He was wearing khaki walking shorts, a royal blue sport shirt, and running shoes. Clear blue eyes sparkled in a face bronzed from the sun. The elder man spoke first, "Good morning, sir." He finished wiping his hands on the tan canvas apron tied snugly around his slim waist and smoothed it back in place. "Welcome to Caleb's Country Corner Retreat. I'm Caleb Johannsen, proprietor." His voice was kind. He smiled warmly and extended his right hand in greeting.

Michael grasped the outstretched hand and gave it a hearty shake. Smile lines on Caleb's cheery face deepened even further. "Michael Nastasis. Pleased to meet you, Mr. Johannsen. This pottery is great. Excellent place you have."

"Why thank you. I'm glad you like it. Course, I'm rather partial to it myself, I guess."

Michael shook his head. "It's hard to believe something so impressive is out here in what seems to be the middle of nowhere. I should have come this way yesterday. Spent the night, instead, at some ramshackle campground down the road. This turn was my last shot before heading back to the interstate."

"Well, I'm glad you stopped. Come on in and have some breakfast. I was just getting ready to sit down myself."

Michael hesitated only a second. "I am hungry. If you're sure you have enough. I know you weren't expecting me, and it's early yet."

"I've got plenty. It's the slow season. If you decide you like the place enough to stay a day or two, then we'll take care of your things. Follow me." Caleb escorted him into the dining room, pulled out an oak captain's chair from the nearest matching round oak table, and helped him get seated. Four blue linen placemats, their heavy weave a subtle but pleasant contrast to the wood grain in the table top, marked the places.

Even while Michael made these observations, Caleb departed and reappeared in a flash at his side. "Here's your menu. I'll be in the kitchen, through that doorway. Call me when you've decided." The spot he indicated was in the corner of the dining room just to his left and had no door. It gave the place a nice, cozy atmosphere. Almost like home.

"Will do," Michael agreed as he scanned the engaging menu. Calligraphy and colored sketches of old-fashioned scenes—a woman churning butter, another making ice cream, a man toting a bushel-basket of fresh vegetables—lent a country feeling. His mouth watered.

"Mr. Johannsen," he called. "Got your pen and paper ready?"

"Sure do. What'll it be?" he asked as he walked towards Michael's table.

"I'll have your 'Homemade, Crunchy Granola, Sprinkled with a Generous Portion of Plump, Fresh Blueberries,' with cream, please, a 'Honey-Bran-Apple-Raisin MegaMuffin,' and a cup of your 'House Specialty, Hot Herb Drink.'"

"Excellent choices. The drink is all natural and caffeine-free, with a spicy, roasted flavor."

"Sounds good."

"Folks love it. I'm sorry, though. I don't have any cream for your cereal. I do have some lowfat milk, if that'll be all right." He tilted his head and raised his eyebrows. "You know, it's better for you."

"Yes, Mr. Johannsen, you're right about that. Lowfat milk'll be just fine."

"Great. By the way, call me Caleb. No need for any 'Misters' around here. I'm a down-to-earth type guy. I'll be back in a few minutes with breakfast. Meanwhile, make yourself comfortable. If you'd care for something to read, you'll find magazines on that rack over there and newspapers hanging on the wooden poles. Feel free to browse."

Michael cringed at the mention of newspapers. "Thanks, Caleb, I'll help myself," he responded. His stomach was already in knots. He silently pleaded, *God, no more headlines, okay?*

For a second, he wondered if Caleb had seen the photos in yesterday's paper. If so, he did not act like he recognized him. He sighed in relief. *Maybe I will have a look at those magazines, after all,* he decided.

He slid back his chair and walked over to the ingenious display. The usual fare of news periodicals, along with some home and gardening magazines, filled the rack. A few on crafts, more on fitness, and a pile of them on religion. And, of course, *Reader's Digest. "Good ole standby, that one,"* he thought.

"Wonder what's in the religious section? Sure are enough of them," Michael mused. He scanned the alphabetized titles: *Charisma. Christian Herald. Christianity Today. Decision. Discipleship Journal. Focus on the Family. Guideposts. Last Days Magazine. Moody Monthly. Today's Christian Woman.*

Caleb interrupted him before he could go any further. He bowed slightly at the table and announced in a theatrical butler's accent, "Mr.

Nastasis, breakfast is served." He broke into a friendly grin and set a generous portion before each of their places.

His guest, returning slowly from the magazine display, missed his attempt at levity. Michael's face was no longer relaxed, but had taken on the beginnings of a dark, brooding scowl. "You must be one of those spiritual health nuts I've read about," he remarked with mild sarcasm as they sat down. "I don't mean to be offensive, but you've got religious magazines galore over there." He hesitated and glanced down at his plate. "And you sure have some unusual items on your menu. Never even heard of, much less tasted, most of them...like tu-fo." His face and nose wrinkled up as he carefully tried to pronounce the strange name.

A merry glint danced in Caleb's blue eyes. Tact was one of his outstanding traits, but he could keep a straight face no longer. He let go a hearty laugh of pure joy. Michael recoiled in surprise and sat straight up in the chair, waiting for Caleb's unexpected fit to pass. "I'm sorry," Caleb apologized. He wiped a tear from the corner of one of his even shinier eyes. "Forgive me. I shouldn't laugh, but you looked so disgruntled, with your comments on my reading material and food. Yet, you couldn't stop looking at your breakfast, sitting there with such a bleak expression on your face and licking your lips at the same time." His tone was teasing. "I'm so glad it didn't spoil your appetite. By the way, it's tofu, not tu-fo. A soybean curd that's very good for you."

Caleb's joy was contagious. Michael's face lost some of its hard edges and his mouth relaxed a little. He leaned forward, sniffing appreciatively the aromatic steam rising from his mug.

"Michael, I guess you could consider me a health nut, of sorts, but religious, I'm not," he said emphatically. "Christian, yes. There's a difference. Would you mind if I say grace before we eat?"

Michael's brow knitted in a puzzled expression. "No, no, go right ahead. I go to church every Sunday."

Caleb bowed his head, while his folded hands rested comfortably on the edge of the table. "Thank You, Lord, for this magnificent day and for bringing Michael here. I ask You to minister to him during his visit and to bless this food which we are about to share. Let our bodies use it well, for our health and for Your glory. In Jesus' name, I thank You, amen."

Michael cleared his throat and shifted in his chair. Something about the prayer made him nervous. For a while, he occupied himself with eating.

"Tell me, Caleb. How did you get into all this, uh…natural stuff?"

"Oh, about twenty years ago, after my wife died of a heart attack and I barely recovered from a near-fatal bout with a tumor, I made a lot of changes in my life. To name a few, I stopped smoking and drinking. Quit eating so much greasy food and concentrated more on wholesome, raw foods. Started exercising every day. Most important of all…because without it, none of the other would have been possible…I quit fighting and accepted the whole truth of the Bible. Lock, stock, and barrel!"

Michael cleared his throat again and changed the subject. "I have to hand it to you, Caleb. This breakfast is pretty tasty. Don't tell me you made the granola and bran muffins yourself."

"Oh, sure. I make as much as I can from scratch. It's a great challenge. At seventy-seven, I feel like a new person…better than most people in their forties and fifties."

"Seventy-seven years old? No kidding. Except for your white hair, you don't look a day over fifty, if that. You must be doing something right," he agreed. "I suppose you'll tell me you're the potter who made all those interesting pieces out front, too."

Caleb smiled. "That is one of my favorite hobbies, besides reading and tending my vineyard. The arbors are out back."

"I'd like to see them." Michael paused to swallow another spoonful of cereal. "I think this place will do me a world of good. The last couple days have been rough. Besides the mess at home, I met the most aggravating little kid. Just when I needed to be alone."

Caleb looked him directly in the eyes. "I can imagine you've had a rough time of it."

Caught off guard by this sudden shift, Michael froze in mid-bite, then gulped and stared back at Caleb. To his relief, he saw only kindness mirrored in the old man's eyes. Neither of them said anything for a moment.

Caleb was first to break the silence. "Even though we had never met, my heart went out to you when I read the paper. It must have been upsetting, to say the least. I almost felt like I knew you."

"Hold on, now," interrupted Michael. "What do you mean, you felt like you knew me?"

"For quite a while now in my prayer times," he continued, "I have felt impressed to pray for someone who would be coming this way. When I saw the pictures in the newspaper, I knew you were the person. That explains why I wasn't completely surprised when you walked in."

Michael, his jaw muscles twitching, stared hard at him. His mouth was no more than a slit accented by two pencil-thin lips. Cynicism was written all over his face, with no attempt to conceal it.

Caleb met his gaze matter-of-factly. "The little kid you mentioned, it wouldn't be Sandy Hawkins, by any chance, would it? Red-haired, freckle-faced little guy about nine-years-old? Helps his mother run a small campground nearby."

"You mean you know him?" Michael could contain his amazement no longer. His mouth dropped open before he caught himself.

"Oh, yes. I love him to pieces, although I haven't known him all that long. He's such a good boy—an only child. There are very few genuinely good kids these days, it seems. So many going astray so young!"

"I'll agree with that." His own two children flashed through his mind. What would become of the now fatherless pair?

"Sandy has worked so hard since his dad died," Caleb resumed after pausing to let Michael's thoughts return. "I try to help him and his mom out as much as I can. Did you know his mom is an invalid?"

"An...invalid?" he stammered. "No, I mean, he never said...at least, I don't think he mentioned." He shoved the fingers of his right hand through his hair. "What's wrong with her? Did she have an accident?"

"No," Caleb answered in a soft voice. "She has advanced multiple sclerosis." His eyes lost their merry glint. Hard as tempered steel, they pierced Michael's heart. "Doctors say she doesn't have much time left."

"Multiple sclerosis...not much time left," Michael's voice faded. He wilted beneath Caleb's penetrating gaze, though his eyes had softened and misted somewhat. Thoughts of Sandy became jumbled with thoughts of his own children. His without a father. Sandy soon to be orphaned. *It just isn't fair!* Icy tendrils of guilt probed the outer reaches of his conscience. Fear reached out to grab him in its clutches, but he slammed that dangerous door shut. "Caleb, I need some time alone. Is there somewhere I can go for a walk?"

"Sure. Come on." He moved his chair away from the table, wiped his mouth one last time, and laid the napkin down next to his plate. Without waiting to see if Michael followed, he led the way through the house.

Caleb fairly bounced along, his steps spry and chipper. Michael, on the other hand, was deep in thought. His head hung down and his eyes focused about a yard in front of his plodding feet. When he reached the porch, Caleb was there waiting for him.

"Look over there. Can you see that path through the grape arbors? It winds through the fruit trees and down to and around the pond." Caleb's enthusiasm was irresistible. Buoyed by it, Michael raised his head and looked where Caleb pointed.

The view was exceptional. Flowers of every variety, even more than out front, brightened the landscape. A vegetable garden, planted in perfect rows, bordered the right. Lush green grass sloped gradually down to the marshy pond in the distance. Fruit trees, their branches hanging heavy with nearly-ripe fruit, created a natural windbreak on the left-most edge of the property, around the pond, and as far as the eye could see.

Also near the pond, at a comfortable stretch from the house, stood a birdbath, surrounded by several strategically situated birdhouses and feeders. As Michael watched, some small birds flew from the tall tufts of marsh grasses and made their way to one of the houses. "Caleb, you have a veritable haven here. This is a nature lover's dream come true! So peaceful... like paradise."

"That's exactly what I felt when I first saw it. The moment I set foot onto this land, I knew this was where I wanted to spend the rest of my life. Of course, it didn't look the way you see it now." His voice faded as he looked off into the distance, remembering the nostalgic moment. "But that's enough talking, I reckon. You wanted to be alone. When you get back, if you like, I'll tell you the story of how I came here, 'way out in the middle of nowhere,' as you put it. For now, it's time for you to hit the trail."

"Sure," agreed Michael. He felt better, and with a full stomach, he was eager to get moving a little. "I won't be gone long. Hey, thanks for the delicious breakfast." He descended the porch steps and waved over his shoulder.

"You're quite welcome," Caleb called out. "Take your time. Enjoy yourself." For a while, he watched Michael follow the path. When he was out of sight, Caleb turned and walked inside and over to his favorite chair. But instead of sitting, he knelt down to pray.

A hundred yards from the house, Michael stopped. He stood with his hands pressed deep into his pockets and stared at the beauty around him. *What I wouldn't give to have ...* He dismissed the thought. *I can't keep what I've got, let alone something like this. Who am I trying to kid?*

He sighed and bent to pick up a blade of the long, green grass. Without thinking, he put it in his mouth and began chewing. Everything was so tranquil, and yet, now that he was alone again, he was troubled by a growing sense of uneasiness. The cheerful chirps of birds flocking the feeders and the gentle sound of water lapping the shoreline interrupted his mood. Despondency's claws continued tearing their way through his calm exterior. Growing more restless, he continued along the trail.

Out amid the grove, beyond the pond, all was silent. All, that is, but the swish of his feet through the ankle-high grass and the buzz of an occasional bee. The temperature was rising. Shade would provide a welcome relief from the encroaching sun. He stopped in the shadow of a large orange tree and leaned his weight against the well-pruned trunk. Pausing to look around, he thought, *Caleb sure takes good care of this place.* Finally, he admitted to himself what was troubling him. It was Sandy.

If only he had known about Sandy's mother. How could he have been so heartless? This was followed by the more truthful, *so what if I had known? Would it have made any difference?* He remembered Sandy's face in the store the night before—a face that formed the picture of childhood innocence as he asked, *"How come yer buyin' so many newspapers? I kin show ya how t'gather kindlin' fer a fire."* One after another the scenes replayed before his mind's eye. *"Are ya sure yer okay? Yer actin' so funny ... maybe I took too long ..."*

The discomforting images pursued him—pulling up in front of Sandy's house and the young boy's words, *"Hope ya sleep good t'night so ya feel better t'morrow."* His hesitant, *"Thanks fer takin' me with ya ..."* It all came flooding back. He remembered, too, his own emptiness. He was so caught up in present circumstances that he could hardly wait to get rid of him. *But I didn't know about his mom,* he rationalized. It did nothing to wipe away the picture of Sandy's trembling chin, his tear-filled eyes, glistening in the dim light from the open car door, or his lonely look as he stood there on the dilapidated porch. He could see him as plain now as he could driving away last night.

Michael shook his head to clear those unwanted thoughts and stepped from the shade. They were still there. *I sure was rough on the kid after I saw that newspaper. It had nothing to do with him, yet he blamed himself for the way I was acting,* he thought. Standing in the sun seemed to shed light on a previously darkened part of his heart. What he saw disgusted him: *Michael Nastasis, big-time success, gets his feelings hurt and takes them out on a dirt-poor kid, lonely for a father figure, who, at the same time, has to be the "man" of the house,* he decided. No, he did not like that picture at all.

His mind continued to race, *The kid did everything he could to be helpful, but did I appreciate him? Yeah, with things like, "That kid is such a nuisance!" or "I should have known the country bumpkin would do something stupid like..."* His temper had gotten the best of him, *"That stupid kid, telling me to pitch my tent up high in the mud. I'd rather have chiggers and ticks..."*

"Why?" Michael cried out now in anguish. "Why?" No one answered. Not even an echo. Just silence, until his conscience revived and reminded him of his earlier cry, *"It's not fair!"* No, life was not fair. He could bear that. What he could not bear was the sad fact that he was very much responsible for some of that unfairness.

All his joy gone, Michael turned toward the Country Corner and began walking back. He hurried, as if trying to flee the picture of young Sandy waving his arms after the car that morning. And his not even stopping to say good-bye.

FIVE

DISCOVERY

THE LANDSCAPE STILL proudly displayed its beauty, but Michael was oblivious. To be free of the ache inside was all he thought about. He realized now where it came from and that he needed to do something to alleviate it. Trouble was, he did not know where to start.

Drawing near the house, he saw Caleb sitting in the shade reading a rather large book. So deep in concentration was he that he never saw Michael approaching. "Excuse me, Caleb. I've gotta talk with you whenever you get a moment. I need to get something off my chest." He glanced down and, as Caleb replaced his bookmark, saw that it was a Bible. Its dark blue leather cover showed signs of wear, but not a page was frayed, nor a corner turned.

"Of course, Michael. How about right now? Come on, pull up a chair and have a seat. You've been gone quite a while. Must have a lot on your mind."

"Well, it's about Sandy Hawkins…sort of." He paused. "But mostly, it's about me, I guess."

"Come on, then. Make yourself comfortable," Caleb urged. "I have plenty of time. What's troubling you?"

"I don't know. I just don't know what's going on anymore. Everything's falling apart, and I've done some terrible things. I never meant to be so hard on Sandy. How did I know that his mother is dying of some dreadful disease? I had no idea!"

Michael sat stock still, his hands balled into fists at his sides. Anguish was plainly etched into his features. He looked up from the floor and squinted into Caleb's compassionate gaze. The least hint of condemnation would have sent Michael scurrying, but there was none. Only understanding.

"Yesterday afternoon, when I pulled up in front of the Hawkins' place, Sandy came running out to meet me. Guess he was afraid I'd drive off. I never met anyone who could talk so fast. I let him talk me into renting a campsite for a couple of days. At first, I thought it would be just what I needed. Boy, was I wrong! Right from the start it was a hassle. I couldn't get the tent set up. It kept collapsing on my head. Then, when Sandy showed up, he promptly let me know I'd picked a bad site." Michael paused, his thoughts drifting, replaying the whole scene again in his mind's eye. Each time it looked worse.

"He only wanted to help, but when I saw that newspaper..." Michael's arm shot out to clutch Caleb's shoulder. "I just couldn't think. Know what I mean? I had to get out of that store."

Caleb nodded, but remained silent, waiting for Michael to continue.

"Sandy was the last person on my mind."

"Mm-hmm." The older man waited a moment. "Michael, listen to what you just said."

"What? All I said was that Sandy was the last person on my mind."

"Exactly. But why, Michael? Why was he?"

Silence.

"Because I was so wrapped up in my own misery, I guess. Besides, what does that have to do with any of this?"

"Perhaps nothing...and perhaps everything," was Caleb's noncommittal response. "Think for a moment about the last time you felt genuinely sorry for hurting someone. I don't mean when you regretted your involvement. I mean sorry for their pain. Can you do that?"

With his eyes wide open, Michael sat back and slouched in his chair. He cocked his head and shook it from side to side. "I don't understand what you're asking. I feel a little bad every time I hurt somebody." He sat up and leaned forward as his eyes found Caleb's. "Wouldn't be human if I didn't, would I?"

Caleb's heart went out to the younger man, who, in his distress, was so vulnerable. Never before would Michael have admitted any such feelings. Until now. He could not. The thick walls of protection encasing his heart were rock solid. Caleb saw through the brittle facade, however. He recognized how fragile Michael was...even more so than the most delicate pottery in his front room. Maybe he could distract him before he clammed up.

"Yes, Michael, you are very human. This may be the first time you've ever realized it, though. But we'll get back to that later. Say, I promised to tell you the story of Caleb's Country Corner Retreat. Still want to hear?"

"Sure, go ahead."

"You've seen the place. I think you understand a little of how valuable it is to me. Have any idea why?"

"Uh...no," admitted Michael. "Aside from the fact that it's beautiful here."

"That's one reason, but there are more. I'll do the best I can to explain. First, let me ask you another question. What do you see when you look at me?"

Michael hesitated, not knowing exactly what Caleb had in mind. He took as long as he could, studying him from head to toe before answering. "I see a man in much better shape for his age than anyone I know. Casual, contemporary dress. Striking white hair and teeth. Nice tan. Warm smile. Bright blue eyes with deep laugh lines." His gaze dropped to Caleb's hands. "And strong, yet sensitive hands."

"That's good, and quite complimentary. Thanks. But everything you mentioned is superficial. Just my outward appearance."

"Well, you asked me to describe what I saw."

"True. The real key to Caleb Johannsen, though, is not in what you see, but in what you can't see." He almost smiled at Michael's perplexed expression. "You have no way of knowing what my life has been like. For seventy-seven years, I (not my outside, but the inner me) have been experiencing life—mountaintops of joy and victory mingled with valleys of fear and darkest despair. I would not be the person I am had I not lived each and every day of those seventy-seven years, even if I looked the same and my name was still Caleb Johannsen."

To Michael, Caleb was speaking in riddles. His normally acute senses, honed to razor sharpness through years of discipline, utterly failed him now. "Just what are you getting at?"

"The importance of invisible things, Michael. How many times a day do you stop to think about the air you breathe? Without it you couldn't live," he snapped his fingers for emphasis, "that long. Yet, you can't see it. Unless the wind blows, you can't even feel it, but it's there just the same. You've got to have air, don't you?"

"Of course," Michael nodded and shrugged his shoulders.

"Much in life is like air. We human beings are dependent upon so many things, most of which we're hardly aware of. If we can't perceive it with our five senses, we think it's unimportant. Or nonexistent." He paused and gazed around. "Take the Country Corner, for instance. I know you said it looks beautiful. And it is. But there's much more to it behind the scenes. This property is especially beautiful and precious to me because of everything you can't see, Michael. Like the turning point in my life this place represents. All I gave up to get it. The many years I invested of myself—cleaning, fixing, planting, pruning—the works. You only see the results. The more I'm in touch with the invisible scheme of things, the more valuable this place becomes. Does that make sense?"

"I don't know. I've never given it much thought before."

"You're not the only one. I believe most of us are turned inside out in that regard. Kind of like sweaters. Imagine us all wearing them with the seams and stray yarn showing instead of the intricate design the manufacturer labored over! Pretty ridiculous, huh?"

Michael nodded.

"Well, many people do the same when they think of themselves merely as external individuals—what they look like, the makeup they have on, the clothes they wear, the houses they live in. In short, how other people see them. We've been taught to judge ourselves by our outer appearance and activities—our profession, involvement in civic affairs at home and abroad. Whether or not we're in the jet set is most important. These criteria all comprise the world's rule of 'who we are' these days. Seldom does it count who's really beneath the skin, but that's as foolish as wearing a beautiful sweater inside out." Caleb stopped and looked into Michael's eyes. He had his listener's attention.

"Internal identity is so different. There, we distinguish who we are in character. We know what we stand for; we know what we believe." He stood up and began pacing back and forth. "This generation would rather pass by people and wonder what brand of clothing they're wearing, which is quick and easy to do, than wonder what they're thinking, what they're feeling, how they're hurting, or what their goals, ambitions, and heartaches are. These are the internal things that make a man." He sat back down and leaned toward Michael.

"Fortunately, God doesn't judge us by the external, but by what goes on inside. With Him there is no favoritism because we happen to be wealthy, good-looking, in shape, intelligent, or successful. In fact, those qualities can even hinder us, if we're not careful. He's most concerned about what is unseen. He looks at the heart. This being true, the internal, unseen essentials should be our primary concern in life. Think about how much satisfaction you have derived from your recent acclaim. It felt good for a while, but what happened when things got tough so soon afterward? The thrill of the applause ended instantly. That's the result of worshiping the transient and the temporal—things you can see."

"All that's great, but what does it have to do with the way I treated Sandy?" he asked defensively. "I don't get your point." Then he paused and sat still for a moment. A glimmer of light began to dawn. "Ahhh..." He nodded his head once, slowly, and then again. "So you're saying that I was cruel to Sandy because I was looking at all the wrong things. The outside. The physical. Things like his poverty and lack of education. Is that right?"

"Yes, that's exactly what I'm saying."

"Okay, okay. Maybe you've convinced me. Say I am looking the wrong way. Focusing on the tangible. With the shape my life's in now, it's hard not to look at the obvious. You read that newspaper article, 'Fame to Shame.' That's me. Humiliated. Slapped in the face with a legal document to keep me from my own house and family. Divorce. How can I not look at all that? Come on Caleb. Tell me...how?"

Michael had a hard time asking anyone for advice. Perhaps he was more receptive to Caleb because he was a stranger and quite a few years his senior. Yet, he could still feel anger oozing from his walled-up heart. His "Come on, Caleb...," already tainted with the foul emotion, sounded as much a dare as it was a plea for help. Caleb recognized the plea. He received Michael's cry and let all else fade away untouched.

"I know it looks hopeless now, but I can assure you it isn't. You may be on the verge of the most significant discovery of your life."

Michael shook his head, disbelief written across his face, and slapped both hands on his knees. "Oh, yeah, this is just great!" With a sigh of disgust, he stood up, stomped to the other end of the porch, and turned around, foldind his arms defiantly across his chest. "Next, you'll be telling me this is all part of God's great and glorious plan for my life. Sorry. I'm not buying that."

"You don't have to buy anything. All I ask is that you listen to what I've learned. Will you?"

He thought for a moment before answering. "Okay, just so long as you don't try telling me God is doing this to me." With that, he let go of the railing and sat back down next to Caleb. Settling himself into the chair, he prepared for what he feared would be some long, drawn out sermon on the virtues of suffering.

"There's no way I can tell you I understand exactly what you're going through, Michael. We're two separate people...of different ages, and with different backgrounds. But I can tell you how I made it through some very tough times in my own life. I had given up. I'd had too many surprises, too many booby traps on my climb to the top. It wasn't fun anymore, and I was tired of fighting."

Michael could relate to that. He began listening in earnest, despite his previous misgivings. The description fit him perfectly, and if Caleb had found a way out, maybe there was hope for him, too. Real hope. Not some pie-in-the-sky fairy tale of the Almighty. When he was a youth in Sunday School, before he knew any better, he might have accepted something like that. Now, when all the important parts of his life were slipping through his fingers like water, he needed something rock solid to hold onto.

Caleb picked up the conversation, gesturing with his hands as he spoke. "I was born into a dirt-poor farming family. Every morning it was cows. Somebody else's, no less. Cows, cows, cows! Mooo...mooo ...mooo... Milking cows, feeding cows, cleaning up after cows, then milking the same cows again, day in and day out. It never ended. I swore that as soon as I was old enough to be on my own, I would never look at another cow!"

Michael let out a laugh, in spite himself.

"I made up my mind there would be no stopping me when I could finally leave home. I did get away, but not until years later. Working days and going to school at night, I learned discipline. It paid off in some respects. Even now, I'm thankful for that part of my early training.

"Soon, I was on the road to success. The drive to win burned as a raging fire in my belly. The only goal I had in life was to be a success—to sit at the top and look down on everyone else. You don't make any real friends like that. At the time, it made no difference. Didn't think I needed any, not with the money I was making. You see, I got in on the ground floor of the television industry straight out of college.

"With some serious research beginning in the field, it was wide open for someone with foresight and the administrative ingenuity to pull it all together. Some folks said I was brilliant. Others said I was crazy. All I know for sure is that I made a lot of money—too much too soon, once the ball started rolling. I may have had the discipline to study a situation and make wise decisions, but I was unable to handle wealth and so-called popularity. Money became my god. Even in my dreams, I would see myself fighting and scrapping my way to the top of the business world. Before long, the dream had become reality.

"I 'had it made,' as they say. Whatever I wanted, I got, one way or the other. From all outward appearances, I lacked nothing. But on the inside, something was very wrong. Try as I might, I could not find peace. The more successful I became, the less I experienced those moments when everything satisfied me. Talk about frustrated!"

"Frustrated I can relate to," agreed Michael, "but just what do you mean when you say 'everything?'"

"Money. Power. Prestige. Hobnobbing with the social elite. I had it all." He paused to look straight into Michael's eyes. "All, that is, but the one thing I really needed."

Seeing Caleb now, Michael had a hard time imagining him frustrated. There was such a peace about him. He sure had a calming effect on his surroundings. The agony of the last few days seemed somehow removed as he listened to Caleb's unfolding story. Part of him wanted to stay there as long as he could—forever—if it would ease his own anxiety. Part of him wanted to run. Instead, he changed the subject. "Did you retire here? You must have paid a pretty penny for this place. I wouldn't mind a few years of minor frustration if I could land a piece of property like this," he admitted.

"It didn't happen so easily. When I was a 'success,' I was more than frustrated. I was miserable. And I made everyone around me miserable."

"You're not that way now…at least you don't appear to be." He slid forward to the edge of his chair. "What happened?"

"I quit."

"You what?" Michael could not believe what he was hearing. "What do you mean, you quit?"

"I quit trying to squeeze the universe into my distorted perceptions of what should and shouldn't be. I quit trying to change everyone around me. I quit thinking I knew everything and didn't need anyone else. Most of all, I quit lying to myself and took a long, hard look at my life. Not all this happened overnight, of course, but it did happen.

"At the height of my sought-after success, something broke inside me. I couldn't handle the stress anymore. The dreams I'd enjoyed while going to school, and early on in my career, turned into nightmares. I'd wake up in the middle of the night in a cold sweat, fear clutching at my guts like an icy claw. I'd see myself on a treadmill. At first, the pace was slow and enjoyable, but it kept getting faster and faster until I was staggering, weak-kneed, with my chest ready to explode…

"Then, on the verge of collapse, I'd catch a glimpse of something ugly chasing me. I knew if it caught me, I was finished, so I'd stagger on a bit farther. But it was useless. It kept gaining on me, getting bigger as it came nearer, until it followed only inches behind. Bam! I always woke up at that point. Never did see exactly what was chasing me. All I know is that it was horrible looking. For months, my nights were like that. My days weren't much better."

Caleb drifted into silence as he remembered the nightmares. He could again feel the dread that plagued him, making him wary of even lying down for a nap. And once begun, they completely undermined the stability of his daily routine.

Fear, pain, and suffering defy the boundaries of race, creed, color, and social status. Now he could understand their razor's edge, but not then. They hurt too much. Once the door to fear was opened, he could not shut it. He saw ghosts everywhere he turned. People he considered friends were friends no longer. No one was above suspicion. He was afraid to look in the mirror—afraid of what he might find staring back at him.

Returning to the present, with a shake of his head and a soft sigh, Caleb focused his attention on Michael. "Things got pretty tough there for a while. Once the nightmares began, it wasn't long before my world started to fall apart. Finally, a couple of business associates decided they no longer needed me and pulled some fast ones to try to buy me out."

"Man, that's awful. The bums!"

"At the time, I felt the same way. I realized then I was not as self-sufficient as I thought. When I cried out for help, people turned their backs on me. What few friends I had, left. Said I was getting my 'just desserts.' Not long afterwards, I got real sick. Doctors didn't think I was going to make it. A team of surgeons removed a large tumor from my brain, but they couldn't tell if they got all of it. Faced with that possibility, you'd think money would lose some of its hold on me. Not true. I hated spending another dollar, even for my own life. One day, deep despair set in.

"Lying in the hospital bed, I started going over the accomplishments of my too few years and wondered how much of a mark I'd leave on the world. For the first time, it became important for my life to have meaning. For somebody to remember me fondly after I was gone. Those strange thoughts hit me out of nowhere. I realized that no matter what I'd accomplished, for me at least, it would all cease the moment of my death.

"You won't believe what happened then. On my bedstand, I found a handwritten note, done in beautiful calligraphy. To this day, I don't know who put it there. No one ever owned up to it. The nurses insisted they hadn't seen anyone go into my area in ICU. Anyway, the note read, 'Not to believe in God is to be condemned to a senseless universe.' It's from the writings of Dostoevsky. That all started me thinking about God. About what I'd do if He did exist . . .

"Michael, have you ever considered the thought of standing before the Creator of the entire universe and giving an account of your life? The very real possibility of the existence of God, and that I might indeed have to do that very thing in the immediate future, scared me more than the nightmares. I had heard enough about God and His standards of righteousness to know that my life fell far short.

"While I was mulling all this over on one of the more painfully lonely days, I had a visitor. He'd been around the hospital on a number of occasions. I just never noticed him before. Turned out he was a Christian. He visited the hospital and shared with patients what, to him, was his most precious possession. I remember looking, through eyes dulled by pain, to see him standing at the side of my bed. He took my hand, smiled the kindest smile I'd ever seen, and said to me, 'Jesus loves you, Mr. Johannsen.'"

The words, "*Jesus loves you,*" struck a chord deep within Michael. Where had he heard them before? *Ralph,* he thought. *That was it. Ralph, the ex-convict.* He told him the same thing the last time they were together. "*Jesus loves you, Dr. Michael...*"

Caleb continued after a slight pause. "Yes, sir. The man said to me, '*Jesus loves you*' in the most reassuring way." He relaxed, leaned back in his chair, and settled himself more comfortably while Michael waited for him to continue. Instead, he sat and waited. The minutes dragged by until Michael could stand it no longer.

"Well, what happened then?" he prodded, but Caleb simply sat, smiling as he reminisced about how touched he was to know that God truly did love him. The concept was utterly foreign to his experience. His image of God, until then, was formed around the distorted relationship he had with his father.

As a child, Caleb never knew what it was like to be hugged or even to be comforted in the night when he awoke with a start from a bad dream. He never knew the joy of riding high atop his dad's shoulders and feeling his protective, loving strength. Of course, his dad was not to blame. He could not pass on what he never had himself, but the end result was still the same. So when a total stranger came in and told him that Jesus loved him, he was quite taken by surprise.

"What happened next?" Michael repeated, his impatience bristling.

"I died."

"What!" That was too much for him. "You died? Well then, who am I talking to?" His tone of voice had risen. It was sharp and defensive, like the tone of someone who felt he was being subtly mocked, but wasn't quite sure, and who didn't like it, nevertheless.

"No, Michael. I don't mean physical death. I died to the old me and became 'a new creation, born of God,' as the Bible says. I chose to believe that God did love me unconditionally. He was offering me a free gift. To reject Him, however, would mean eternal separation from Him. At the moment I realized the truth, I thanked Him for dying and rising again to save my soul. I'd had enough hell on earth. Oh, I felt such peace! I *knew* I was forgiven. That's what I meant by 'I died.' I became a born-again follower of Jesus Christ. A Christian. When I did, I found not only the Lord, but life itself."

"And that's what gave you peace? That's what took away all the nightmares and fears? Just becoming a Christian...nothing else?" Michael asked in open disbelief.

"Yes, believe it or not. But that was only the beginning. The next twenty years of walking with Jesus began with the first step. Each day has been another step of a journey into eternity." Caleb lapsed again into silence.

This time Michael did not interrupt him. He was thinking. Oh, how he wanted such peace, but it sounded too simple...almost too good to be true. Much of what Caleb described fit him to a tee. He wanted success. As far back as he could remember, that was what motivated him. He could not stand for anything to come between him and his work. It had seemed all worthwhile at the awards banquet, but no longer.

And what Caleb had said about discovering that God loved him tugged at his own need, deep within. Michael imagined himself a guitar string being stretched and tuned by a master musician. His whole life, he had been a member of a church. Most Sundays you could find him in his regular seat—left-hand side, third pew from the front, on the aisle. He rarely absorbed much from the service. And certainly, he did not feel loved by God. If someone loved you, wasn't he supposed to do good things for you? Anything good that had ever happened to him was a result of his personal effort, he thought. He shuddered to think what would have become of him had he not fought so hard to get ahead. No, it couldn't be as easy as Caleb said.

"Come on," Caleb startled Michael out of his reverie. "I've kept you here on this porch long enough. You haven't seen the grape arbors or been to the potter's wheel, and it's past lunch time already. I'd say you're about ready for a bite to eat."

"To be honest, I haven't even thought about lunch. Hearing about your past kept me spellbound. Now that you mention it, I could use some more of that homemade health food of yours. First, though, can I ask you just one more question?"

"Fire away."

"I've gone to church most of my life, yet it hasn't had nearly the effect on me that you've described. I'm still miserable and my home life has disintegrated. What's the difference?"

"Faith, Michael. The unseen essential."

"Just faith?"

"That's right. Too many say they believe in God, but they don't. What they mean is, they admit that Someone probably created the earth, but they refuse to believe they can know Him intimately. Nor do they want to. True, most people do have faith in something—themselves, another person, their bank account, their talent. Human beings can't live without faith of some kind. Yet, they're completely unaware that the foundation of their belief isn't the least bit secure. It can crumble and vanish in an instant. I'm talking about faith in One who is faithful…One who changes not. And if I could use a single word to sum up the initial step of the unseen essential that makes the difference between a changed and an unchanged life, it would be this—*agreement.*"

"Agreement? Sounds so…ordinary. Almost like a business contract. I don't see how that can change my life."

"Believe me, it can, Michael. You may have gone to church for years, yes, but have you ever agreed with God? Or are you still at odds with Him? That's kind of like being on the opposing team. You may have been trying to come to Him on your terms instead of His. There's a verse in the Old Testament, Amos 3:3, that says it better than I can. It goes like this in the King James Version, 'Can two walk together, except they be agreed?' Think about that for a while. Let's get something to eat. We can talk more later."

SIX

THRESHOLD

MICHAEL AND CALEB enjoyed a light lunch together. The crunchy, raw vegetable-tofu sandwiches on stone ground wheat bread and fresh fruit for dessert were new to Michael. He was quiet as he nibbled on his sandwich. Mostly, he was pondering the word *agreement*. He thought of people he agreed and disagreed with, and why. Stephanie, for one. They had been arguing a lot. The biggest disagreements in his life, though, had been with his father. They never saw eye to eye on anything. His dad criticized him no matter what he did or how well he did it. He was never satisfied. How this fit into agreeing with God, he had no idea. Somehow, he sensed it was important.

After lunch, Caleb led the way to his workshop, where he did most of his pottery making and repair. Peace and orderliness permeated the place. The bench was clean and all the tools hung in rows. Two vessels lay near the wheel itself. They were unfinished and appeared to have been set aside for some future work.

"Michael," Caleb began. "See those two pots over there? I didn't work the clay enough to remove all the lumps before I started shaping. I didn't catch my mistake until the pots were nearly finished. That's why I stopped. I couldn't put them in the fire like they were, or I would have ruined them for good."

"They aren't already?"

"Far from it. I'll soak them in water to soften up the clay, and then I'll be ready to start over. Nothing lost but a little time, and there's plenty of that around here. Of course, it would have been nice to have caught the flaw the first time. You and I are those pieces of clay, and God is the Potter…except that He never misses a single flaw. He hasn't given up on man any more than I've given up on my pots. Agreement with Him is the first step toward getting 'repaired.'"

Michael ran his hand over the marred vessel. "You've mentioned agreement several times, now. Be more specific, would you?"

"Sure, I'll get right to the point. You have never agreed with God. You have been His enemy, so to speak. In a lot of ways, you're like I was, Michael. I worked so hard trying to convince the world that I was wonderful. All I wound up doing was destroying myself. The way you fought to be successful, struggling your way to the top despite the odds, reminds me of my early days in the television industry. I didn't see the truth until years later, when the Christian stood at my hospital bedside. He shared with me something that Blaise Pascal said…that God created man with a 'God-shaped void' within him. In my ignorance I was trying to fill that 'God-shaped void' with human-shaped materials. I think you've been trying to do the same thing."

"You may be right. But I don't understand how I've disagreed with God."

"Okay, let me ask you a question. Do you consider yourself to be a good person? Not just a 'nice guy'—that's different—but a good person?"

"Of course I do," he replied somewhat haughtily.

Caleb looked at him with compassion, noticing his agitation at the question of his goodness. He remembered his own similar fear. Then, slowly and carefully, he chose his words. "Think back, now, to the way you told me you treated young Sandy. You poured your heart out earlier regarding what an insensitive brute you were to him. Tell me, do you consider that good—acting thoughtlessly to an innocent child—partially because he doesn't have as much 'class' as you do? And because you were having your own private pity party?"

Michael winced. He dropped his head. Caleb had him. For a long while he stared quietly at his shoes, still caked with the now-dried morning mud he had forgotten about. He blushed, whether because of his dirty shoes or Caleb's pointed accuracy, he wasn't sure.

"No, Caleb, I wasn't nice at all to Sandy. But...you've gotta take into consideration what's happened to me lately. Doesn't a person get a little slack once in a while? Usually I'm a pretty likable guy." He stopped short and swallowed hard. "Well, I guess Stephanie, for one, wouldn't agree with that, huh?"

"At the moment she doesn't think you're Mr. Nice Guy. That's okay. You're fast approaching the starting point of agreement with God's Word! His standards are way different from yours. He says that not a single one of us is good. We can't make ourselves good, either. No way. Try to see it from His point of view. His is the One that matters."

Michael knitted his eyebrows and nodded slowly.

"You've probably sat in the congregation of your church and heard the message of salvation many times. Then again, maybe you haven't. Some churches don't know what salvation means. John 3:16 says, 'For God so loved the world that he gave his one and only Son, that whoever believes in him shall not perish but have eternal life.' Could it be that you never experienced any lasting change because you never considered yourself to be 'perishing?' That's the way I felt."

Michael stared hard at him and didn't say a word. Caleb pursued him.

"Tell me, what kind of feelings does the word *sinner* bring to mind? Would you classify yourself as one?"

"Absolutely not!" he protested. "A sinner is someone evil who breaks the law and hurts people. I don't do that." Pride seeped into his voice. His thoughts drifted to the only convict he had ever met. Well, ex-convict. Now *Ralph* was a sinner, though he had long since given up his sinner's ways by the time they met.

"A sinner, Michael, is more than someone who deliberately hurts others, though that usually is the end result of sin. Contrary to popular belief, criminals are not the only sinners. According to the Bible, a sinner is anyone who descended from the first man, Adam. That doesn't leave much room for exceptions. And the word *sin* means more than wrongdoing in the usual sense of the word. It means more of a 'falling short of the mark,' like an arrow having been shot at a target but falling to the ground—short of the bull's-eye for lack of strength. In that respect, we have all fallen short of the mark. Always will, too. Not just through our own misdeeds, but because we are born with the 'sinful nature' of Adam."

"Caleb, that's hard to swallow. I've never met the man who supposedly blew it in some garden thousands of years ago."

"No, but his nature was passed down to you through the generations. You inherited it, somewhat like you inherited your olive skin and dark hair from your ancestors. For years, I totally disagreed with God on His most basic premise when I fought against admitting I was a sinner. Romans 3:23 says 'all have sinned.'"

He rubbed his chin as he searched for the right words. "Whether I believed I was or not didn't change the facts one iota, any more than whether or not I believed in the law of gravity would change the facts. It is a law that's built into the universe. Let's say I jumped off a ten-story building. Would it make any difference if I decided I didn't agree with the law of gravity when I jumped? I would still perish, wouldn't I?" He paused for Michael to let that sink in.

"Obviously, Caleb. Well, unless you had a parachute...or a hang glider. Or even a net down below."

"Right. I would need something outside myself to save me, because the law of gravity is unyielding. When the Christian fellow came into my hospital room and began telling me of Jesus' love for me, in spite of my sinfulness, it cut right through all my carefully maintained facades of self-righteousness. Love has a magnificent way of doing that."

All the while they were talking, they had been standing in front of the potter's wheel. Michael imagined God's hand, like the extremity of some giant, searching for a flaw, then crushing him to powder against a spinning piece of steel. It sent shivers down his spine. That did not sound like love to him. "Caleb, can we go outside for a bit? This old potter's wheel makes me nervous," he added with an embarrassed chuckle.

"Sure, if you'll tell me how a potter's wheel can make you nervous." Squinting against the afternoon sun, Michael followed him around to the side of the building where the grape arbor stood. "Come on, out with it. What's with the potter's wheel?" Caleb asked.

"It's silly, but I kept imagining God reaching down to crush me like one of those flawed pots you showed me. That's like my father claiming he loved me, yet going for months without talking to me because I didn't meet one of his outrageous expectations. If God is like that, I don't *want* to know Him." He reeked of bitterness as he spat out the words.

"Michael, Michael," Caleb said, turning to face the younger man and grasping his shoulders firmly, giving them an encouraging squeeze, "your father was only a man. You can't let his weaknesses influence your perception of God. God is God. His love for you is not dependent upon anything you do or don't do. He loves you and me merely because He chooses to...on the merit of what Jesus did." Caleb's face tightened and his eyes narrowed. He spoke with intensity.

"You must understand that the laws of a just, holy God are uncompromising. They are more unyielding than the law of gravity. Whoever tries to defy them is crushed in the long run. No one can ever measure up to God's standards. That's why we all need a Savior. Then, the potter's wheel, instead of being an instrument to crush us because of His ruthless demand for perfection, becomes an example of His patience with those He has chosen to love. God does love you, my friend. I know that with the situation you're in now, it might be hard to believe, but it's true. Looking only at the crushing blows of circumstances causes you to come away with half a truth. He proved His love on Calvary two thousand years ago."

Michael listened intently.

"When I finally grasped this fact, it staggered me. It's a good thing I was lying down in that hospital bed. God wanted me to be close to Him! Yet, He knew it was inconceivable because of that original sin of Adam in me. So He did the only thing that could make it possible for me to come to Him. He paid for my sin with His own blood. Remember John 3:16? He loved me so much, He died for me...and He died for you. We both needed it. He died for the world, too, but most of the world refuses Him. They don't believe they need to be 'saved' from anything. In fact, in their arrogance, they scoff at the idea. They think they're good enough to work their way to heaven. Or they're good enough to avoid hell. What a rude awakening they'll have one day. In other words, they choose to stay at odds with God.

"Instead of simply agreeing with the value He has already placed on them, despite their sin, they try to prove their self-worth over and over again through accomplishments and possessions. What an exercise in futility! When situations change, out goes their sense of self-worth. Finally, their lives have no stability at all. My own need to prove myself lessened when I realized that God loved me enough to suffer and die for me when I wouldn't give Him the time of day. God's love never changes. Once you begin to know Him, you'll understand better what I'm saying."

Agreement, to Michael, meant completely accepting something for what it was. How could he agree with something he knew so very little about? But Caleb's arguments had touched the core of some crucial doubts, and in spite of his earlier denial, he felt drawn by them. He was being told that the first step out of his present darkness was coming into agreement with God. But yet, to really love God and to trust Him with his life, he needed to know Him first. He was confused.

"Aren't you taking an awful lot for granted, Caleb?" he asked teasingly. "I never said anything about agreeing for certain, did I?"

"No, you didn't." With a twinkle in his blue eyes, he dropped his hands from Michael's shoulders. "At least you haven't said anything yet." He grew more serious. "Don't put off the most critical decision of your life. It's nothing to play around with. Adam agreed with Eve about the fruit instead of with God. Look where it got him…and us."

"All right, already. I'll admit, I'm accepting more than I ever have before. I do want the peace you spoke of…the peace I see in you. It seems to fill the whole place here. You say I can have it, too, if I start agreeing with God? I'll be honest with you, Caleb. A month ago I wouldn't have listened to half of what you've been telling me, much less believed it."

"Then that explains why God didn't bring you here until now. He knew you weren't quite ready. But, today, you listened. God's Word explains how faith comes—by hearing the Word. And the Word spells it out very plainly in 1 Corinthians 15:3–4, 'that Christ died for our sins.' You've heard what He has to say about your sin, His love, and your need to be rescued. I've told you what He's done for me." Caleb paused and looked at him for a sign that Michael was still absorbing what he was saying. He was pleased at what he saw. Michael seemed to be deep in thought, but a brightness shone in his eyes, hinting at something good taking place within. Indeed, that was just what was happening. Caleb stopped there. He knew Michael would never be pushed simply for the sake of convenience. Experience had taught him that God was fully capable of completing what He'd begun. He was in His hands now.

Without saying another word, Caleb resumed a measured pace. The view from that perspective was breathtaking. Each passing year served only to heighten his appreciation of the beauty of God's handiwork. The two men began there at the side of the building where the grapevines grew in rows along the gentle rise of the land. Caleb bent over to examine the grapes hanging in clusters from his meticulously trimmed vines. On each one, the grapes grew thick and heavy, causing the branches to hang down low to the ground. It would soon be harvest time. And, oh, how he loved the taste of fresh grapes! He could feel the cool juices tingling his taste buds already.

Michael came alongside, only listening to the soft sound of their footsteps. His thoughts ranged far and wide over the last thirty years of his life. It was true, what Caleb quoted about emptiness inside. What was it... "a God-shaped void?" Even before being faced with the loss of his wife and children, that empty ache was there. He could almost ignore it by submerging himself in his work. Almost, but not quite. There was still a part of him, like a dull toothache, that nagged at him, destroying his peace.

"Caleb, so much of my life is in turmoil, where do I start? You said Jesus changed you. I know He wants to change me, and I think, my situation. But where first? It's overwhelming. Discouraging, as a matter of fact."

"Don't let it be." Caleb walked to where the ground once again began its gentle sloping. "Look out over there—the vegetable garden, the grove of fruit trees, those lovely grapes, the pond stocked with fish, the birds enjoying the feeders and bath. What kind of shape do you think this place was in when I bought it?"

Michael surveyed the view. "I don't know, but it couldn't have been that bad."

"Well, you're right," Caleb admitted, "nothing is ever as bad as it seems once we begin agreeing with God. But this place was pretty rough...terribly overgrown. I was able to see past the results of neglect to the possibilities. Don't you think God can do that with you? Your circumstances seem dark now, and you may not feel you have faith enough to survive. We all have times like that, even after we've been walking with the Lord for years."

He reached into his back left pocket and produced a worn, miniature New Testament. "Here is a passage of Scripture to always remind you of agreement. It's the same one God used to confirm His desire to give me this place for a retreat. It's in the gospel according to Matthew." He began reading from Matthew 13:44, "The kingdom of heaven is like treasure hidden in a field. When a man found it, he hid it again, and then in his joy went and sold all he had and bought that field."

"In God's eyes, Michael, you are that hidden treasure. Jesus left all the glory He had in heaven to buy you back from Satan. You are worth Calvary to Him, and so are we all. Agree with that and you won't have to suffer from low self-esteem again. There's another side to it, though. He is also your hidden treasure, and He gave the Holy Spirit to live within you. Believe Him. He'll help you cut through the underbrush of your failures. In your weakness, He is strong. He does His part. You do your part.

"Let me put it another way. What did you do in college when you had an exam coming up? You did your part by studying. To have showed up unprepared and then ask God for a perfect grade would have been presumptuous. However, if you had asked Him to guide your preparation for the exam and to keep your mind clear, that would be a more reasonable way of working with Him. His part and your part. You could then rest contentedly, knowing He would provide, whatever the outcome. The same is true with the challenges you face in your personal life."

"Test-taking, I know about," nodded Michael. "I lost count of how many I've taken." He hesitated. "Guess what I'm going through now is another kind of test." For the space of a dozen heartbeats, he paused, then turned to face Caleb. "I do need your help." Tears glistened in his eyes.

"You'll get whatever help I can give you, but all I can do is point you to Jesus Christ. I can't fix your marriage or even bring you to your children. He can. Turn to Him. His way is the only way." Soon their steps had carried them to the crest of a hill, up to a white latticework gazebo. "Care to sit? It's such a beautiful sight from here. You can see all the land and the sunset. It's a wonder to behold. When I want to be reminded of the awesomeness of God's love, I come here."

"You're so sure of His love, aren't you? There doesn't seem to be any room for doubt in your mind." Michael hesitated. His head hung low. But then he squared his jaw with determination and looked full into the startling blue eyes of his new friend. A bit sheepish at first, he offered, "I...I guess I'm ready, Caleb. I do want what you have." Once he'd gotten it out, all trace of hesitancy left his voice. "I need to know the peace of God, too."

"Then come to Jesus. Simply agree with what you do know of Him at this point. Remember though, you can't enjoy the peace of God without first coming to know Him. The gift is inseparable from the Giver." Caleb was emphatic.

"That doesn't change anything. I still need that assurance. You're right about me being a sinner who needs to be saved. I'm a mess. As for His love, I can't really feel it, but I guess I'll just have to take your word...no, His Word...for it." Michael paused, groping for the right phrases. "I've listened to all you said, and I'm not stupid, but...well, I just don't know how to start. Will you help me?"

This was a turning point for Michael Nastasis. He and Caleb knelt down together. With no outside pressure—only the gentle tug of the Holy Spirit—he confessed his need of a Savior and thanked Him for the forgiveness of his sins. Where years of church attendance and misconceptions had proved fruitless, pure love conquered. In that instant, from unbelief to belief, and from death unto life, as Caleb led him in a profession of faith, he became a new man. A born-again Christian. He accepted the biblical account of Jesus Christ—that He was born of a virgin, lived a pure and sinless life, died on the cross, was buried, and then rose from the dead three days later to be seated at the right hand of the Father. All this would save Michael from eternal separation from God. He believed the gospel in 1 Corinthians 15:3–4.

Along with an intellectual assent to the truth, Michael agreed in his heart. He wondered why he had not seen the truth years ago. It made so much sense, which surprised him. One of the few Christian books he ever read, *Kingdoms in Conflict,* by Chuck Colson, came to mind. Chuck said that faith did not require a person to give up a rational mind. Michael had doubted it at the time he read the book, thinking, "*Sure, it would take a real fool to 'turn the other cheek' in today's society. He'd get eaten alive.*"

Somehow, Michael no longer considered it foolish. The first indication of his change of heart was his uneasiness towards his previous thoughts of the foolishness of turning the other cheek. He knew he had been wrong.

As they rose from their knees, their eyes were misty. Caleb extended his hand to shake Michael's and spoke first. "Welcome to the family of God, son!"

He smiled. "Thanks...Dad. Faith...I have it now, right?"

"Sure do. Say, do you remember my sharing Romans 10:17 from the New King James Version, 'Faith comes from hearing, and hearing by the word of God?'" Michael nodded. "The same Jesus you just acknowledged as Savior and Lord is the Word made flesh! That's only the beginning. Faith you need to live by grows as your knowledge of Scripture increases."

Caleb threw his arm around Michael's shoulders and gave them an encouraging squeeze. "What do you say we head on back? I've got some things there I'd like you to see."

"Sure. Lead the way." Caleb let go of Michael's shoulders and turned to follow the well-worn path to the house.

"Tell me, Michael, deep down inside...how do you feel? Not that you should judge by your emotions, but I'm just curious."

"I don't feel like the same person. It's almost as if I've been living with a five-hundred-pound weight strapped to my back and didn't even know it. The weight's gone, Caleb. As sure as I'm talking to you, it's gone!"

"That's just one of the results of agreeing with God. A lot of that weight came from the inner conflict between the desire to conform to the world's expectations and to your own. Agreeing with God calls a peace treaty—peace of mind and peace of heart."

"I feel free, too."

"Mm-hmm. A sense of freedom is another result of salvation. By faith, you have been forgiven and made righteous in Christ. But...in turn, out of gratitude, you must learn to forgive all who sin against you, no matter how badly they hurt you. Agreement will strengthen your family relationships, especially the one with your wife." Caleb paused so he could ponder that one. "When you turn to the Bible for direction, you'll find that it doesn't *suggest* that husbands and wives live at peace with each other. It commands it!'

"Whoa, hold on there, now. I'm not the one wanting the divorce," objected Michael. "What can I do?"

"That's where faith comes in. If you have done any wrong to her, make it right. Ask forgiveness for whatever you may have done to hurt her. And, most important of all, believe God. Take Him at His Word. *Search* the Bible for specific promises about the sanctity of marriage. He will lead you if you keep an open heart, because marriage is a covenant similar to the covenant God makes with His people. He will never divorce you. For the time being, let's leave that topic there. We'll try to get back to it, okay?"

By this time, they had reached the door to Caleb's workshop. "Feel any better about the potter's wheel?" asked Caleb with a smile, his blue eyes sparkling.

Michael glanced over at it. "You bet."

"Good. Well, it's time I did some work around here. I've been blessed by our time together. You're welcome to hang around while I work on straightening up those damaged pots and see what else I can come up with."

"Thanks, but I think I'll go on in. You said there was something you wanted me to see."

"Oh, that's right. Make yourself comfortable. I'll run in and get it." Minutes later Caleb returned with a manila envelope and notebook under his arm and a Bible in his right hand. It was not the same Bible he had been reading earlier, but it could pass for a twin. The only telltale difference was its less-used condition. "Here...my friend and new brother in Christ," he said warmly, extending the Bible to Michael. "This is yours to keep. And here's the paper I've been working on for some time now that I'd like you to read over. It may answer more of your questions. When you get some quiet time, check it out." He handed the envelope to Michael, who received it with a nod of his head and a soft thanks. "If you need anything, I'll be out here for a couple hours. Once I get started, I lose track of time. Don't hesitate if something comes up, okay? Just make yourself at home."

"Sure. I'll be fine." Michael turned and walked back to the main house. Instead of going in the back door, he wandered around to the front. He wanted to get another look at the place from there. Something about Caleb's Country Corner Retreat appealed to him way down at the center of his being. What it was, he had no idea.

SEVEN

CHANGES

Fingers of red streaked the evening sky. From his room's balcony, Michael enjoyed the heavenly display as the sun neared the horizon. He started skimming through the contents of the manuscript Caleb had been working on. "It may answer more of your questions," he had said. That was enough to spur Michael to reading. The first heading sparked his interest, and he set out in earnest to digest the contents of the paper.

KNOWING AND GROWING

Knowing God forms the basis for agreement with Him, but is also the end result. Nurturing our identification with Christ sets the stage for us to live godly lives. This is where the problems of sin can be dealt with and where we are made righteous in Him. Because we have accepted His mercy for all our behavior—past, present, and future—we take on His peace and His power.

Ah, he thought, *this is what Caleb was talking about earlier.* With increasing interest, he continued.

Maturity in Christ often has little to do with a person's physical age. In 1 John 2, John differentiates between three specific stages of the spiritual maturation process in which agreement plays a vital role. The first stage is for those who are new in the Lord. He expounds, "I write to you, dear children, because your sins have been forgiven on account of his name" (1 John 2:12). Adolescent Christians comprise the second stage. "I write to you, young men, because you have overcome the evil one" (v. 13). The third stage is that of a mature Christian adult. "I write to you, fathers, because you have known him who is from the beginning" (v. 14).

John speaks of the "little child" as one who knows the basics of faith. He simply understands that his sins have been forgiven. All future spiritual growth must be built upon this important foundation. "Young men" are those with more experience who have overcome the wicked one. And how do they overcome the wicked one? By abiding in God's Word. The Word is the source of their strength. The path of spiritual victory is to live by the power of the Spirit, appropriating the daily intake of God's Word. We must meditate on it, believe it, savor it, embrace it, treasure it, hide it in our hearts, and obey it. The Word of God is God's voice to our souls, and it is attended with the same power that God evidenced in the creation of the world in Genesis 1. This "Life in the Word" is a vital element of spiritual growth. Finally, John says the criteria for spiritual fathers is that they know God. Note carefully that fathers are secure and selfless enough to "grow others up." This is perhaps the greatest need in the church today.

Michael set the paper down and looked out at the ever-changing sky. He thought, *That's what Caleb is to me—a spiritual father. He's saying I'm a child because I've just realized my sins are forgiven. I guess he must be trying to help me mature, since he knows God and I don't. Interesting. I've never thought of myself as needing to "grow up..."* Michael shifted in his seat and continued reading:

To know God and feel comfortable with Him is to become familiar with Him, but how do we become familiar with the One who, with a word, framed the heavens? How do we approach

One whose face we are not permitted to see? It should be more than obvious that this can be no ordinary friendship.

To love someone, whether spouse, children, or friends, implies that we think about them often. It requires no effort to see their faces in our mind's eye. We know each one's features in detail. Knowing what they look like enhances our feeling of knowing them and being close to them. Writers throughout the Bible yearned to see the face of God. Yet, this desire will not be attained until they, and we, are with Him in eternity. (See 1 Corinthians 13:12; Revelation 22:4.)

When Moses asked to see God's glory, He responded by saying that no man could see His face and live (Exodus 33:20). Though we truly love Him and long to commune with Him, we, like Moses, wish we could first see His face. Just a glimpse. For now, He is invisible, but there is still a way we can know Him. Jesus! He is the perfect image of the invisible God, and by reading His Word, we can know God's nature and His thoughts.

What do Christians mean when they say they have a "personal relationship" with the Lord? Is it possible to have a personal relationship with Almighty God? Presumptuous some would think. We don't have the same luxury as the Old Testament patriarchs—Abraham, Isaac, and Jacob, or even Moses—who heard God speak out loud to them and who experienced His power firsthand. So does that leave us out in the cold? On the contrary. Our potential is even greater because His Spirit lives within us as born-again Christians.

Michael mused aloud, "That's why Caleb made sure I had a Bible—so I'd be able know God better. My church hardly ever used one. As for this agreement thing...well, I can agree with God in the areas I know of now—the basics. It must be a lifelong process of learning and agreeing, then learning and agreeing some more. So...I've just started. The more I know Him, the less He and I will be at odds, I guess." Picking up the pages to bring them into a better light, he continued reading:

SELFISHNESS, A STUMBLING
BLOCK TO GROWTH

Many of us go through life trying to climb to the top of our professional fields. We want to be the very best. Science, medicine, economics, business, or education...it matters little. The race to the top is the same, regardless. Fighting and elbowing our way to the pinnacle of our respective pile, we wind up on the bottom of life because we're missing the very center, which is Christ. We must come to a point of agreement where we understand who He is, who we are in relation to Him, and what He considers important. Climbing to the top or having the most "toys" is not what pleases God.

Oftentimes, our line of sight is fixed only on the horizontal. Today's philosophies train young people early to value things more than people. We all focus on what we can acquire rather than on what we can give. Such an attitude of consumerism has become a way of life, crossing the boundaries into Christian camps. It has insidiously wormed its way in and destroyed the church's sense of values concerning this most important of all relationships. Many of us want to know exactly what the church can do for us before we join. Before some of us will even give our lives to Jesus Christ, we want to know the complete "benefits package," as we would before accepting an employment opportunity. From that moment on, we pray, asking Him to give, give, give. Selfishness reigns. How many people go to church just to share or, better yet, live their lives filled with a desire to give to God? Not many. Can we expect to grow close to Him when we haven't the faintest idea of what it means to be in a relationship with Him—the Creator of heaven and earth?

While Michael read, the sun settled completely out of sight. So caught up in the words unfolding before him, he never even noticed the time slipping by. His own susceptibility to a consumerist mentality was apparent. Just that afternoon he had fallen prey to it, and he recoiled at the thought. In essence, he had told Caleb he would agree with God so he could have peace of mind. Not because God was God, but just for what he could get out of Him. Not good. Reading Caleb's paper was almost like reading about his whole life, especially the part about fighting his way to the top. He could see the need for some drastic changes. Turning the page to see what the next section held in store, he read the heading, "Doubt and Unbelief." That was a good stopping point for the moment. He laid the manuscript on the desk and made his way downstairs.

Caleb closed his workshop with the onset of darkness. He preferred to work in the light of day. It seemed to him less harsh, softer somehow than artificial fluorescent light. Silly? Probably. Nevertheless, he humored himself and used this as his cutoff point. Over the years, it had become ingrained into his daily routine.

Often, his time at the potter's wheel served a dual purpose. While reworking the not-quite-ready clay, he prayed and meditated on Scripture. Today, his prayers centered around the new Christian in his care. How he wanted to save him from the pain of all he was going through! But to do so would not serve God's greater purpose for his young life. Whatever the future held for Michael Nastasis, the present was God's time, and His alone, to set him on the right path. He would only get in the way and hinder the Lord's work, so he prayed that Michael would receive with an open heart. By the time he closed up shop and showered, Michael was waiting for him in the front room. He was ready with questions, too.

"How'd your work go?" he asked with a measure of concern. "Did you get the two flawed pieces straightened out?" The answer was important to him. Perhaps he was unconsciously comparing himself to one of them.

Caleb reassured him, "The work went swell. They're coming along just fine. How'd it go with you? Did you get settled in upstairs?"

"Mm-hmm. I chose a room with a good view of the setting sun, like you suggested. It was beautiful. Say, let me ask you something." He paused for a reaction. When all he got was a twinkle from Caleb's blue eyes, he continued, "You wrote that paper, correct?"

"Yes, along with some input from others. It's a theme that has been on my heart and in my prayers for some time, but I give the Lord credit for anything worthwhile."

"Do you meet many guys in my situation?"

"No. Why do you ask?"

"Well, if I didn't know better, I'd swear you were writing about me. That's impossible, and yet..." Caleb let the silence build, knowing there was more to come. "My consumerist nature showed this afternoon. You probably think I was pretty selfish, when all I wanted was God's peace, huh? I'm kind of embarrassed."

"Oh, don't be...not with me anyway. Talk to the Lord about it. That's between you and Him, you know."

"Okay, I'll try." He hesitated. "Another thing. I've hardly mentioned Sandy all day, and that was why I originally wanted to talk to you."

"Whenever you get ready, I'm ready. I'm not going anywhere."

"It's just that...well...I still feel bad about the way I treated Sandy. Talking to you and reading your paper made me think more about my selfishness. Do you realize my entire life has been motivated by a desire to succeed to build up my own ego? What was it you wrote about? 'Those who scramble to the top actually wind up on the bottom of life.' Something like that, wasn't it?" He paused, dropped his gaze to his tightly clasped hands, then looked up, imploring Caleb. "But what else is there? If you take that drive away, there's nothing left...

"And after seeing my photo on the front page like that, I kind of went into shock. I had one thought—I was ruined! I think I was afraid—afraid of losing my grip on life. That was all I could think about. I never stopped to consider Sandy." Ashamed of his actions, yet willing to admit them, he looked up at his friend. Caleb sat silently—listening. Not a word slipped by him, but now was not the time either for lecturing or preaching. It was a time for accepting. Michael searched his friend's expression. The least hint of condemnation would have been enough to inhibit him. Like before, there was nothing but loving acceptance. "I know you feel badly about how you treated the little guy, but it's forgiven, as far as God is concerned."

Thus encouraged, Michael continued, "Well, what do you think I should do about Sandy, though? I don't want to just go off without at least trying to explain and tell him I'm sorry."

"Good point. I'm glad you came up with the idea yourself—it shows spiritual growth. Here's a suggestion: I'm planning to go over to the Hawkins' next week. Their house needs painting, as I'm sure you noticed. We've already scraped off all the loose stuff, so we'll start applying the primer. A few shutters need tightening, and there are some other odds and ends to do. Care to come along? You'd get a chance to talk with Sandy and make your amends." He stopped and chuckled. "Then again, you might not get a word in edgewise! He does love to chatter. Meanwhile, until next week, spend as much time as you can reading your Bible and getting to know God better. That, my friend, is of the utmost importance."

Michael smiled and nodded. The two men sat quietly, listening to the night sounds of the country. "It would be easy to get to know God out here. It's so peaceful. I haven't heard a single roaring truck or screeching siren all day, and I haven't missed either one." He sighed. "You know something? In all the years I went to church, no one ever told me to read the Bible. When I did glance at it now and then, I could hardly understand a word. Where's a good starting place?"

Caleb, hands folded together under his chin, straightened and turned to Michael. "I'd say the book of John. Before you leave, I'll put together a few suggestions for some regular Bible reading, plus a passage or two for study. I like to refer to the people in them as the 'Olympians of Faith.' The Word is filled with stories of men and women who knew what it meant to live by faith. Read their stories. Study them. Feed on them. Each one contains a message just for you. God has taught, comforted, and encouraged me as I studied the lives of those proven faithful in the past."

"I'll need encouragement, that's for sure."

"True. I think you'll enjoy Hebrews 11, the 'Roll Call of the Faithful.' It discusses many of these great spiritual athletes who discovered true knowledge, friendship, and power. Victory was not an instant accomplishment for any of them. They conditioned and strengthened themselves in much the same way as modern athletes train for competition. Each one exhibited a day-by-day commitment, and yet, when their lives were over, they had this testimony—they were found faithful."

"Okay, Caleb. It's a deal—the book of John and Hebrews 11. I'd planned on turning in early, but I'll get started reading, now that you've pointed me in the right direction. First, though, I'm ready for some more of your home cooking. You may make a health nut out of me yet."

———

Supper was another culinary delight. Maybe it was Michael's new start in life, but even the foods tasted fresher—the tangs tangier and the spices spicier. Crisp raw vegetable salad, tossed lightly, baked fresh yams, steamed broccoli, and swordfish steaks, marinated, then grilled on a little hibachi made up the menu. As Michael watched the swordfish sizzle, his mouth watered from the zesty aroma. He could hardly wait to taste the meal. When all was ready, he was not disappointed. It was delicious and satisfying.

After dinner, they cleaned up the dishes together and enjoyed the camaraderie. When all was put away and they were comfortably settled in the study, they prayed, giving thanks to God just for being who He is. They prayed for specific situations, too—the restoration of Michael's marriage, his children, his future at work, Sandy and his mother, and guidance for themselves.

Deep peace flooded Michael's spirit. Obeying the urge to start reading on his own, he excused himself for the evening. Once he was situated at the desk in his room, he began at Hebrews 11:4, "By faith Abel offered God a better sacrifice than Cain did. By faith he was commended as a righteous man, when God spoke well of his offerings. And by faith he still speaks, even though he is dead."

From a second notebook Caleb had given him as a study help, he started to read:

> Abel, the first of the Old Testament Olympians, provides a prime example of someone who agreed with God. God commended him not only because of his sacrifice, but because of his faith. From antiquity to eternity, Abel has a message for believers. To have acted "by faith," he must have heard God speak on the importance of offerings. How else would he have known that only a blood sacrifice would do? The Bible declares that faith comes in one way only—by hearing the Word of God. From this, we can deduce that both Cain and Abel heard God. He would not have rejected Cain's offering, otherwise. Abel moved beyond hearing. He believed without question. Without hesitation. And he demonstrated his belief through his actions.
>
> Another message speaks from eons past. Abel offered acceptable and proper worship because his animal sacrifice was something for which he could take no credit. In contrast, Cain's

offering was only from the land over which he had labored. (Remember that God had cursed the land after Adam and Eve sinned in the Garden of Eden.) God's approval cannot be earned through any work of the flesh. "Only by faith!" cries the righteousness of Abel to our present generation. Faith accepts God at His Word.

To worship God as He desires, we must choose to present our bodies to Him as a "living sacrifice," Paul writes in Romans 12. If our obedience is but mere formality, an attempt to gain acceptance through a multitude of works, shouldn't we, too, be rejected by the Lord? Are we any better than Cain? No, unless we, like Abel, worship Him correctly on the basis of a blood sacrifice. We don't need animals anymore—not since Calvary. Just wholehearted faith in the blood sacrifice of Jesus Christ on the cross. The choice is ours—today, tomorrow, and every day for the rest of our lives.

Michael stared long at that last line. He was going on forty-years-old, and today was the first time he had truly come into agreement with God. Yes, he had made the right choice. Tomorrow was another day. He would make tomorrow's choices tomorrow. For the moment, he rested in the assurance that he had made at least one right decision.

Things were beginning to grow clearer in Michael's mind. He knew he wanted Abel's kind of faith and shuddered at the thought of being rejected by God. "Help me, Lord," he prayed, "to believe Your Word. I want to be like Abel, not Cain." The peace of God filled him, and for the moment, all fears about the future vanished in its wake.

He set aside the notebook and manuscript on the desk, then dressed for bed and crawled between the cool, soft sheets. Propping himself up on his pillow, he opened the Bible that Caleb had given him to the gospel of John. Motivated from his reading of Abel, he read with expectancy, "In the beginning was the Word, and the Word was with God, and the Word was God." A couple of chapters later, he fell sound asleep with the open Bible lying on his chest.

Morning light filtered through the partially opened shades. Back at the desk, Michael looked up from his Bible. Normally not such an early riser, he had been up and reading since the first hint of dawn brightened the morning sky. The joy of yesterday's decision and new knowledge lingered. Even with his life at its most trying point, he woke up with a smile on his face and a hunger in his heart.

Reading those first chapters of John before going to sleep had unlocked a new door that opened wider now. Insight pierced areas hidden behind impenetrable walls. Jesus was no longer some vague person from centuries past who claimed to be God. He was God—with skin on. So precious to Michael was the sense of being protectively enfolded in the arms of the Almighty, that it drew him onward, stoking the fire of zeal for his Lord.

While Michael was in his room reading, Caleb was downstairs reading and praying. Much of his prayer time concerned Michael. Experience had taught him that the new Christian would face many challenges and difficult decisions in the coming days. How he approached them would determine future patterns. He could run to God or he could slip back into old habits. Caleb, knowing the need, interceded for him. Like Jesus praying for Peter, he did not ask God to spare Michael from any of the testings, nor the attacks of Satan within those trials. Satan desired to sift him as wheat, hoping he would walk away from his newfound faith. Caleb prayed—oh, how he prayed—that Michael's faith would not fail. He would become a mighty man of God, if Caleb had any say in the matter.

Later that morning, after a light breakfast and a brief introduction to the joy of running (Michael walked most of the way), he expressed the desire to get back and face whatever awaited him at work. "No sense delaying the inevitable," he remarked glumly when Caleb asked him if he was ready.

"True, Michael, but remember, don't be discouraged by appearances. You have the same Holy Spirit within you that raised Jesus Christ from the tomb. Listen to Him. Obey Him, and you will see circumstances and situations change. More important yet, you'll change in response to them."

"I know... I read my Bible last night and again this morning, and I did

notice something. Jesus was in control everywhere He went. He never
forced anyone; He just met them at their point of deepest need. Then he
called them and they followed." He sighed and shook his head. "Still, I
can't say I'm looking forward to going back to work. Kinda dreading it,
in fact."

"That's understandable. Your old ego suffered a pretty tough blow."
He paused and thought a moment. "Say, would it help any to hear about
a couple of guys who faced their own threatening situation with courage?"

Michael nodded halfheartedly. "It sure wouldn't hurt."

"Well, in my opinion, these two stand among the Olympians of Faith.
Ever heard of Joshua and Caleb?" He cocked his head and raised his
eyebrows.

"Joshua, vaguely. You're the only Caleb I've ever heard of."

"Wait 'til I tell you about the guy whose namesake I am. Maybe he
and old Josh'll encourage you. Let's start with our talk yesterday on
agreement. Joshua and Caleb agreed with God. It was their trademark.
They believed He would do just as He had promised, and they acted
upon their faith. Literally, it saved their lives.

"Joshua was born during the years of bondage to Egypt and grew up
under Moses' leadership. He witnessed firsthand the power of God in
the parting of the Red Sea and water springing from the rock to satisfy
the thirsty multitudes. He led the men into a victorious battle against
their enemy at Rephidim, while Moses held up the rod of God. All these
miracles took root in the fertile soil of Joshua's heart.

"Not too long after this victory, Moses chose twelve spies to search out
the Promised Land of Canaan in preparation for conquest. Joshua and
Caleb were included in the twelve-man crew. They entered Canaan and
saw that it did, indeed, overflow with milk and honey. The only trouble
was that giants were included in the package. Ten of the twelve spies
chose to be moved by what they saw, as if God had been misinformed
when He promised them the land. They ignored God's commitment
and brought back such a discouraging report that they persuaded the
rest of the Israelites to rebel. Those ten, and the entire generation that
had come out of Egypt, died without ever entering the Promised Land.
Why? Because of their refusal to agree with God.

"Even in the midst of such rebellion, God had his faithful remnant.

Joshua and Caleb stood as two rays of light shining forth in the darkness of doubt. They saw the same giants, but chose to believe God anyway, going so far as to bring back huge clusters of grapes to show the people. Those two agreed that what God said was already an established fact. He had promised them Canaan; therefore, it was theirs. Caleb told the people in Numbers 13:30, 'We should go up and take possession of the land, for we can certainly do it.'

"Follow that same path, Michael. During the drive home, meditate on that verse as well as 2 Timothy 1:7, 'For God did not give us a spirit of timidity, but a spirit of power, of love and of self-discipline.' Agree with Him first. Then ask Him to help you meet your colleagues."

Michael hesitated. "You make it sound so easy. Wish you could go and face all those gawking people instead of me." He got up from the table and headed upstairs to pack. At the foot of the staircase, he stopped and turned to Caleb. "I didn't mean to be so abrupt. Sorry. Guess I'm kind of tense. Just last night before I went to bed, I prayed for the same kind of faith Abel had. I hoped I wouldn't be like Cain. Or worse yet, like those who saw Jesus' miracles and still refused to believe. Looks like I need a good dose of Joshua and Caleb's courage, too. Right now I feel as full of unbelief as the ten spies."

"There's a difference between unbelief and doubt, Michael. Some doubt is natural for a new Christian and could even be considered an essential component of the thought process. Can you imagine any adult believing everything he was told, without question?" He shook his head for emphasis. "When you find yourself beginning to dispute the things of God, however, it's usually because you don't know who He is or have forgotten His faithfulness in past situations. That's what happened to the Israelites in the wilderness. They had seen the Red Sea part, had eaten manna from heaven daily, and had witnessed many other miracles, but they still questioned His ability to sustain them in times of trouble. And talk about incessant complaining! Too bad they never learned the lessons of praise and thanksgiving—focusing on the eternal, unseen things of God and rejoicing in Him. Praise dispels doubt."

"You mean, that's all I need to do if I ever start to doubt?" Michael wondered in awe.

"There's a little more to it than that, but gratitude does play a very important role." Caleb got up and joined him at the stairs. He clapped his hand on his shoulders. "Come on, pal. No sense standing here. I'll give you a hand getting your things together. We can finish talking up there."

Michael put his suitcase on the bed and snapped open the locks before pursuing the subject he was mulling over, "But then what's the difference between doubt and unbelief?"

"Well, I think of unbelief as a willful refusal to believe. Doubt wants to believe, tries to believe, but fears at the same time. Unbelief encompasses a state of mind closed against God and a disobedient attitude of heart." He looked him straight in the eyes. "Isn't that where you were for many years?"

"Yeah, guess so."

"Well, doubt lies somewhere between unbelief and faith. Os Guiness, in his book, *Doubt,* notes that it represents a kind of spiritual sickness. But when you're spiritually healthy, you have faith."

"Well, even a pretty healthy person catches a cold now and then..."

"Right. Part of our struggle with doubt stems from this: faith sometimes appears irrational to the five senses that we've depended on to guide us most of our lives. Rational knowledge looks on the concrete reality of something and believes only because it has seen. True biblical faith simply sees the unseen things of God and knows they're every bit as real as the visible realm. 'We walk by faith, not by sight,' the Word says."

"Tough to do for a dyed-in-the-wool pragmatist like me. One day at a time though, right?"

Caleb grinned his response.

As Michael finished packing, he leaned his weight on the suitcase to close it and clicked the latches in place. Still bending forward, he looked across the bed. Caleb seemed like he had more to say. He did. "Now, I don't mean to imply that you should dismiss doubt with a quick brushoff just because it's a normal part of growth. Doubt contributed to the fall of Adam and Eve. It plays an integral role in 'spiritual pride, moral evil, psychological alienation, and intellectual confusion,' as someone once said. Need I say any more? That just about covers everything that can ever go wrong."

"I'll say!"

A knowing smile played back across Caleb's face. "So, what do you think about next weekend? Are you sure you can make it back to help out at Sandy's?"

"Definitely. Is there anything you need? I could pick it up on my way back," he volunteered.

"I've got a list downstairs. You can look it over and see if you want to get any of the items. I'm sure Sandy and his mom will appreciate whatever you can do."

"All right, then. Let's go take a look at it," Michael urged. Caleb led the way downstairs. They checked off the list together and divided the items between them. Soon, they were shaking hands good-bye. "I'll miss you, Caleb. How can I ever thank you for what you've given me?" His voice trailed off with just a trace of tremor.

"The only thanks I ask is that you keep your eyes on Jesus."

"I hear you. See you in a few days. Take care of yourself." Caleb raised his right arm, index finger pointing heavenward. "I will, but He does a much better job. Yes, Michael, do keep your eyes on Him! So long for now. Drive carefully, you hear?"

EIGHT

UNTANGLING

Mɪᴄʜᴀᴇʟ's ꜰɪʀꜱᴛ ᴛᴀꜱᴋ back in town was to find a place to stay. He didn't want to burden any of his friends, so after he dropped by Pat's to leave a short thank-you note and return the camping equipment, he began scouting around for a decent furnished apartment. Much sooner than he expected, he found a suitable one with all the conveniences of home, including a spa and swimming pool. Spacious on the inside, it had a second bedroom that he decided to use as an office and study area.

Time passed quickly, almost in a blur for him. Yet, it passed smoothly. He could sense the Lord behind the scenes. As Caleb suggested, he tried to maintain a thankful attitude. Aside from occasional bouts of self-pity, even in his hurt, he gave thanks. He could not have explained why, but the more he praised God, the less he hurt. Peace comforted him in his loneliness.

Finally, the day arrived for him to return to work. He had chosen it with much thought, knowing that every Wednesday morning, beginning promptly at 8:30 a.m., Dale held a department head meeting. It was a time to air difficulties and submit progress reports and proposals. Most of all, it helped Eagle Aeronautics' employees maintain a sense of unity. Each knew that his or her ideas would be considered and, if valid, implemented. Michael had always held a place of prominence at the meetings. Others valued his opinions for their no-nonsense approach, though at times he came across like a velvet-covered sledgehammer...without the velvet.

That morning found Michael up at dawn, reading his Bible and praying for what he was preparing to do. Fear gnawed his heart. He could feel it trying to overtake him, but he was somehow removed from its power. In the past, he would pump himself up to a fever pitch in order to conquer his fear of looking foolish in front of others. This time he did something different. He admitted his weakness in prayer. Calling upon God, he received peace and strength enough to carry out his plan. He was a new creation, according to the Word. It said that old things had passed away. Michael believed this and knew it was time for a change at work. His uncaring ways and cold manners would have to stop, and the sooner the better. Time to right the wrongs.

He looked at his watch. It showed 8:15 a.m. He took a deep breath, then slowly exhaled. Adjusting his tie and shifting his sports coat to make it as comfortable as possible across his shoulders, he was ready. "Okay Lord, it's You and me," he prayed. "Lead on, Boss." He opened the solid mahogany doors to the conference room and took another deep breath. Looking neither to the left nor right, his stride casual, but purposeful, he entered the room. Dale looked up...and froze. His mouth parted a fraction in surprise. Michael, his features set with solid determination, nodded his head once in greeting as he continued to his regular place.

His motion triggered Dale. He jumped up and came around the conference table. "Welcome back!" he greeted him. With head tilted and one eyebrow arched, he looked Michael over with a discerning eye. Standing face to face, they shook hands. Dale's obvious pleasure and genuine warmth surprised him. "Are you back to stay?" Dale asked. "You still have some vacation left, you know."

"I know. We'll see," Michael replied. "We'll see how things go." Dale was not quite sure what he meant, but kept silent.

The meeting began with the reading of the previous week's report and a review of recent developments. Following those, Dale asked Michael if there was anything he wanted to add. He replied, "There is, but it doesn't pertain to the business of Eagle Aeronautics, in the strictest sense of the word." He looked to Dale, who nodded, giving him the go-ahead.

Never one to pull punches, he came right to the point. "Up until now, I have not been easy to get along with. I've had a chance over the past few days to step back and take a long, hard look at myself, both here at work and at home." He stopped and lowered his gaze to the tabletop. A second passed, then another. With a slight catch in his voice, he continued, "I'd like a fresh start with each of you, but first I've got to clean the slate. I owe many of you an apology." Looking first to Dale, and then, one by one, to each of the others seated around the long table, he came full circle until his eyes locked onto Dale's. "Will you forgive me for the insensitive way I dealt with you all in the past..." His voice trailed off. There was total silence, but for the tick, ticking of the clock. "And give me a chance to start over?"

He sighed. Deeply. *There,* he thought, *it's done.* He stood mute, emotionally naked in front of his peers. Vulnerable and at their mercy, he truly wanted their acceptance. He always had, but until now, was too well-insulated to admit it. He had prayed for the strength to carry out what he knew had to be done. Now he waited.

For some time, he was not sure how they would react. No one moved. Silence reigned...until Dale cleared his throat. It shattered the quiet. Then he spoke, "What brings this on, Michael? I don't know what I expected, but it wasn't this." Dale paused to look at the others. They nodded their assent. All propriety cast to the wind, Dale slid back his chair and stood. In three strides, he was around the conference table and facing Michael. He reached out, grasped both his shoulders, and said, "Of course, I forgive you." A hearty chorus of "That's right" and "You bet," interspersed with hearty backslapping and an occasional hug, filled the room.

Any plans for a business meeting collapsed while each one present made a point of personally thanking him for his openness. They offered to help in all sorts of ways. For the first time at work, he felt wanted. Just for himself and not for what he could accomplish.

This marked another turning point for Michael. He established a new routine at work, even though it felt awkward for a while. Instead of skipping meals or eating alone in his office while he worked on some project, he purposely went to the cafeteria. He knew that there had to be a complete break from his past habits. To his surprise, he enjoyed his co-workers' company.

Friday afternoon came quickly enough, and with it an expected call from Dale. Would he mind staying late... and maybe coming in on Saturday and Sunday? Dale blinked in bewilderment at Michael's answer, "Sorry, boss, it's cost me too much already. I've made plans that can't be broken." He heard the harsh edge that crept into his voice, and not wanting to be too abrupt, he explained about Sandy and Mrs. Hawkins and his promise to help Caleb fix up their house. Dale listened, confused by so many sudden changes in his employee. He wondered what on earth had gotten into him.

Quitting time arrived. Michael was deeply engrossed in his work. An old habit reared its head—the temptation to continue was great, but he resisted. Within a short while, he was on his way home. A hot shower, clean clothes, and an hour later found him on the road to Caleb's. His anticipation mounted. How good it would be to see his new friend again!

While he drove, the words of Scripture with soft background music poured out of his cassette player. The tape greatly enhanced the trip, he decided. Still very much an efficiency expert, he had grown dissatisfied with wasted travel time. Then, browsing through the local Christian bookstore earlier that week, he had found a version of the Bible on cassette. Now he smiled inwardly, pleased with his latest discovery.

Dusk had fallen by the time he pulled into Caleb's parking lot. Even before he shut the car off, his mentor appeared on the front porch. He recognized Michael and hurried out to greet him. They shook hands vigorously as Caleb commented, "It's good to see you, buddy. I'm so glad you were able to get away."

"Wouldn't have missed it for the world."

Caleb smiled. "Me either. Did you have a good week?"

"Great. I'll tell you all about it as soon as we get squared away. The trunk is full of things for Sandy and his mom, but that can wait until morning. No sense moving it twice." He grabbed a lone suitcase and garment bag from the back seat. "I'll follow you." They reached the porch, then Michael stopped. Tilting his head to one side, he looked at Caleb. "There's something so special about this place." He shrugged his shoulders and followed Caleb inside.

Later, seated comfortably in the study and sipping one of Caleb's hot spiced drinks, Michael related his week. He started with how God provided such a nice place for him to live and concluded with his last-minute temptation to revert to his workaholic tendencies. Caleb was most interested in the episode of the department head meeting at work. He listened in silence the first time through and then, once Michael finished, moved to the edge of his seat and asked him to recount it one more time. Interjecting a question here, a comment there, he nodded his head all the while.

" And that should bring you up to date," Michael finished.

"I'm proud of you. Not everyone would have been able to make themselves so vulnerable that soon after giving their lives to Christ." Caleb's eyes twinkled, with flecks of silver dancing in the blue depths. "Yes, son, I'm plum proud of you. That was the right thing to do."

"Thanks. Say, I've been reading the material you gave me, and I've got a bunch of questions for you." He shared how the story of Cain and Abel had such a strong impact on him and also how he set out to take God at His Word—in short, to agree with Him. The dilemma over wasted driving time came up, too, and how he had solved the problem with the Bible on cassette.

Caleb's delight broke into a grin as he exclaimed, "That's an excellent idea, Michael!"

"It's working out well. I listened to the book of Romans on the drive here…several times as a matter of fact. You said the fifth chapter relates to agreement, didn't you? I don't think I understand how."

"Want to take a look at it together?" asked Caleb. He stood and walked to where his well-worn leather Bible lay. Putting on his glasses, he picked it up tenderly, turned a few pages, and began reading at the beginning of chapter 5. His voice flowed with feeling, sincerity evident in every word:

> Therefore, since we have been justified through faith, we have peace with God through our Lord Jesus Christ, through whom

we have gained access by faith into this grace in which we now stand. And we rejoice in the hope of the glory of God. Not only so, but we also rejoice in our sufferings, because we know that suffering produces perseverance; perseverance, character; and character, hope. And hope does not disappoint us, because God has poured out his love into our hearts by the Holy Spirit, whom he has given us.

You see, at just the right time, when we were still powerless, Christ died for the ungodly. Very rarely will anyone die for a righteous man, though for a good man someone might possibly dare to die. But God demonstrates his own love for us in this: While we were still sinners, Christ died for us.

Since we have now been justified by his blood, how much more shall we be saved from God's wrath through him! For if when we were God's enemies, we were reconciled to him through the death of his Son, how much more, having been reconciled, shall we be saved through his life!

"I could listen to you read the Bible forever. It's so...so...well, I can't describe it. I just know you believe every word. It gives me such confidence."

"That's great, Michael, because I do believe every word. Do you have any idea yet how this passage applies to agreement?"

"Some...I think I have a better idea now...along the lines of what you've been telling me. It's only because of Jesus that I'm no longer God's enemy. I'm justified and reconciled to Him, by faith. That's the whole foundation of Christianity, isn't it?"

Without hesitation, Caleb responded, "Yes. Martin Luther, founder of the Protestant Reformation that changed the course of church history, proclaimed, 'Justification by faith!' to the salvation-by-works oriented church of his day. Romans 5:1 supports him, 'Therefore, since we have been justified through faith, we have peace with God through our Lord Jesus Christ.' Think of justification like this: in our new life, it is just as if we had never sinned. We have agreed with the power of the blood of Jesus to cancel our debt. Paul says in this passage that even the attacks of the enemy can work to our good. Sometimes life can get tough, but those are the times when God pours His loving grace into our hearts by the Holy Spirit within us."

"Yes, I'm beginning to see that. But what is the truth about the grace of God?" Michael asked. "If I'm saved by grace, and there's nothing I can do one way or the other to earn it, what's to keep me from falling back into my old ways after I'm saved?"

"Nothing but the love and grace of God," Caleb answered. "Nothing else is needed. Still, the message of grace, as beautiful a message as it is, can be misconstrued. When taught and believed correctly, it leads to peace and comfort…and holiness…by bringing us close to our Lord. Balance is the key. Some teach that there is no longer any need to live a life of holiness, because Jesus already paid the debt for sin—past, present, and future. Their philosophy of grace goes something like this, 'I don't have to be a legalistic Christian fanatic. I have liberty under the new and better covenant, so I can enjoy myself. It's all under the blood. My faith is there, anyway.'

Michael laughed, "Even I can see how that can't be the true message of grace. It doesn't sound right, although it's certainly more appealing."

Caleb got up. He paced back and forth as he continued, his voice growing more and more intense. "The Word of God is explicit in its warnings against false doctrines, especially in these last days. We must pray for discernment and heed the words of 1 John 4:1, 'Do not believe every spirit, but test the spirits to see whether they are from God, because many false prophets have gone out into the world.' Most people have trouble with anything abstract. Faith, because it is unseen, does fall into that category. Any teaching on faith must be based on the complete Word of God. Look at the abundant life teachings and prosperity messages. Those are valid truths promised to us because of Jesus' victory on the cross, but they must be balanced and tempered with the rest of the Word. As disciples, we are also willing to suffer for His name's sake…

"True faith in the Lord, Michael, is an entirely different undertaking from what I call the 'Name it and claim it' doctrine. The by-products of the two teachings differ, as well." His pace quickened. "Too often the 'Name it and claim it' philosophy is tied to a desire for worldly prosperity—greed, in other words. It's easy to believe. Most people want to hear that kind of message, and plenty of eager teachers stand willing to oblige them. They proclaim, 'You're King's kids…you ought to live like royalty!' Perhaps they forget that the King of the universe was the Servant of all.

Jesus' primary concern was spiritual prosperity, which comes through that unseen essential of faith…often during our toughest times of lack." He stopped and turned to face Michael. "Now please don't take all that to mean you have to run out and become an ascetic. You know, seek personal poverty and failure so you can be closer to God. That's extremism. You simply strive to love and serve Him with everything you have in you…and all you possess."

Michael shook his head in wonder. "You make it sound so simple. I've had worldly prosperity, and it did hinder my faith in God. When everything was going fine, no one could have convinced me of my need. I basked in a false sense of security. It seems so clear now. Makes me wonder why I didn't see the answer myself instead of bothering you with questions."

"Don't be silly, Michael. You're doing the right thing. When you approach a new subject, the first thing you do is gather facts. The more you know about a matter, the easier it is either to agree or disagree with the findings. Regarding God's truths, as you begin living them out, strong feelings develop toward them, and they become part of you. It's a three-part progression—facts, faith, feelings. Make any sense?"

"It's making a whole lot more sense than I ever thought possible. I've only one more question for now." He grinned at Caleb, a sheepish look on his face. "I know there's more to this faith thing than agreement. Mind telling me the next step to the unseen essential?"

"Ha!" Caleb let out a hearty chuckle as he put his hands into his pockets. "I should keep you in suspense 'til morning!" He paused to gauge his reaction and rocked back and forth on his heels. When Michael's eyebrows raised a notch, Caleb chuckled again. "No, I couldn't keep you waiting all night. Dependence is the second step, but that's all I'll say for now. There'll be plenty of time tomorrow, once you and Sandy have had a chance to patch things up." A slight yawn escaped him. He smiled. "That sound okay?"

Michael was tired, too. It had been nonstop at work all day. Then there was the drive. "Sounds fine to me," he agreed. Maybe he could read up on dependence before going to sleep. It was sure to be in Caleb's notes, somewhere.

Caleb interrupted his mental planning. "Before I head off to bed, I've got to ask you one more question." Head canted to the side, he waited for

Michael's assent and then continued. "Did you try to find a way to talk to your wife? You've mentioned everything but that."

Michael dropped his gaze to the floor and hesitated on the edge of his seat. How could he admit to Caleb that he had not mustered the courage to find a way to contact her or get the restraining order lifted? He had wanted so much to hear the sound of Stephanie's voice. Each time he had reached for the receiver, his hand started shaking. Every tremor sent icy claws raking his insides. "No, Caleb…didn't hear a word," he replied with forced calm. Uncomfortable with his own lack of honesty, Michael stood. "Well, good night. And thanks for inviting me back."

"My pleasure. Wait until we've finished the work at Sandy's," he chuckled again. "You may not feel so grateful then."

Michael sat at the desk in his room and arranged his study materials neatly. His extreme sense of order, so vital during his years as an engineer, was still evident. There, just to the left of center, was his Bible. To the right of center was a writing pad and pen. At the far corners were Caleb's notebook and manuscript. He wondered what Caleb meant by *dependence*. Before retiring, he needed to find out.

"Dependence." He spoke the word aloud. "What a strange subject in a walk of faith." His mind conjured up images of dependency as he knew it. None had the least bit of appeal. Drug addicts scraping for their next heroin fix. Winos wandering along dismal streets, groping for spare change to buy a bottle. Babies crying for mothers to change their diapers. Elderly nursing home patients waiting to be fed. Paralysis victims reduced to the status of "vegetables." *Ugh! Who wants all that to get faith? Not me. No, thanks.* He knew he would have some pointed questions in the morning.

He searched Caleb's notebook for *dependence*. There. Pages loaded with one reference after another. Despite his misgivings, he settled down to some serious reading:

> Sincere head and heart agreement with divine truth leads to dependence on the Lord. He is Jehovah-Jireh, the Lord our Provider. By His own name, He promises to provide for every need.

Seeing this to be true, wisdom dictates our total dependence
upon Him. As His dearly beloved children, even the times we
make a decision without His counsel—and goof—He continues
providing. He does not withdraw His love.

Michael thought, *That's good to know.* Yes, he, too, could testify to the
truth of God's provision. Since giving his life to the Lord, his needs had
been met every step of the way. Some of his desires went unfulfilled for
the moment, but not a single need. *This dependence thing is looking better*, he considered in silence, then continued:

Before we develop a working dependence on the Lord, we often
must be broken. Self-will, so opposed to God's will, declares its
mastery of the soul. Let one ounce of independence remain,
however, and its insidious spread, like an unchecked malig-
nancy, will destroy godly dependence and breed rebellion.

Peter, the most outspoken of the twelve disciples, is an excellent illustration of brokenness leading to dependence. If ever we
wanted an example to prove that God does not choose us for
who we are, but for who we can become, then Peter is the one.

Michael flipped the page. Mixed among the notes were references to
a tape series by one of Caleb's favorite preachers, Dr. Charles Stanley.
Charles Stanley. I've heard that name. He sat thinking about where and
then turned back to the notebook.

Peter—impulsive, coarse, self-centered, strong-willed, and
independent—hardly qualifies for high honors. Despite his
obvious weaknesses, he was included with James and John in
an inner circle with the Lord Jesus. He was even privileged
to be present during His transfiguration. Jesus saw through
Peter's human frailties, as He does all of ours. He chose Peter
because he was a man through whom He could work. The Lord
selects His workers today on the same principle. He always
looks at the heart.

A study of Peter's preparation for the ministry reveals a beautiful example of brokenness. God brought him through a process that transformed him—body, soul, and spirit—from a life

of self-centeredness to one of joyful submission to the guiding presence of the Holy Spirit.

Dependence does not come without a struggle—a fierce struggle for the independent, successful individual. First, God focuses on an area that needs work. Often, His choice does not coincide with ours. We would keep our strengths and build up our weaknesses, but our strong points are where we are most susceptible to independence and pride. An acknowledged weakness can be more readily turned over to God than a strength. It is too easy to want to rely upon our strong points.

So, the Lord pinpoints a problem that may be hindering what He desires to accomplish in and through us. It can be an attitude, habit, relationship, or anything we are attached to that stands between us and Him. Usually, He spots something especially dear to us.

Lifting his eyes from the page, Michael leaned back in his chair. He raised his arms over his head and stretched, easing the tension in his back and neck muscles, and mused aloud, "Something dear to us." Caleb had certainly struck a nerve on that one. "Is that what that humiliating newspaper fiasco was all about? I sure do value my career and my professional image..." He marked his place and closed the notebook.

His mind wandered. He wanted to be dependent on God if it was an important part of faith, but deep down though, he cringed at the thought. All his life, he had made his own way. "A self-made man," many called him. He strove to be independent, not dependent. Inwardly, he rebelled. Peter's example gave him a thin ray of hope.

The urge to read was satisfied for the time being, so he got ready for bed. Uneasiness settled upon him, but he could not locate its source. Childhood scenes flickered on the fringes of his consciousness. Slipping between the sheets, he prayed for God to keep him spiritually hungry. He would need that focus to go through brokenness.

Dawn arrived. Michael was already up and reading his Bible. He had slept fitfully until the early morning hours when, tossing and turning, he struggled through dreams he couldn't remember. A night's sleep did little to dispel his disquietude. It had all started with those comments on dependence and brokenness. If it meant more pain... He wanted to agree with what he had read, yet something inside him balked at the idea. Confused by his mixed emotions, he prayed that God would restore his peace of mind as he searched the Scriptures. He started with a couple of chapters from the gospel of John. Then he read from the book of Romans, inspired perhaps by the tapes he had listened to while driving out to Caleb's. Collecting his thoughts, he began reading again at the first verse of chapter 6:

> What shall we say, then? Shall we go on sinning that grace may increase? By no means! We died to sin; how can we live in it any longer? Or don't you know that all of us who were baptized into Christ Jesus were baptized into his death? We were therefore buried with him through baptism into death in order that, just as Christ was raised from the dead through the glory of the Father, we too may live a new life.

Michael recognized the same idea of holiness that Caleb had described in his notes. Eyebrows knitted together, forehead furrowed in concentration, he paused and spoke aloud, "'That we too may live a new life.' That means I have a choice whether I walk in newness of life or not. How do I, though? That's the question." He lowered his gaze back to the passage and continued.

> If we have been united with him like this in his death, we will certainly also be united with him in his resurrection. For we know that our old self was crucified with him so that the body of sin might be done away with, that we should no longer be slaves to sin.
>
> —ROMANS 6:6

That was the secret. He could walk in holiness because he was free from the power of sin, and he was free from the power of sin because the old Michael was dead. He looked up and stared off into space. A sudden thought startled him. His frustration level mounted. *But if I'm dead, how can I accomplish anything?* he wondered. As soon as the question surfaced, the answer followed, and he spoke it aloud slowly, so he could grasp it. "By faith, I've got to depend on what Jesus accomplished on Calvary. That's the only way." Pieces clicked, like the tumbler of a giant combination lock falling into place. He sighed with relief. He was beginning to see how dependence fit into the greater picture.

Birds chirped their morning greeting outside his window as he finished reading the sixth chapter and continued on into the seventh and eighth. "Therefore, there is now no condemnation for those who are in Christ Jesus, because through Christ Jesus the law of the Spirit of life set me free from the law of sin and death" (Romans 8:1–2).

He stopped, eyes drawn back to the phrases "law of the Spirit" and "law of sin and death." It was new to him. The only law he remembered from the Bible was the Law of Moses, and he was not sure he knew what that entailed. But this... being free from the law of sin and death because of the law of the Spirit of life. He wished Caleb were right there. He resolved to bring it up at the earliest opportunity, then continued reading. "All things work together for good to them that love God" (Romans 8:28). *Now that's a comfort,* he thought. *I do love God...more and more each day...so He will work all this out for my best,* he decided. There was so much to learn. It was enough to occupy his thoughts, and by the time he closed his Bible and stood to get ready, all trace of anxiety had departed. "Thank You, Lord," he said softly. "Now I'm ready for the day."

Later, sitting with Caleb at the breakfast table after their morning run, Michael brought up the subject of his reading. "Can you help me understand this thing about the two laws in Romans 8?"

Caleb grabbed the pitcher of fresh-squeezed orange juice and poured a glass for each of them. He set the pitcher down and cleared his throat, then mulled over the question. The usual sparkle dancing in his blue eyes grew in intensity. They looked like they glowed. "Think of the Constitution. Do you know how many times it's been amended?"

"A bunch, that's for sure."

"That's right. Once a law is brought into effect, it can never be simply erased. It takes a second law to do away with, or alter, the first one. The realm of the Spirit is similar. Everything about the old Michael Nastasis lived under the old law and worked death. Everything about the new man, who has Jesus Christ living in him, works life. A holy walk of faith is possible because of the new law of the Spirit of life in you."

"Whew! That's heavy."

"But it flies, son. It flies." Michael, still a little confused, looked at him, so he continued. "You're an engineer, my friend. When you design an aircraft, it must conform to certain basic principles, or laws. Gravity says planes can't fly. You can believe the Wright brothers heard that often enough. But given the proper thrust and lift..." He laughed. "Look at me, telling an aeronautical engineer the principles of flight. But you get the idea, I'm sure."

"I think so..." Michael stopped. Eyes squinting in concentration, he was quiet for several minutes. Then he added slowly, "Gravity must be like the law of sin and death. It keeps things earthbound. And the law of the Spirit is like the law of aerodynamics that maintains a plane in flight. Keeps things heavenbound..." He paused and grinned wide. "I get it! The law of sin and death is still in effect today, just like the law of gravity..." He jumped up and waved his arms, spilling his orange juice all over the table. "But the law of the Spirit supersedes the law of sin and death...given the right formula, which is Jesus! Right?" They both burst into hearty laughter as they sopped up the juice with their napkins.

"Exactly, Michael. Very good insight! But our fuel tanks can still run empty, which can be pretty serious in mid-flight. I guess you could say that we keep the fuel flowing through constant dependence on Jesus."

"That's great, Caleb. I see it now. It sure threw me when I first read it. Thanks a bunch."

"My pleasure. You came up with some pretty good stuff yourself there, pal."

He smiled his appreciation. He felt a bit awkward with the compliment so he changed the subject. "Say...we're supposed to be over at Sandy's soon. Does he know I'm coming with you?"

"No, I haven't mentioned it to him. I thought you might like to surprise him."

Michael nodded. "Yeah, that would be fun. Good idea." He thought of his own children. He missed them...missed hearing their laughter as they watched the Saturday morning cartoons. Stephanie might have told them he asked about them. He hoped so.

Caleb noticed the faraway look in his eyes. Not wanting to interrupt, he waited and took another sip of orange juice.

Suddenly, "I forgot to tell you I wrote to her," popped out. Caleb did not need to be told who "her" was. "After the meeting," Michael continued, "I wrote a long letter to Stephanie. I told her what happened the last time I was out here—my decision to start agreeing with God. I apologized for hurting her. Poured my heart out, then asked her to forgive me." Michael hesitated, toying with the last bits of cereal in his bowl, then looked across the table. "Do you think I did the right thing? Do...do you think she'll even read it?"

Caleb wanted to encourage his friend, but even more he desired to be truthful. He chose his words with care. "Yes, in time. I believe she'll read your letter, but she may wait a while. And even if she does read it, she may not yet be willing to forgive you." He watched Michael's shoulders slump in disappointment. It was not the answer he wanted to hear.

Michael took a deep breath. His eyes darted around the room before settling on Caleb. In a moment, he squared his shoulders and straightened up in his chair. "It hurts, but I have to go on."

"Of course you do. God knows your heart, Michael. The important thing is that you've admitted your shortcomings and asked her forgiveness. Now it's up to God. He is the One who can draw you back together. In His time, in His way. It would be easy to tell you, 'Yes, she'll forgive you and ask you to come home.' But I won't. You must depend on God to fulfill His Word."

"Ah, dependence again. I read about that and brokenness last night." He bristled slightly.

"What did you think of it?"

"Do you want the truth?"

Caleb answered without hesitation. "Of course!"

"No, thanks...on the brokenness. I've been through enough already. That was my first reaction. After this morning, well..."

"For now, that's good enough," Caleb reassured him. "There are times I still feel apprehensive about the things of God. Agreeing with Him is a lifelong process. We're the ones who lose when we delay, though." He looked at Michael, a smile playing at the corners of his mouth. "Are you ready to get started for Sandy's?"

"Sure am."

"Good. Let's unload the stuff from your trunk into my truck. We can talk more along the way, if you want."

But that was not the case. Both Michael and Caleb were quiet during the trip. Michael, now that he was not driving, took advantage of the opportunity to study the countryside. He welcomed the momentary diversion. Everything looked new, somehow more alive, this morning. Cows ambled along to an unknown destination, all moving in a care-free, yet orderly fashion. Farther down the road, dew sparkled on fields of waist-high grasses glistening like diamonds in the sunlight. He was awed at the beauty of nature.

Sensitive to Michael's mood, Caleb drove in silence. All the while, he prayed under his breath...for Sandy and his mom, and for the new Christian beside him.

NINE

MENDING

CALEB AND MICHAEL, bouncing along in the pickup truck, rounded the last bend in the road. Caleb slowed to make the turn into the narrow driveway. That was all the announcement they needed. Sandy threw open the screen door and rushed out. In one giant leap, he was down the stairs and running. He came to a dead stop, ten feet from the truck. He started to wave, his mouth open to shout something, but did neither. His eyes were glued to Caleb's passenger.

Michael recognized Sandy's confusion. He looked like someone who wanted to give away a present, but hesitated because he was not sure it would be accepted. That confusion cut Michael like a knife. It reminded him of the many times as a child he wanted—no, needed—to throw himself into his father's arms, but did not. The very rejection he feared with his dad he had caused in Sandy by driving away and leaving him the week before. It did not have to continue, he decided.

Sandy stood frozen in place like a statue as Caleb rolled to a stop. Michael opened the door, jumped out, and stood beside it. His eyes were fixed on Sandy, even as the young boy's eyes filled with tears. "Uh...hi, Sandy," he muttered. He scratched the back of his head. "I'd like to help, too...if you'll have me, that is."

Sandy's eyes opened wide and he took a deep breath. "Wow!" His whole face lit up like a Christmas tree. He broke into an ear-to-ear grin. "Oh, Mr. Michael, I'm so glad ya come back. I never thought I'd see ya agin," he cried, running into his widespread arms. They held each other tight.

After a brief hug, Michael unwrapped his arms from around Sandy as he set him down. He crouched low, dropped to one knee so he could see eye-to-eye with the young boy. "Sandy, I treated you pretty bad last week. I want you to know it had nothing to do with you. I was very upset because of some problems at home." He sighed. "I took it out on you, and that wasn't fair. I didn't mean to hurt you, but I did." He felt a little clumsy, but knew he was doing the right thing. "Will you forgive me... please?"

Sandy's grin faded. He grew pensive. He stared Michael straight in his eyes and nodded slowly. "Yep, Mr. Michael, I felt real bad." He looked down as two tears splashed onto a tennis shoe full of holes. His toe pushed a stone from side to side in the dirt. "But I fergive ya." He looked up and smiled, unable to restrain his joy any longer.

By this time Caleb, who had been silently watching the drama unfold, stepped forward. "Hi, young man. How's my special guy?"

"Howdy, Mr. Caleb. I'm doin' fine... now." Sandy reached up to hug him, then grabbed his hand and turned to hold out his other hand to Michael. "C'mon in and say hi to Ma." After some friendly greetings, they wheeled her chair out under a shade tree near their work area. The fresh air would do her good. They hoped being outside by them would make her feel more a part of things.

Morning passed in a flash. The task and the laughter kept them busy and made time move too quickly for all of them. Only one thing threatened their fun—Sandy's mom sitting on the sidelines in her wheelchair. Caleb prayed with her, and soon she dozed off.

Shortly after lunch, Michael missed the nail he was aiming at and whacked his thumb hard with the hammer. "OUCH!" Blinded by sudden pain, he lost his temper and let out a few choice swear words in front of the others. He felt humiliated beyond description. If there had been a hole big enough for him to crawl into, he would have, gladly. Caleb tried to console and encourage him, but to no avail. Michael's bruised ego hurt worse than his throbbing thumb.

During a short early-afternoon break, Sandy asked Caleb to tell him a Bible story.

"Hmm, let's see…" He stopped to think and then began, "Sandy, do you recall the thief who was crucified beside Jesus?" Turning to his other side, he asked, "How about you, Michael?"

They nodded, Michael with less enthusiasm.

"Maggie?" She blinked her answer.

"Not everyone is as fortunate as he." All three listeners raised their eyebrows at that one. He continued his story:

> Few people can give their hearts to Jesus and be with Him in paradise the same day. Chapter twenty-three of Luke tells how during those last few hours on the cross, one thief agreed with God and acknowledged that he was a sinner who deserved to die. He asked the Lord to remember him when He entered His kingdom. Jesus promised not only to remember him, but assured him that he would be in paradise that very day. Imagine—agreement to paradise in a matter of hours!
>
> And then there was Joseph who didn't have it so easy. When he was a young man, God spoke to him in two dreams, showing him that he would be raised up to a place of importance above the rest of his family. If God showed you something like that, you'd be excited, wouldn't you?

Sandy, wide-eyed, could only bob his head up and down vigorously. He inched closer in anticipation of what was coming. Caleb often told him stories of Bible characters, and he always listened with rapt attention.

> Joseph got overanxious, plus maybe a little proud, and revealed his dreams to his family. His brothers had always been jealous of him because he was his father's favorite son, and when they heard the dreams, their jealousy intensified. Soon after that, his brothers tricked Joseph and sold him into Egyptian slavery. Did he give up? No. Did he lay around and pout, grumbling about the accommodations? Absolutely not. He became the most diligent slave in his foreign master's household, and he was rewarded by being raised to a place of importance.
>
> Still, Joseph was not in a position of authority where the Lord could fulfill his earlier vision. Did God just promote him then? No, sir. The master of the house had a wife who thought Joseph

was pretty good-looking. Over and over, she tried to get him to give in to her wiles, but he remained faithful...both to God and to his master.

When she couldn't have her way, she lied to her husband and told him that Joseph attacked her. Can you imagine that? Well, there's an old saying: "Hell hath no fury like a woman scorned," or something like that. It sure was true of Potiphar's wife. Her husband had Joseph thrown into prison, of all places. He was trapped.

Even in prison, Joseph worked hard and was promoted once again. Because of his faithful service, he became overseer of the prison, but it did little toward helping him get released. For his freedom, his return to his family, and the eventual fulfillment of God's prophetic Word, Joseph could do nothing but depend on God. He had no alternative. It was depend or die.

God had a plan and a purpose for Joseph. He supplied him with the necessary spiritual gifts all along the way. His training period started way back when he was still a child. Years later, right there in prison, God used that same gift to help two of Pharaoh's former right-hand men to understand their dreams. What God revealed to Joseph—that one man would be restored to his position, the other, executed—came to pass!

Of course, the day arrived when the head honcho himself—Pharaoh—had an upsetting dream that none of his magicians could understand. Word got back to him about a Hebrew prisoner's amazing ability to interpret dreams. The Lord's gift made a way for Joseph, just as the book of Proverbs promises. He told Pharaoh the dream and its interpretation. In turn, Pharaoh made him the second highest official in Egypt. In that position, Joseph prepared the foreign nation for the coming famine and saved his own family from starvation as well. They all wound up bowing down to him, just as the dream of his youth had shown him.

So Joseph came to understand God's sovereignty through times of pain, persecution, and success. Wherever he was, he served diligently...from lowly slave to chief administrator. He didn't give in to regrets, tears, or resentment because of what happened to him. If he did, it wasn't for long. Total dependence enabled him to live a life of faith, in spite of hardship. Remember though, Joseph did not depend on the gift, but on the Giver.

"Caleb," Michael asked, "how long did all this take? I mean, from the time his brothers sold him until he became Pharaoh's right-hand man… how long was it?"

Sandy kept quiet, but he listened to every word. His eyes darted back and forth between the two adults.

"Thirteen years," Caleb added.

"Thirteen? That would be terrible."

Caleb nodded. "Yes, it sure would seem like it…from the time Joseph was seventeen until he was thirty years old. God protected him during setbacks and disappointments, but he also cooperated. He saw things from God's eternal viewpoint and refused to let human limitations distract him. God had shown Joseph what the final results would be, and he believed Him." Then Caleb tapped his chest with his fingers. "For us, too, dependence on God and faith in His Word can turn trials into a virtual hothouse of spiritual growth. Endurance, fortitude, integrity… they abound in such a climate. God wants mature saints who will bear much fruit for His kingdom."

Michael looked to Sandy, winked, and turned back to Caleb. "Thanks for a great story."

"You're welcome. My pleasure."

Sandy piped in, "Yeah, Mr. Caleb, I love Joseph. He's my favorite, I think."

Caleb grinned at him. "Sandy, you say that about every Bible character." Then Caleb brought them back to the work at hand. "Now, what do you say we get going with that painting? The sealer should be dry by now, warm as the sun is…and with such a pleasant breeze."

"Guess we better," agreed Michael. He made as if to jump up and run. "Last one to the paint shed gets to clean up!" With a shout, Sandy leaped to his feet and took off like a flash.

Although they worked all afternoon in the hot sun, the camaraderie kept their minds off the heat. Every so often they checked on Maggie. Michael felt like either a big brother or a father to Sandy. He could not figure out which and wondered how the boy looked at it. All he knew for sure was that Sandy thoroughly enjoyed himself. He worked hard, too.

"It's for Ma," he would say as he looked over at her. Then he kept going more fervently than ever.

They called it a day just before sunset and enjoyed the heavenly panorama as they sipped on cool spring water. What work remained would take no more than half a day. There would be plenty of time to complete the job following the Sunday morning worship service.

After cleaning up and getting everything ready for the next day, they wheeled Mrs. Hawkins inside. While Michael, nursing his throbbing thumb, sat awkwardly across the room, Caleb spent time with her. He was so patient, in spite of the difficulty in understanding her. Her words were slurred from the effect of the multiple sclerosis on her muscles. Caleb seemed to empathize with her thoughts, feelings, and pain. When he finished ministering, he prayed. Once again, she drew strength immediately.

Her next words were to Michael. "Take care of my boy," was the garbled phrase Caleb interpreted. Rather than reach out to her, he wanted to run. He wrung his hands and tried smiling assurance to her, but it looked as forced as it felt. And he could hardly look her in the eyes. He breathed a sigh of relief when at last they left for Caleb's. He knew he should not have felt like that, yet he did. No two ways about it.

Later that evening, Michael confessed as much to Caleb.

"What do you think brought out all my awkwardness around Mrs. Hawkins?" he asked. They were, by now, back at the Country Corner relaxing on the porch. Caleb, sitting with his Bible open on his lap, said he didn't have a clue.

Michael had his Bible, too. He held it, still closed, in his hand. There was something else bothering him. He related the feelings he had experienced with Sandy earlier—the overwhelming desire for Sandy not to feel rejected because of the past weekend.

"Think for a minute, my friend. Can you remember anything from your childhood that might account for these feelings? God may be shedding a little light on something that, if it isn't healed, could hinder your walk of faith."

He frowned, eyes squinted. "I'm not sure I know what you mean, Caleb."

"Do you remember feeling rejected any time in the past? If you do, then maybe there is some correlation between then and now. Of course, it could be just an isolated incident and nothing to worry about."

The air was growing cool, so they headed inside. Michael sat down on the couch next to Caleb. He ran his hand through his hair, smoothing it in place, then cupped his chin in his right hand, resting his head. He chewed on his fingernail. After a moment, he stood up, walked three steps, and about-faced. "There is something. I can remember a time or two when I felt rejected by my parents, especially by my father. I tried reaching out to them for attention. It never came, though."

"Michael, please don't think I'm prying, but would you tell me about one of those incidents? I have my reasons for asking."

"Sure, I don't mind. It happened so long ago, it doesn't bother me anymore." Caleb said nothing, only raised an eyebrow. "The one that stands out the most was when I was about four or five. My parents used to take me shopping with them whenever they went." He started a slow pace back and forth. "One day I heard them talking about going, so naturally, I expected to go along. I waited and waited for them to tell me to get ready. Instead, they asked me to go to the backyard to look for something. I agreed, but tried to hurry so I could get ready. While I was out there, a noise in the front caught my attention. All of a sudden, I had a queasy feeling in the pit of my stomach." He paused, threatened by those same emotions. His forehead felt hot and his hands, clammy.

"I ran as fast as my little legs could carry me. Down the hill and around the side of the house to the front yard, I ran. By then I was screaming at the top of my lungs, waving my hands over my head. I remember thinking, *They're leaving me… they're leaving me…* I got there in time to watch them back out of the driveway and head on down the road…

"Things get blurry from that point, but I do remember walking back around the side of the house. I was crying hysterically. My reaction was all out of proportion to what happened. It was more than the shopping. I trusted them, and they betrayed me—at least, that's how it seemed. I thought they were trying to get rid of me, leaving me forever. You wanna hear the irony of it all?" Michael's laugh was tense. "They were shopping for my birthday present. A big, beautiful telescope. Just what I wanted. But almost a week passed before my birthday came and I found out why they didn't want me tagging along. It was one of the worst weeks of my life." A tear rolled down his cheek.

Caleb was silent for some minutes. He tried fitting what he knew of child raising into the situation he had just heard. His friend's personality was beginning to make sense. Michael interrupted his thoughts.

"All the time I was growing up, I don't remember my parents ever telling me they loved me. They never hugged me, but if I asked, they'd give me a good night kiss on the cheek." His voice rose in pitch. "I tried so hard to please them, figuring if I did, they'd love me." He wept softly. "Straight A's in school didn't move them. I was supposed to be the best." He spoke louder, almost spitting out the words. "But let those grades drop one iota, and I was an absolute failure in their eyes." He squinted, and looked at Caleb. "Leastwise, that's the way it seemed then."

"Do you still feel that way?"

"Oh, I don't know," he responded half in disgust. "Sure, I guess they loved me, but it would have been nice if they had shown it a time or two."

Caleb patted Michael's knee and interjected, "I'm very sorry you felt so unloved, my friend. I'm as sorry as I can be. I went through similar feelings as a child. If you had been secure about your parents' love for you, you would never have assumed they were trying to get rid of you and leaving you forever." He sighed. "That rejection has affected you ever since. Maybe it wasn't entirely their fault. People can only pass on what they've been taught. That may have been all they were ever shown when they were young."

A sudden thought struck Caleb. "How affectionate did you act towards your children? And your wife?" He could tell from the shocked expression on Michael's face that he, too, had trouble in that area.

Caleb's voice was gentle and kind. "You know, Sandy's open affection caught you off guard today, but you responded quite naturally. So there's great hope for you. Michael, my boy, your own hurt as a child can be transformed into a tremendous blessing. Personal pain can be an instrument of healing for others...if you give it to the Lord first. The choice is yours. But you're accountable now for how you react to your past."

Caleb paused and then spoke in hushed tones, "Listen to these words: 'Forgiveness...is the fragrance the violet sheds...on the heel that has crushed it.' Mark Twain wrote that saying. Jesus practiced it— almost two thousand years earlier—and He said we must forgive if we want to have evidence that we are forgiven." They sat silently for a while, except for a few periodic sniffles. Caleb handed Michael his handkerchief and reached over to give his shoulder a caring squeeze. "Growth is tough sometimes, for sure. I know it is. Say, before it gets too dark, I'd like to check out something on the side of the house again. How about it? Feel like taking a walk around there, buddy?"

He blew his nose. "Lead on. I'm right behind you."

"Great. Let me turn the floodlights on. They'll help some."

As they walked, Caleb asked him if he knew about the basics of pruning plants. "Like a hedge, for example. The more it's trimmed and shaped the more it fills out. It grows thicker and fuller, which is usually the gardener's desired result."

"Yeah, I know. That's how I keep my rose bushes looking so good and full of blooms. Well...used to keep my rose bushes, I should say."

Caleb continued, "Grapevines are the same way, and so are most, if not all, fruit-bearing trees. When I got into the hobby of growing grapes, I learned a few lessons. It was easy to see why the Bible refers so much to vineyards and grapevines. For one, they involve a life-long investment. Their fruit-bearing span can be as long as forty years. Patience is a must.

"For three years, you cannot let a single bloom come to fruition. And just a couple of branches are allowed to shoot off from the main trunk. During each of those three years, everything else is pruned. That produces a healthy, fruit-bearing vine, once it gets past the three-year mark." He paused, his blue eyes glistening. Being a grape grower was clearly a labor of love.

They reached the side of the house, and Caleb stopped in front of the arbors. "Pruning never ends. There's always a stray branch needing a good clip or two. Here, look." He pointed out the heavy-hanging clusters. "Feel the size of these."

Michael reached down and grabbed hold of a bunch. The cool grapes felt smooth, firm, and plump to his touch. "Man, these are fat!"

"That's right, and they would never be as full if I hadn't pruned the vines. The sucker shoots have to be removed or they'll take nourishment away from the producing areas. They're good for nothing. Got to go! Same with us. We all have old 'sucker shoots' from the past hindering our progress."

Michael nodded slowly. He understood.

"Now feel right here." Caleb placed Michael's right hand around the thickest trunk and his left around the smaller one extending out from it. They both had rough and smooth spots, but the big one was solid. "Tell me...how long would this branch live if I cut it off from the main vine?"

"Not long...hours maybe."

"How many grapes would ripen?"

"Get serious. Not a single one. They'd shrivel up and die."

"That's right. Branches are totally dependent on the vine to bring them nourishment enough to produce grapes. According to the Bible, we Christians are spiritual branches who have been grafted into the true Vine—Jesus Christ. Each one of us should develop huge bunches of ripe fruit of the Holy Spirit. On our own, not only will we fail to produce any healthy spiritual fruit, we cannot even live. It is that important to be one hundred and ten percent dependent upon God! Listen to what the Word says in one of my favorite passages, John 15." He began reciting from memory:

I am the true vine, and my Father is the gardener. He cuts off every branch in me that bears no fruit, while every branch that does bear fruit he prunes so that it will be even more fruitful. You are already clean because of the word I have spoken to you. Remain in me, and I will remain in you. No branch can bear fruit by itself; it must remain in the vine. Neither can you bear fruit unless you remain in me.

I am the vine; you are the branches. If a man remains in me and I in him, he will bear much fruit; apart from me you can do nothing. If anyone does not remain in me, he is like a branch that is thrown away and withers; such branches are picked up, thrown into the fire and burned. If you remain in me and my words remain in you, ask whatever you wish, and it will be given you. This is to my Father's glory, that you bear much fruit, showing yourselves to be my disciples.

As the Father has loved me, so have I loved you. Now remain in my love. If you obey my commands, you will remain in my love, just as I have obeyed my Father's commands and remain in his love. I have told you this so that my joy may be in you and that your joy may be complete. My command is this: Love each other as I have loved you. Greater love has no one than this, that he lay down his life for his friends.

As Caleb finished reciting, Michael shivered. Yet, he felt hot at the same time. The shadows deepened as the two men walked toward the back of the house and on inside. They settled themselves in the study. Both wore pensive expressions. Michael was thinking about the huge grapes hanging on the vines. *Dependence.* Maybe it wasn't such a bad idea after all. If he could keep his eyes on the end result and not on the trimming taking place, he would be all right.

"Does that help with the concept of brokenness?" Caleb asked. "God never breaks any of us just for the sake of breaking. He always has a good reason. Brokenness is a tough subject...but so needed in removing that independent spirit rampant in the church today. Take Peter, for example. I assume you had a chance to at least skim through the section about him."

"I did. It's what started me thinking along those lines."

"Did you read the entire section?"

"Some, but not all, "Michael admitted. "I'll try to finish it later."

"Good. Peter is one of the best examples of what God can do in and through a man who is totally dependent on Him. You can conquer the fear of rejection you described a while ago if you become absolutely dependent on God. He, who is perfect love, chases all fear away. You can't have both. Peter had another problem, too. Did you read enough to notice how Jesus had to deal with his pride? Whenever you read about him, you see one thing happening."

"Peter was the one who tried to walk on water, right?"

"That's him. In the middle of the storm, waves crashing all around and over the boat, the disciples saw someone walking on the water toward them, but they weren't sure if it was Jesus or a ghost. Peter cried out, telling the Lord, that if it was really Him, to call him out on the water, too. Jesus said, 'Come,' and Peter did. He actually walked on the water, until he took his eyes off the Lord. When that happened, he sank. He'd have gone down clear out of sight, but he cried out again to the Lord and was rescued."

Michael laughed. "I can see it now. Peter throws his arms up and hops out of the boat. He's probably thinking, 'Watch me, fellas! Here I go!' And then, plop...down he sinks. Jesus has to escort him back to the boat looking like a half-drowned rat." He shook his head. "Talk about humiliating."

"That, my friend, was one of the chisels Jesus used to break Peter's prideful spirit. You hit it right on the head when you said 'humiliating.' Each time Peter bragged about his intentions, he blew it. 'Just call me, I'll walk on water. I won't have You washing my feet. I won't let them kill You. I'll never leave You, Jesus. Count on me, I am the rock.' Old, prideful Peter." He paused for emphasis. "Yet, look how mightily he was used once he learned to depend on God. That reminds me of something I read somewhere. It takes more than a rose petal to polish a precious stone. Sometimes we need to be polished in more abrasive ways to bring out our hidden beauty and create a gem of value. The rose petal is one extreme. The hammer and chisel, the other. Only our Creator knows which is appropriate for each person's character."

"Do you think God has targeted a faulty area in my character?"

"Yes, sir!" he teased, his blue eyes twinkling.

"Well, you don't have to agree so fast." Michael thought for a few moments. "Do you think it might have something to do with my fear of rejection and failure? My need to be successful? Or my independence and pride?" Caleb did not respond. After a minute or two, he stood up. "The Lord knows you best, son, but I think you're on the right track. He does pinpoint strengths as well as weaknesses, I can assure you of that. Let's ask Him, shall we?" They prayed together and then relaxed in the twilight.

So much had happened so fast. Michael wondered how he could remember everything. He wanted to absorb all he could from Caleb… from his writings and from his life. A lot had sunk in already, but there was much more.

"Caleb, before we call it a night, tell me something. In this dependence and brokenness stuff, what part do I play? I mean, can I speed things up?"

"What part do you play?" Caleb echoed softly. "It's more than a part you're playing, Michael. You are the part. It's you God is interested in much more than any part." He paused, carefully choosing his words. "But you can quicken the process by surrendering your will to His. If God has zeroed in on areas in you, and you think you know what they are, then you're well on your way. Believe He has allowed the circumstances in which you are to be broken, even arranged them. Often He lets us work ourselves into a position from which only He can deliver us.

"Whatever the situation, He chooses the exact instruments He needs and uses them with utmost skill. Were we to make the selection, it would never hurt and would accomplish even less. Sometimes His tools are pointed and sharp. Pain and suffering may accompany them, but He knows exactly how much each one can take without breaking his or her spirit. He's after our stubborn self-will. His sole purpose is to drive out whatever hinders our relationship with Him." Pausing a moment, Caleb sat up and turned his piercing blue eyes on Michael. "What tools might He be using in your life?"

"You've got to be joking," exclaimed Michael. "Look what's been happening. Divorce pending. Restraining order. Newspapers. Do they qualify?"

"I'd say they do. Now let's get back to dependence on Jesus. That's the goal of brokenness. Some people have the ability to make dependence almost look easy. Like great big bunches of grapes on the vine, they are living testimonials of 'abiding in Christ.' They come from every religious and denominational background, from rich and poor families. No matter what the circumstances of their lives, they cannot be shaken from the Vine. I know one woman who went through the most horrible trials early in her marriage. Those years drove her to her knees, drove every ounce of pride from her character. She depended on Jesus to help her raise her family. Everyone around her was strengthened and encouraged by her pronounced faith in the Lord."

"Caleb, that's all well and good," protested Michael, "but how can I have faith like that? I sure need it now." His eyes followed his right fore-finger as it traced a spiral pattern in the wood of the coffee table. He looked up, questions written across his features.

"One day at a time, my boy. Especially for those of us who were taught to be independent and non-submissive. We have a hard time learning to depend on the Lord. I was that way, Michael. You've already heard a little of my business ventures. For too many years, I depended on nobody but myself. Weakness was something I despised. Not for the life of me could I understand anyone wanting to be broken. Even years after giving my heart and life to God, it was still a struggle to believe that 'in my weakness, He was strong.' Thank the Lord I learned the blessedness of total dependence before it was too late. It hurts to think how headstrong I used to be.

"Perhaps, if I'd heard a message or two on brokenness from the pulpit, it would have made the learning easier. Even today, that word is not in vogue among most Christian circles. That's the reason there are so few examples of true faith in the church anymore. Trials come, and people are either overcome with fear or embittered. How can we discover God's faithfulness if we get mad and rebellious at every opportunity to step out in faith? We grow when the odds are against us."

"I see what you mean," agreed Michael. "My marriage—whatever's left of it—is one of those opportunities, isn't it?"

"Yes, and recognizing that is the key to where you are right now," Caleb added. "If you would have continued hanging onto the hurt, or had grown bitter towards your wife, you could not have received from God the forgiveness you so desperately needed. I won't be so foolish as to tell you that the problems of life aren't important; yet, on a comparative level, they're little more than tools. Your attitude towards them determines whether you will be changed into a winner or a loser.

"By choosing to draw near to God, you've allowed Him to work His will in your heart. Not everyone wants to become dependent on Him like you do, Michael. One woman I know comes from quite a religious family. From the time she started school until she graduated from college, she made straight A's. Today, she's always doing something for somebody, and there's not a visibly evil bone in her body. With all of this, she is quite proud and independent. A true Pharisee. Her accomplishments stand in her way. Because of them, she cannot see her own needs. Her self-sufficiency hinders any reliance on Jesus Christ. As much as this hurts me, because she's my friend, I can't become dependent for her."

"Or for me."

"Right. Remember, there is only one way to speed up the learning period. By submitting and committing your will to God. Not once, but each day. Make every decision based on what pleases Him instead of yourself. It's a lengthy process—longer for some than for others. Look at the Bible characters. For many of them, it took a lifetime."

"Whew! That long?"

"It's up to you. It took Peter three years of walking with Jesus in person to prepare him for the role he was to play in the early church. Even after the day of Pentecost, when he and the other believers were filled with the Holy Spirit, he had to depend on the Lord. You and I are no different...

"But be on the lookout, Michael. Satan's workings are so subtle. He can lure believers into even becoming proud of their seeming dependence. No matter how skillful the disguise, pride will extend the process of brokenness. Anytime you confront an obstacle, you face two choices. On one hand—reliance on God. On the other—pride. It will have you react in anger, bitterness, and selfishness. Or it will tell you that you can handle it yourself if only you try harder...next time."

"Boy, Caleb, pounding my thumb with the hammer this afternoon showed how proud I am...and how little it takes to make me lose my temper. Pretty disgusting. I wanted to look good in front of you and Sandy. When I think of how angry I got after the restraining order and newspaper article...I couldn't face it, but I hurt so bad, I cried. Hadn't done that since I was a kid." He was silent a long moment. When he continued, his voice was little more than a whisper. "My anger sure got away from me again today." He shook his head slowly from side to side.

"You're growing. Don't let setbacks discourage you. Repent from your heart and get on with it."

"Yeah, I guess so. I just thought I'd come further than that."

"We all encounter struggles in our faith walk in one way or another. For example, I face a constant challenge to maintain a scriptural balance in certain areas—like the delicate one between brokenness necessary for great faith vs. great faith's resulting 'prosperity.' We should seek neither extreme—asceticism nor hedonism. We seek Jesus. The apostle Paul found the happy medium. He learned to rejoice, both in times of want and in times of prosperity. I've never been in prison like Paul. I can't imagine how hard it would be to sing songs of thanksgiving in there."

Michael's head jerked up. His eyes focused on Caleb. "I met someone after he got out of prison. I didn't know him while he was inside the fence, but if anyone could have rejoiced, he was the one." He stood and stared out the window. The silvery moon was reflected off the pond's surface. As his thoughts returned to Ralph, he wondered if he really was able to be happy while he was in prison.

"What happened to your friend?" Caleb asked after a minute, drawn by the finality in Michael's tone.

"He died." The words landed with a thud. Michael continued to stare out the window at the flickering silhouette on the water. "Something happened to him in prison. He worked with some sort of chemicals or something, and he got real sick." Michael turned around to face Caleb. "Ralph was always so full of joy, right to the very end of his life. Guess he had the kind of balanced faith you're talking about, huh?"

"Sounds like he did. But he probably wasn't always that way, even after he accepted Jesus. Didn't he grow into such tremendous faith?"

Michael stopped to reminisce about his few conversations with Ralph. "Come to think of it, he did mention that for years he was up and down in his walk with God. One day hot, the next day cold. On again, off again...while he was in prison. His faith depended on the circumstances at hand. Something changed him though, once he got so sick. Then he had no choice but to depend on God. Big difference, huh?"

"Mm-hmm. One is mature faith, like those sweet, juicy grapes outside, almost ready for harvest. They've been attached to the vine a lot longer than the small, hard, sour ones. Right, pal?"

Michael nodded.

Suddenly, Caleb jumped up and broke into song on the rousing chorus, "Abiding in the Vine, abiding in the Vine, love, joy..." He even clapped and gave a couple of hops from one foot to the other while Michael looked on and laughed. It lifted the heaviness that had started to settle over them. When he was done, he said, "Well, it's been a long day. How about if we 'hit the sack,' as Sandy would say?"

He yawned. "Sounds good to me. By the way...what time does church start in the morning?" He walked to the coffee table and bent to pick up his empty mug.

"Ten o'clock sharp."

"Okay, I'll be ready. See ya in the morning," he called as he headed upstairs. He was tired, but did not think he could get to sleep just yet. There were still too many unanswered questions. His talk with Caleb helped. Their conversations served to arouse an even stronger longing for more of the truth.

TEN

HOPE

In his room once again, Michael knelt at the side of his bed. How he wanted the calm assurance he sensed in Caleb! He had moments of calm and moments of assurance, but never both. And they were fleeting. No price seemed too high to possess such faith. Never one for fancy prayers, he poured out his heart to God. "Father, I love You, but I still have so many doubts and fears," he prayed. "And lots of faults for You to work on... Thank You for forgiving my loss of temper today and help me to get it under control. Do with me as You will. Teach me to depend on You completely. Teach me Your love, Lord Jesus, to love others as You love me..."

Michael rose slowly, his knees stiff from their unaccustomed contact with the floor. He smiled and reached for his Bible. While he was praying, he kept remembering bits and pieces from a story he heard years ago. Opening his Bible, he flipped through the pages. "Wow, here it is!" he exclaimed, elated at finding it. He sat on the edge of the bed and began to read in Mark 5:24:

> So Jesus went with him. A large crowd followed and pressed around him. And a woman was there who had been subject to bleeding for twelve years.

She had suffered a great deal under the care of many doctors and had spent all she had, yet instead of getting better she grew worse. When she heard about Jesus, she came up behind him in the crowd and touched his cloak, because she thought, "If I just touch his clothes, I will be healed." Immediately her bleeding stopped and she felt in her body that she was freed from her suffering. At once Jesus realized that power had gone out from him. He turned around in the crowd and asked, "Who touched my clothes?" "You see the people crowding against you," his disciples answered, "and yet you can ask, 'Who touched me?'" But Jesus kept looking around to see who had done it. Then the woman, knowing what had happened to her, came and fell at his feet and, trembling with fear, told him the whole truth. He said to her, "Daughter, your faith has healed you. Go in peace and be freed from your suffering."

Those words took on a sudden, new meaning. He could see the poor woman's total dependence upon Jesus. After everything else failed, He was all she had left. Yet, it was not a passive, "woe-is-me" dependence. What had he read..."people crowding against him?" That did not stop her from pressing in to reach Him. Somewhere, she must have heard about Jesus. Otherwise, why would she believe He could heal her? Yes, she had heard plenty and had sought Him with determination. Nothing could have kept her from reaching the One she depended on to meet her needs.

Michael felt one piece being nudged into place. He saw a facet of dependence that had previously eluded him. It contradicted all his prior conceptions. The woman with a bleeding disorder did not portray clinging, leech-like wimpiness. Her struggle to get through that crowd to touch even the hem of Jesus' garment required more than choosing to believe He could heal her. She backed her choice up with action.

"Lord," he prayed, as he closed his Bible and laid his right hand firmly on top of it, "Thank You for leading me to this passage. I don't yet understand all You're trying to show me, so please, Lord...teach me. Help me to be dependent on You and do my part at the same time." As he got ready for bed, he felt assured of more illumination to come. Expectancy, a sudden flame kindled by light from the Living Word, intensified. And with it came peace. He soon fell asleep.

Michael rose early the next morning. The sense of anticipation was still with him. His first waking thoughts focused on the similarity of his past to that of the woman he read about. He saw her twelve years of fruitless searching for health as his years of groping after success. Neither of them were better off for their efforts. But he, too, had finally heard…deep down where it counted…about Jesus. He and the woman both needed healing—she, physically, he, emotionally and spiritually. She had come to Jesus. He was still learning to lean.

Dependence meant a whole new way of life, but he wanted it now more than ever. The inner joy he felt confirmed his choice. He went downstairs and, seeing Caleb, could not wait to share his latest discovery from the Word. During their morning run, he had ample time. Breakfast was a delight, but he ate little—a few bites of wheat toast and honey and an occasional sip from his hot drink. His vegetable omelet went almost untouched.

Caleb's blue eyes crinkled with laughter at Michael's enthusiasm. The two men shared equally the expectancy of good things to come. Despite the circumstances, Michael was learning to believe God for good. That belief came from no natural source. Caleb knew that God, by His Spirit and through His Word, had done what only He could do. Heaven-sent joy buoyed them along as it purged some of Michael's fears and doubts about the future. For the present, that was enough.

"By the way, can you be ready in half an hour?" Caleb asked finally.

"Sure. I thought the service didn't start until ten o'clock. What's the rush?"

"I'm sorry. I forgot to mention that I pick up Sandy and his mother on the way. It takes a little while to help her with the wheelchair. Besides, I have to be there early to take care of some last-minute details."

Michael's eyebrows arched in surprise. He liked to take his time getting ready. A question formed, but he said nothing. He was getting used to being surprised by Caleb.

Forty-five minutes later, the two of them parked alongside Sandy's front porch. His red head popped through the doorway, followed by his slender body in a navy blue suit. Michael blinked. His mouth dropped open and closed, as if he were about to say something and thought better of it. The boy who was standing on the porch and holding the screen door open for them bore little resemblance to the ragamuffin he'd first met. Except for the hair. Even though it had been carefully wet down, the cowlick in the back defied any amount of combing.

"G'mornin,' Mr. Michael. G'mornin', Mr. Caleb," Sandy called to his two friends. "Ma's ready. She's been waitin' fer ya."

"Good morning, Sandy," the two chorused.

"Well, don' jes sit there. C'mon in," excited little Sandy encouraged, his enthusiasm at the bursting point. Only the blue suit, a gift from Caleb, held him in check. Still, he did a slow jig, dancing back and forth from one foot to the other.

Michael chuckled, seeing the struggle going on in front of him. "Hold on, buddy. We're coming," he called out before the little boy in Sandy could win out over the young man dressed in his Sunday best. Michael thought of his own children and shook his head to rid it of unwelcomed emotions. *Something good is coming,* he reminded himself. He was determined that nothing would keep him from receiving it.

At the door, he stopped to greet Sandy and wait for Caleb, who was two steps behind. Sandy held the door with his foot and reached out to hug the older man. Then Michael and Caleb followed his gentle tug on their arms as he led them around the hallway and into the living room.

Much of what Michael had seen yesterday of the sparse furnishings inside the Hawkins' house had failed to leave an imprint on his memory. He saw why. The mismatched assortment looked like a collection of donations from several well-meaning families...after careless children and untrained pets had long since left home. "Junk benevolence"...was that the term for it? A way to redecorate and have the old stuff hauled away for free. He felt a twinge of guilt for some of the shabby items he had sent to charities in the past. And all the while, patting himself on the back for his generosity.

Caught up as he was in his thoughts, he failed to notice the faint whir of the approaching wheelchair. Sandy's mother appeared, escorted by Caleb. Suddenly, it was as if the sun had sent a ray shining into the very center of the room. Michael noticed her, seemingly for the first time. He saw a pretty woman, wearing a golden yellow dress that set off shiny chestnut-brown hair cascading over her shoulders. Her long curls partially concealed the brace that kept her erect. Even the cushions on the armrests of her wheelchair had been covered with matching yellow and green material.

In age similar to Michael, she was a woman who had lost both her husband and her future. When she looked up at him, her green eyes sparkled as she smiled a faint "Hello." Michael was unprepared. Never had he paid much attention to the handicapped. They existed, but their plight failed to impact him. Today, Sandy's mother broke his heart. Into his joyful spirit flooded a river of compassion, the likes of which he had never experienced.

He cleared his throat. "Good morning, Mrs. Hawkins," he greeted her as Sandy let his hand go and crossed the three steps between them to take his place at her side.

"You kin call her Maggie, short fer Margaret Elizabeth. Don't she look purty?" Sandy asked proudly. He put his arm around her neck, his cheek against hers, and hugged her.

"She sure does," Michael replied. "You both look great. Maggie, your dress is beautiful, and Sandy makes a perfect gentleman in his blue suit. You've got two mighty handsome escorts this morning." Michael stopped speaking. He noticed the sudden moist glint in her eyes and was afraid he had said something wrong. He felt awkward, out of place. Did it show? Caleb stood behind them and winked, nodding his head in encouragement. It was not enough. Michael felt like shouting, "Dear God, why do Your children suffer like this?" At this moment his pain for them overshadowed any he had left for his own situation. *If only I could help...* He offered a silent prayer for them.

Caleb coughed. The tension eased. Their attention focused on him. "Michael, if you'll lead the way out, I'll bring up the rear with our leading lady."

"Sure thing," he agreed, dipping his head to Sandy and Maggie. After Caleb carefully maneuvered out to the car, helping make Maggie comfortable and stowing her wheelchair in the trunk, they were off to

church. Songs of praise rang from the car stereo and from the car's passengers as they made the brief trip. Except Maggie. She could only smile and bob her head.

Michael, not knowing what to expect, anticipated a quaint, white wood-frame country church, complete with a tall steeple, graveyard out back, and a plump, pleasant-faced preacher. *After all,* he thought, *hardly a soul lives out here in the country.* He could not have been more wrong. The local population may have been limited, but people drove from miles around.

"Where in the world did this huge place come from?" Michael asked, amazed.

"It's not in the world, buddy," Caleb teased.

"But it's right..." and he paused, looking at Caleb and then Sandy, who giggled. He reached over to Sandy in a futile attempt to smooth his unruly red hair.

"Actually," Caleb continued, "you're right. We're in the world, but not of it, as Scripture says. Isn't that right, Sandy?"

"Yes, sir. It says so in Second C'rinthians." He looked to his mom and smiled, squeezing the hand he held with such love. "The sixth chapter... near the end, I think."

"Good, Sandy. Very good. Your studying is beginning to pay off," Caleb commended the youngster. He scanned the partially filled parking lot, and as he did, his eye caught Sandy's in the rearview mirror. He winked. "Verses seventeen and eighteen. 'Therefore,'" he quoted as much for Michael's benefit as Sandy's, "'come out from them and be separate, says the Lord. Touch no unclean thing, and I will receive you. I will be a Father to you, and you will be my sons and daughters, says the Lord Almighty.'" Caleb finished quoting and shut off the car engine at about the same time. Michael sat, still amazed that a church, or for that matter any building of that size, could be located in the country and still draw a crowd. "Well, we're here, folks," Caleb said. "I'll be going off for a bit once we get inside. Michael, there are some friends I'd like you to meet, if you don't mind waiting some after the service."

"Of course not," he responded with a look towards Sandy's mother. The mixed sense of grief tugged at him again. "I'll be fine." Looking from Maggie to Sandy, and back again, Michael ached to do something to encourage them. He hesitated a second when he thought to act, and the moment passed. Before regret could settle, Caleb was out the door. In a flash, he retrieved the wheelchair and came around to Michael's side to help Maggie.

Michael, with his limited exposure to invalids, did as much to hinder as help, but his heart was in the right place. Caleb's experience more than balanced his lack. Michael took note of this. He noticed how Caleb maneuvered the wheelchair inches closer with the toe of his right foot and how he lifted her into it with such tenderness that not a crinkle showed in her green-trimmed, yellow dress.

Sandy lifted his mother's hair and strapped her in her brace, so she would not fall forward. Then he ever so lovingly arranged her hair on her shoulders again. Michael turned away. He wanted to cover his eyes to hide the tears that threatened to spill forth. Only Caleb noticed, but said nothing. Instead, he urged Michael, "Down in front to the left of center is the wheelchair section."

"Don' worry, Mr. Caleb," Sandy called out from beside his mom. "I'll show him jes where t'go. We won't git lost."

"Okay, Sandy. I'll trust them both to your care." Caleb winked at Michael over the top of Sandy's head. "Just as soon as I can, I'll be up to join you." He said this last as he held the door for the others. Safe inside, Caleb, with a hand on Sandy and Michael's shoulders, stood smiling. He stooped down to Sandy's mom, and as gently as a butterfly dancing on a rose petal, kissed her forehead. Then he turned and strode off around a nearby bench.

"C'mon," Sandy said, with a tug on Michael's left hand. "He'll be back real quick. You'll see. Let's go git our seats." Michael agreed, gave Sandy's hand a hearty pat, and turned to grasp the handles on the rear of the wheelchair. Guiding it with care down the aisle, he took note of the multitudes beginning to stream through the open doors.

Many nodded greetings to Sandy and Maggie. Several stopped to say "Hello" or bend and give her a hug, and one mussed Sandy's red hair even more than it was already. He took it good-naturedly. "Mornin', Mr. Shaw," he called, while ducking out from underneath the man's huge paw of a hand. "This here's Mr. Michael. He's a good friend," Sandy said proudly.

"Pleased to meet you, sir," boomed Mr. Shaw as he leaned down and whispered to Sandy's mom, "Good morning, Mrs. Hawkins. It's mighty good to see you in church today." Then he rose and remembered to extend his hand to Michael, who gave it a firm, hearty shake. "Name's Shaw, Bob Shaw."

"Michael Nastasis."

"Well, it's a pleasure to meet you, Michael," the bear-like man declared. "Any friend of Sandy and his mom is a friend of mine. If you need anything, come and get me. I'll be with the ushers at the rear. Just relax and let the Spirit of God minister to you."

Michael watched him amble up the aisle, greeting people as he went. He smiled and turned to catch up with Sandy, who was already leading the way to their seats. "Here ya go, Ma," Sandy motioned, patting the armrest to the *Reserved* section.

They had time, in the thirty minutes before the service, to prepare, each in his own way. For the most part, Sandy made sure his mom was comfortable. Michael watched the people filing in to be seated. He could not explain the feeling, but he felt good about being there. The sense of expectancy that he experienced earlier had returned in full measure.

Finally, lights dimmed in the sanctuary and brightened on the platform. A brilliant choir of voices burst forth in joyous songs of praise. They sang one piece after another. Soon, throughout the sanctuary, all who could stand did so. A thousand voices joined with the choir to sing the high praises of God. Michael had never heard anything like it. He wondered for a moment if he was in heaven, so fully was he caught up in the joyous freedom of worshiping God. Tears filled his eyes, but he did not even notice.

When he thought he could not stand another minute, the music softened. Like a breath of cool fresh air, peace descended. Across the building, people knelt. No one directed them, but almost as one they bowed before God. Music from a huge pipe organ undergirded the harp-like arpeggios of a grand piano. Out of the hushed background arose a rich baritone voice. In a free-flowing style, a man sang the old hymn, "I love to tell the story of unseen things above...of Jesus and His glory...of Jesus and His love...I love to tell the story, because I know it's true...it satisfies my longing as nothing else can do...I love to tell the story...'twill be my theme in glory...to tell the old, old story...of Jesus and His love." A shiver ran down Michael's spine as he listened.

Many remained kneeling. Some dried their eyes. Others raised their hands. A few sat quietly. Sandy nudged Michael with his elbow, leaned over, and whispered, "That was Mr. Caleb. I'd know his singin' anywhere." Michael's mouth dropped open in surprise. *Caleb sings like that? He never mentioned he was a singer,* Michael thought. He was in such awe at what he felt. He was speechless.

Very soon, Caleb, his face radiant, returned to sit with them. Sandy leaned over and whispered to him, "I heard you singin', Mr. Caleb." He nodded, smiling, and put his finger to his lips in a "Shh" gesture. Sandy grinned proudly at Michael and nudged him again with his elbow.

Then the minister stepped forward. His slight body and graying hair disguised an inexhaustible energy. After calling the people to rise for prayer, the pastor tapped his Bible twice with his open right hand. "I have a message straight from the throne of Almighty God for you," he began. Every eye settled firmly upon him, following the rise and fall of his half-open hand. "The Holy Spirit keeps bringing me back to this message. We all need certain things. Water to drink. Food to eat. Air to breathe. Try holding your breath for a minute. Unless you're in shape like Caleb over here, even holding it a few seconds is hard." He paused and let his eyes scan the eager faces before him.

"Just this morning, the Lord reminded me of something. Have you noticed how the human body can survive longer if it's deprived of tangible substances, such as food and water, than if it's deprived of something as intangible as air? Think about it. Weeks without food. About seven days without water. But minutes, mere minutes, without oxygen—and the brain starts dying. Like air, faith is a critical substance. You can't see it. You can't touch it, but it is real, nonetheless. And just as vital to your existence. Why? Because 'everything that does not come from faith is sin,' Romans 14:23...and 'the wages of sin is death,' Romans 6:23. The Amplified Bible defines faith this way in Hebrews 11:1, 'Now faith is the assurance (the confirmation, the title deed) of the things [we] hope for, being the proof of things [we] do not see and the conviction of their reality [faith perceiving as real fact what is not revealed to the senses].'

"Another Scripture passage backs up what faith is and carries it a step further—to what faith does. Turn with me in your Bibles to Second Corinthians, the fourth chapter and verses thirteen through eighteen." He turned to Caleb. "Would you read for us, brother?" Caleb stood and cleared his throat. He began reading:

It is written: "I believed; therefore I have spoken." With that same spirit of faith we also believe and therefore speak, because we know that the one who raised the Lord Jesus from the dead will also raise us with Jesus and present us with you in his presence. All this for your benefit, so that the grace that is reaching more and more people may cause thanksgiving to overflow to the glory of God. Therefore we do not lose heart. Though outwardly we are wasting away, yet inwardly we are being renewed day by day. For our light and momentary troubles are achieving for us an eternal glory that far outweighs them all. So we fix our eyes not on what is seen, but on what is unseen. For what is seen is temporary, but what is unseen is eternal.

Caleb paused and looked at Maggie seated in her wheelchair. She smiled peacefully and blinked her eyes in agreement.

The pastor strode from behind the pulpit to stand on the edge of the platform and declared, "'Our light and momentary troubles are achieving for us an eternal glory that far outweighs them all.' Are any of you afflicted? Persecuted? Then you're among friends. The question is, 'Where do you go for comfort?' Don't be drawn by the delicacies of the world. They only go rancid. Don't look to the waters of the world. They dry up. Forget about that change of climate. It may alleviate your hay fever, but do nothing for the real you. Look to Jesus." He paused and pointed up, then continued, his voice gaining strength, "Look instead to Jesus—the Author and Finisher of your faith." His voice rose another notch. "Look to Jesus the Christ...

"Look through every situation with the eyes of faith. Find Him in the middle of every circumstance. Cry out to Him when your heart is heavy and Satan's lies would bury you in despair...when he tells you that God doesn't hear you. Or that He doesn't care about you. Cry out—Jesus!" His voiced boomed, "because Je-sus-is-Lord," he proclaimed, as he froze in that position with his right arm raised and index finger pointing heavenward. Shouts of "Glory!", "Hallelujah!", and "Praise God!" rang forth from around the building.

"Declare His sovereignty in everything. Sign up for God's team and not the devil's. Line yourself up with Him. Scripture tells us that 'the righteous one will live by faith,' and that 'without faith it is impossible to please God." I believe that the desire of most of your hearts is to be found pleasing in His sight.

"Ah, yes...faith. So elusive to some. So vibrant to others." Pausing, the pastor stepped back from the edge of the platform. He walked to his right and stopped in front of Caleb, Michael, Sandy, and his mother. To Michael, it seemed that he was the focus of the pastor's attention. "Biblical commands to have faith and to believe prove that faith is not just an option. It's a mandate from heaven. A man without it is more in danger than a man with no air to breathe." He moved across the front of the platform, eyeing the congregation to drive home his point as he did so. "Faith—the invisible quality—is that important."

That was the preamble to the morning's message. Not one to be bound by a strict program, Pastor Fontaine knew the leading of the Holy Spirit. Michael sat transfixed. He watched every move the pastor made. It was not what he had come expecting, but it was just what he needed...and the message was only beginning.

"Today we are going to read of a man full of faith. A man who knew the glory of God. His name...Moses. He was a descendent of the priestly line of Levi. The faith of Amram and Jochebed, Moses' parents, may have insulated them from the idolatrous rites of their Egyptian captors. None can determine the exact degree to which many of the Israelites were affected by such heathen goings-on, but one thing is certain—those two remained faithful to God.

"Faith kept Amram and Jochebed when they were forced to hide Moses. Faith kept them when they set him adrift down the river Nile. And faith kept them when Divine providence brought him back to be nursed by his own mother." He paused, but quickly resumed his vigorous walk. "Today, people set their babies adrift in a river," he stopped and turned, his gaze slowly sweeping the people hanging onto every word, "and they don't even know it.

"This river is not from God. No, my friends, it is not the mighty stream that flows from His holy temple, restoring life to whatever it touches. I speak of a river of death, issuing straight from Satan's kingdom and flowing over the banks of wicked principalities and rulers in high places. It threatens to drown all who are snared by its seductive current. Its name? Secular humanism: faith in man—worship of self as the supreme being.

126

"Where are humanism's shrines? The media—television, radio, films. Print. And institutions—schools, government. God forbid, even churches have been infiltrated by this philosophy of 'You're the center of your own universe, so if it feels good, do it.' Saints, do you want your children protected when they're out in the world? Then guard your home with prayer. Be selective when it comes to the programs you watch in your home. And above all, strive to depend on the Lord in all you do.

"Do you think it was easy for Moses' parents to let their infant go floating down the river? They loved him. He was a beautiful baby. But they had no other choice if they wanted to protect him from Pharaoh's baby-killing rampage. Of course it wasn't easy, but their security was rooted in God. He brought them through when no one else could have.

"Moses learned this lesson, too. In the courts of Pharaoh, he was schooled in the wisdom of Egypt...and he excelled. But there came a day that his training forced him to make a choice. He saw an Egyptian beating a Hebrew slave, and one thing came to his mind—revenge! Trained as a warrior, he made a decision, then acted. The Egyptian was dead!

"Moses, the murderer. Do you hear me, my dear brothers and sisters? Murder in the first degree." His voice softened. "But was this what God, who looks upon the heart, saw in Moses for the rest of his life? Let's look in the book of Hebrews, chapter eleven, verses twenty-four to twenty-seven. If you would read it, good brother." Caleb stood and read. His clear, strong voice carried throughout the church:

> By faith Moses, when he had grown up, refused to be known as the son of Pharaoh's daughter. He chose to be mistreated along with the people of God rather than to enjoy the pleasures of sin for a short time. He regarded disgrace for the sake of Christ as of greater value than the treasures of Egypt, because he was looking ahead to his reward. By faith he left Egypt, not fearing the king's anger; he persevered because he saw him who is invisible.

"Brother Caleb," Pastor Fontaine asked, "did you read anything about murder?"

"No, sir. Not a word."

"But you did read, 'By faith Moses,' and again, 'by faith,'" declared the preacher. "God saw not a murderer, but His humble, chosen deliverer, who would leave the pleasures, the position, the wealth, and the esteem of Egypt...because he had faith. Moses saw the invisible.

"Of course, forty years in the Sinai desert were needed for God to weed out of Moses the ways of Egypt. That, my dear brothers and sisters, is when Moses learned another key element of faith: it took more than a blood sacrifice to get the job done. And it takes more than believing in Jesus' death on the cross for you to walk by faith today." This caused a few raised eyebrows among the congregation. "Don't get me wrong... you're called saints, but you still need Jesus. Admit it. Once and for all, you do have to quit arguing with God before you can ever begin to have faith. But move on. Like Moses, learn to count on God. Rely on Him for everything, because He's quite a reliable Father. Caleb and I have had some good talks about this aspect of faith. He calls it dependence. It's the same thing. Dependence on a dependable Lord. And you've got to have it...unless you want to spend forty years wandering around the desert. You choose."

When a moment of much head-shaking passed, he continued. "Countless times in counseling, my heart has been broken by just these kinds of choices. Husbands get disillusioned with their wives. Wives feel betrayed by husbands. These aren't unsaved folks, now. These are Christian, God-fearing people. They know what Scripture says about marriage—how holy and precious it is in the eyes of God. If you asked them about that, they would readily agree.

"But...when it comes to the practical application of their faith...in other words, waiting and relying upon God to restore their marriage for them...hah! That's another story. They refuse to believe. Instead, they seek immediate divorce and wander around a spiritual desert until they either learn to depend on God..." He paused, lifted His Bible with his right hand head-high, and walked to the center of the platform. Every eye watched that Bible, held two feet above the pulpit for the space of two hastily drawn breaths..."or they die!" The Bible fell. The crack it made hitting the pulpit sliced through the silence. "It's that simple, people."

Michael listened with renewed interest to the rest of the message. In principle, the pastor was saying the same thing as Caleb. Biblical heroes of faith still speak today. Faith is a process. And he would have to learn to walk his talk. It was clearer now, in a special way, and was beginning to be more a part of him. He identified with Moses and the choices he made, but would he, Michael, be willing to suffer more affliction, if need be? He wanted to say "Yes," but wanted even more to be honest.

He heard how Moses, skilled in the wisdom and knowledge of Egypt, made excuses to God when He first called him to work. Said he couldn't speak very well and was afraid to go back alone. The burning sun and the blinding sandstorms cut and shaped this man until all was gone but his burning need for God. Greater was it than even the fear of an unresolved murder hanging over his head. *That*, Michael thought, *was dependence.*

Michael got excited when he heard how God provided for Moses. He did not send his servant to Pharaoh powerless. Or alone. On the contrary, Moses gained all by losing all. He acknowledged his need. God supplied His power.

The word *power* interrupted his thoughts and captured his attention. "Yes," continued the pastor, "power comes from the throne room of heaven for a purpose. Moses received power to witness to Pharaoh. You and I receive power to witness to the world, and God brings deliverance for His witnesses. He did it for Moses, and He'll do it for you. It may not come according to your time frame, but it will come.

"When Moses marched into Pharaoh's court and commanded, 'Thus saith the Lord God of Israel, Let my people go,' I'm sure he expected Pharaoh to do just that. You can read the account in the fifth chapter of Exodus." The pastor marched to the edge of the platform and pointed first to Caleb, then Sandy, his mother, and finally, Michael. "Well, is that what happened? Pharaoh replied, 'Yes, of course, Moses, whatever you say.'

"No," cried the pastor, "he did not. He retorted, 'Who is the Lord that I should obey his voice to let Israel go?'" The pastor's penetrating voice dripped with cynicism. "'I do not know the Lord and I will not let Israel go.' That's how Pharaoh responded to Moses. Then he forced the Israelites to work under worse circumstances than ever. So where was God's power I mentioned? History's final chapter wasn't written yet, brothers and sisters. In the end, praise His glorious name, the Lord destroyed the powers of Egypt. Their strength, their false gods, and their hope...wiped out. By then, Pharaoh did know who the Lord was. Yes, he certainly did." Pastor Fontaine stopped short and waited. Then he wiped his forehead with his handkerchief and picked up his pace.

"Imagine Moses' astonishment when the plagues struck the Egyptians at the words he spoke, while the Israelites remained untouched! How must he have felt, striding boldly among the plague-infested, pestilence-riddled heathen? Frogs. Flies. Lice. Rivers of blood. Darkness so thick you could feel it, enveloping a people who worshiped the sun. That was only the beginning. For a finale, how about the death of all firstborn children and animals in one night…in every household throughout Egypt? As Moses stood watching one false idol after another fall before the true God—his God—do you think he even remembered the pain of those forty wilderness years? Probably not. Indeed, Moses' faith had grown by leaps and bounds during that time, and he was seeing the results." The pastor stopped in front of the pulpit, picked up his Bible, and made a sweeping motion with his arm.

"God desires each one of us to continue growing in faith and knowledge of Him. So endure the wilderness. Step out in faith and depend on His care. That's where the Father is leading." The pastor started walking again, but at a slower pace. Back and forth, gazing steadily upward. In an instant, he stopped and turned to the congregation.

"How do you live your lives? Do you base your decisions, plans, hopes, and dreams as if the One living within you…" (he pointed to several people he knew well: Caleb, the organist, two men in the choir) "as if He is greater than the one in the world? Do you have a God-given vision for your life? Anybody?" He waited as a number of hands went up. "Is it limited by your puny human strengths and weaknesses? If so, start over. This time, listen to the words of encouragement that Jesus had for His disciples—all of them. He said in John 16:33, 'I have told you these things, so that in me you may have peace. In this world you will have trouble. But take heart! I have overcome the world.' Hallelujah! He overcame, people. He overcame because He always did those things which pleased the Father. Can we do any less? Of course we can, but not if we want to hear, 'Well done, good and faithful servant. Come and share your master's happiness!' Those words are limited to people full of faith.

"So then, my dear brothers and sisters in Christ, let's review, for a moment, what we've learned so far about our walk of faith. First, decide to line yourself up with God's Word and His promises. Get on His team and quit being at odds with Him about everything. Stop trying to make up your own rules. That's a sure way to lose the game of life. Priority #1 is accepting your own need of a Savior—a Deliverer. Second, learn to follow and rely on Him. Knowing that His name is Jesus is not enough. You need to know for yourself that He is a dependable Provider. Run to His Word, don't walk, if you feel depressed and full of doubt. When the day comes that everything crumbles around you, and you find yourself helpless, surrender...surrender...*surrender* to your God. Cling to Him. In spite of appearances, He knows what He's doing. Faith is often perfected in the Spirit's "School of Hard Knocks."

"The Israelites had no excuse for their lack of faith in God. They had their dependence on Him demonstrated time and time again. Food, water, and battles with their enemies made it plain that they could do nothing successfully on their own. The rod of God, symbolic of the Lord Jesus, had to be held high to part the Red Sea. It had to be held high to defeat the people of Amalek in their first wilderness battle. Israel saw all of this, but at the border of the Promised Land, they fell short.

"Jehovah God had never once let them down. So, what were a few measly giants compared to the Red Sea? Yet, their hearts grew faint. They trembled, refused to depend on God, and sealed their fate. Hear me, brothers and sisters, I'm about ready to close," the preacher explained, "but this is important. Your works, not just here in church but in your day-to-day lives, demonstrate your faith to the world. Others cannot see faith. They may as well try to catch the wind. Won't you let them see visible evidence of your dependence on God? In these last days, they will need it. Desperately.

"Stand to your feet, please," he continued. "I believe God is calling each one of us to a deeper walk of faith this morning. I know He's been speaking to me." Michael lent his silent agreement to the pastor. There was such peace and a gentle tug on his heart. He wanted to relinquish his heart afresh to God, to his Father, and give Him complete control of his life. Big things. Little things. All of it. And as the pastor led the congregation in a prayer of commitment, Michael did just that.

Around him, many others prayed. Some wept, their tears spilling unashamedly. Others knelt, leaning their heads on the pews in front of them. The sound of the piano and organ, a gentle thread linking the people, floated through the building. After some minutes, Michael could not tell how many, the tone of the music changed. It gathered strength, ordered as it was by the Holy Spirit, until all were singing to the chorus, "Give Thanks."

ELEVEN

LESSONS

LATER, ON THE ride to Sandy's, Michael relived the service. In those final moments, he felt transported to the very gates of heaven by the magnificent instruments and uplifted voices. The presence of God was so strong, yet gentle, as He ministered to His people. It formed a stark contrast to the church he had attended all his life. Why, he was not sure.

During a couple of minutes alone with Caleb as Sandy made his mom comfortable, Michael questioned him about the contrast and was surprised at his reply. "Faith. Faith is the difference."

"Just faith?"

Caleb laughed at Michael's open-mouthed expression. "You know, you really shouldn't let your mouth hang open like that. You might get away with it back in the city, but you've got to be more careful out here in the sticks. Never know what might fly in!" he teased, the corners of his mouth turned up in a smile. "Getting back to your question...true faith is the key." He paused, trying to frame the right words. "First, it's your new faith. The Spirit of God is alive within you now. He wasn't before, because you didn't know Jesus...

"Also, it's Pastor Fontaine's faith and his own close relationship with the Lord that allows him to be anointed. God uses dependent, trusting souls who willingly submit to His discipline. And who learn to discipline themselves."

Michael nodded and smirked. "Guess that's not true of all church leaders, huh?"

"No... unfortunately. But be careful how you say that, Michael. The body of Christ has suffered some gaping wounds and we're still healing. Much of the trouble today's pastors and evangelists get into stems from lack of discipline—physically, mentally, and spiritually. When obedience precedes service, like in our pastor, God uses him. Pastor Fontaine is not perfect, by any means. Nor are we. He is human, but he's a sincere man of God.

"One more reason for the difference you sensed in church today is the faith of those around you. The greater their faith and the more willing they are to be in God's presence, the more He responds." Again Caleb paused, this time to make his point. "Ultimately, the anointing is up to God, but He never fails to respond to true faith."

"He sure did today," Michael agreed. "That was awesome. I wish..."

Caleb understood the faraway look in his friend's eyes. It was his desire for his family to be in church with him. Caleb reached over and gave his shoulder a hearty squeeze. "Keep praying, son. Don't give up...Say, here comes Sandy. Are you ready to wrap up this little job?"

With an effort, Michael forced his thoughts back from their wishful wanderings to the task at hand. Just a couple more hours of painting, some small touch ups, and their work would be done for the weekend. The house was shaping up, looking more lived-in than run-down, and he felt good about being a part of it. A warm glow spread over him. "Yep, I'm ready, pal," he replied. "Ready as ever."

Squinting into the Monday morning sun, Michael's concentration was divided between his driving and the people in his life, of late. He thought about Maggie Hawkins and wondered what would become of Sandy if something happened to her. A hard lump formed in his throat, making it difficult to swallow. The boy was too young to be on his own. Well, there was always Caleb.

Michael's friendship with him weighed on his thoughts. It was ironic. His own father would be the same age as Caleb if he were still alive, but they shared little else in common. Whereas his dad was distant and cold, Caleb was warm and compassionate. His dad had been impossible to please. Caleb, on the other hand, could find pleasure in the smallest things. He desired excellence, but not as a condition of his love. *Yes,* Michael thought with a smile, *I sure could get attached to that old guy.*

Such was his state of mind as he parked the car in front of his apartment and gathered his things. By then it was midmorning. He got out, took a deep breath, and walked toward the front door. The street was deserted except for one lone man dressed in blue-gray pants and a light blue shirt. He was stepping out of a small white truck. Michael squinted at the side of the vehicle. Written underneath a blue eagle was *U.S. Mail.* That reminded him of his letter to Stephanie. He wondered if she had responded yet…or if she even would.

After depositing his bags in the bedroom, he could stand the suspense no more. He headed out to the mailbox and sorted through the few pieces of mail as he ambled back to the house. His breath caught. A letter from Stephanie! He recognized her elegant handwriting on a pastel pink linen envelope. With trembling fingers, he separated it from the assorted advertising flyers and held it before him. His heartbeat quickened. *At least she answered,* he reasoned. He set the envelope down, poured a glass of juice, and strolled out to the porch for some fresh air. He inhaled deeply. "It's a nice day," he spoke aloud as he went back in. Torn between fear and anticipation, he made a decision—fear was childish. He slipped his finger beneath the flap of the envelope and with one smooth motion, tore it open and removed the letter. He unfolded it. Eyes glued to the too few lines of handwriting, he felt around him for the back of the kitchen chair. Grasping it with his right hand, he slid it out from the table just far enough to squeeze in and sit down. He read with caution:

Michael,

> *I wish I could tell you this separation hurts as much as you described in your letter, but I can't. I'm numb from hurting so much for so long. Now all I feel is relief. For your sake, I'm glad you're willing to admit your part in the failure of our marriage. That did come as a surprise, but doesn't change a thing as far as I'm concerned.*

Whatever "spiritual experience" you may have had, Michael, simply happened way too late for us.

Stephanie

The white hot poker of each word burned deeper and deeper, searing his very soul. He could not tear his eyes away from those last few words. *Too late... too late... too late...* grew into a chant, as its singsongy sound echoed through his mind. Michael was stunned. He buried his head in his arms on the table top, but the words continued, *Too late... too late for us... too late... too late...*

"Lord," he cried, "I prayed. Caleb prayed. I thought You answered prayer. How could You let this happen? And Your Word... it says You hate divorce... let man not separate what You put together." His voice rose until he was shouting. "We're one flesh, Lord. You said so!" His bitter cries of anguish brought forth no response. Even worse, he was questioning God. Face to face with his lack of faith, the hurt mounted. All his hopes disintegrated, dashed like a broken vessel on the rocks. Waves of remorse washed away his recent joy. Despair swelled its way out of some hidden darkness that desired to drown him in its icy depths.

It almost had him. For hours, he sat in a daze. At last, he lifted his face from numbed arms, pushed away from the table, and stood. With nowhere to go, he plodded on leaden feet into the bedroom and collapsed face down on the bed. He covered his ears with his hands to muffle the mocking phrase, *too late... too late... too late.* It did not help. Eyes squinted, he lifted his head and shouted, "STOP!" Almost out of breath, he opened his eyes and spied his Bible on the end table.

Just seeing it helped. Some of the despair lifted, but not enough. He still wanted to give up. Then softly, so quietly as to pass almost unnoticed, he sensed Someone calling him. Not in an audible voice, but in the depths of his being. "*Michael...*" the voice summoned. "*Michael...*"

"Oh, Lord," he pleaded. "What have I done?" Confronted further with his lack of faith, the ache in his chest intensified. He felt choked and gasped for air. "Jesus... Lord Jesus," a cry for help escaped through barely parted lips.

"Trust Me, child."

"Lord, I want to trust You, and I thought I was, but now..." Again, Michael sensed the Lord saying to him, "Trust My love for you. It has not changed and never will. Look what I did out of love for My church. I shed My blood to cleanse her. I gave My life that she might live. I sent My Spirit that we might be one. You, too, are a part of My church, Michael, and I will never leave you. I know your loneliness, for it is Mine. I know your grief, for it is Mine. I know your sorrow, for it is Mine. Trust Me beyond sight. Trust Me beyond reason. Trust Me. I am the Potter. You are the clay. Let Me mold and fashion you. I will not force you in any way. You, My child, must not only allow Me, but invite Me. Only trust Me."

Total silence filled the room. Michael held his breath; even his heart skipped a beat. He was awed. God wanted his trust, yet He would not force him to give it. Time slowed, waiting for Michael's decision. For an instant, he glimpsed the urging voice's limitless depths, and he recognized its source—*love*. Michael surrendered. Suddenly, peace filled him, filled all the empty places, and overflowed. The ache in his chest ceased. Anger, fear, hurt—all vanished. "Thank You. Thank You, Lord," he repeated again and again. "I know You waited so long for me...I can wait, too."

The following weeks revealed a new pattern. The courts lifted the restraining order and granted him visitation rights with his children, so every Saturday morning, he went by the house to pick them up. Always, Stephanie greeted him with the same cold, stone-faced expression. All her attention was focused on the children. He was given stern warnings to take care of them and to be back at the appointed time.

Dropping them off again after spending the morning together— walking through the park to feed the ducks, visiting the local zoo, or the annual fair—always left him feeling dry and hollow. Their questions of "Why, Dad?" and "When are you coming home?" tore him apart. Time after time, God came to his rescue, and he usually found a way to encourage them, if not himself. From there, he would drive out to Caleb's to spend the rest of the weekend, where they would talk by the hour or go over to Sandy's to help around the house. Michael grew closer to all of them. In some ways, they managed to fill the void left by the family he no longer had.

Time proved to be the greatest factor in Michael's growing dependence on the Lord. No amount of skill brought, in his opinion, a satisfactory response from Stephanie. He was forced to depend utterly on God and to believe that what He had promised, He would do. There was one other alternative—quit waiting and find someone else. But that was not an option. The eventual manifestation of God's faithfulness opened the gate for him to pass through to the next step of faith.

Dependence in the absence of alternatives may have been all right for starters, but God desired more. Caleb began encouraging him to move forward and graduate from what he called his "limited base of operations." Michael harrumphed at this, not wanting to accept the possibility that he was limiting himself. They had just finished replacing some rotten floorboards on the Hawkins' front porch and were enjoying a few moments' rest, when he thought to ask Caleb to explain himself further.

"You're a father, Michael," Caleb began. "What if your children obeyed you because they had no other choice? If you knew that, on the inside, they were still rebelling and would rather be doing anything else, how would that make you feel?"

"Not very good. Angry...and hurt."

"Wouldn't you rather they obey you out of love?"

"Of course." Caleb smiled at him, knowing light was dawning.

"God is similar to you in that respect, Michael. He wants your trust, your devotion, and loving obedience. Now that you're discovering His faithfulness, He wants you to take the next big step and trust Him, even when you don't have to."

What had begun as instant liking for Caleb blossomed during those weeks. Caleb helped Michael stay grounded in God's Word. All the knowledge gained through years of walking with the Lord was at his disposal. He learned to trust his older friend with his innermost struggles. Slowly, tentatively, like a timid bather testing the water temperature before taking the plunge, he began opening his heart.

God was the strength and the foundation of their relationship. Their shared experiences encouraged them both...like the time Michael related how he had already been called by the Lord to trust Him. Caleb was overjoyed that Michael was learning to hear God speak to Him. The Lord's words about the Potter and His clay opened the door for him to teach more on one of his favorite subjects. For that, he escorted Michael back to his workshop.

As little as Michael knew about pottery making, he knew even less about preparing clay. "That is every bit as important," Caleb explained, "as the manner in which it is worked." He described the many stages clay goes through before it becomes a vessel fit for the potter's use. One by one, he gently placed various lumps of clay, all in different stages of the process, into Michael's hands. "Feel the difference," he directed. Michael shivered from the clay's cool temperature. Then Caleb suggested he read further on the subject in Frank Damazio's book, *The Making of a Leader*, and a few other sources.

Michael did just that. Much to his surprise, he found the topic fascinating. He had always known that clay first had to be dug from the earth, but thinking of himself in that manner lent a new perspective to recent months. It took the disaster he'd made of his marriage to break up the ground enough for him to be lifted out. Those first days with Caleb—getting started reading the Word—were the equivalent to the washing and soaking process, the second step that clay underwent immediately after being dug from the earth.

Looking to what lay ahead in the next several stages, he understood why God had called him to trust Him. Stage three was the one where the potter began to beat upon the clay, working it with his hands. Clay had no choice in what a human potter did with it. He, Michael, had been able to choose whether to surrender to the Lord or not. God had asked, and he had accepted. His place now was in the Master Potter's hands.

During the fourth stage, the potter used a thin wire to work all the air bubbles out of the clay. *Sounds like real fun*, Michael thought as he read on. He actually cringed imagining a cool, thin piece of metal going through him. He managed a wry smile before mumbling, "Well, at least You're still working on me."

In the fifth stage, after all the bubbles were gone, the clay was placed on the center of the potter's wheel for further development. Another not-so-gentle stage, the sixth, followed. The clay would then be stretched apart, pulled up and down, and formed into whatever shape the potter had in mind.

Conforming to the potter's image of what it should be was not the final stage yet. After being placed up on a shelf, the damp vessel had to dry out and harden, during the seventh phase. Michael sensed how difficult that must be for someone called to the ministry. To look and feel ready to be used and yet be forced to be shelved in the shadows, waiting and watching. He wondered how many ministers failed at this point.

From what he had heard of all the ministries crumpling of late, he reasoned that far too many had never allowed themselves to undergo the eighth and final stage of preparation. "And no wonder!" he exclaimed out loud, after reading about the long, very slow process of firing in the kiln. At temperatures up to one thousand degrees centigrade or even higher! Then Michael realized something about God's Word. In his excitement, he ran downstairs to share it with Caleb. "Every vessel or pot is meant to carry something, right?" Caleb nodded, so he continued. "And every born-again believer is an earthen vessel holding a treasure—the Holy Spirit, true?"

"Exactly," Caleb assured him.

"Well, you said men and women of God are praying for a great outpouring of the Holy Spirit on the church in these last days. But if God did fill His vessels with that river of living water, too many would not be ready for it. The church needs the fiery furnace before the filling!"

Caleb slapped his knee and laughed with delight. "That's wonderful insight! You're right on target. As with clay, the fire in the furnace builds strength. Without it, a vessel is good for little more than a showpiece. Let the pressure rise, and it will collapse and crumble." He paused. "Many Christians fear fiery trials. Of course, I'm sure you recognize that you're included among those who need the furnace before the filling." Michael's face sank and his enthusiasm waned a little. Carried away as he was with this insight, he almost forgot that he, too, would have to pass the test.

The next week flew by. Midday sunshine streamed through the passenger window as Michael turned off the interstate and started the last leg of another Saturday afternoon trip to Caleb's. That morning with the children had proved interesting, to say the least. It started with a visit to the local planetarium for a show entitled, "Creation."

As the house lights dimmed and the pinpoints of light began appearing on the domed roof of the auditorium, the commentator explained how the universe was expanding at a tremendous rate. With the aid of computers, they were able to portray the sky as it looked during any period since the moment the universe began. However they managed it, the effect was stunning. "Oohs and aahs" punctuated the stillness as thousands of years passed across the "sky."

Later, Michael explained the Big Bang theory to Stephen. He told him how the Bible says God created the heavens and the earth, and that what scientists call the Big Bang was, in reality, God saying, "Let there be light." The children listened with thoughtful expressions, and he assumed that would be the end.

Stephen and Michelle were quiet most of the drive back home. That was not unusual; it was hard for all of them to say good-bye. As they neared their street, Stephen spoke up. "Dad, God made all of this," he said, waving his hands around the front seat, "just by telling it to?"

"That's right, Stephen. He made all this and a whole lot more we can't see." Michael waited for the next question, but when it did not come, he glanced at his son. Stephen was fiddling with something in his two small hands, but it was hidden from view as his hands continued twisting and turning.

Michael parked the car in the driveway. As he did, Stephen stopped what he was doing to look up. Michelle, too, looked his way, chin quivering and eyes moist with unshed tears. It was Stephen who spoke first, "Dad, if God made everything and He can do anything He wants, He can even put you and Mom back together, can't He?" The words spilled from him like water from a dam too long held back. Michael reached out and enfolded his son with his right arm. With his left hand, he reached over and gently cupped Stephen's chin. "Boy, Dad," he sniffed, wiping his tears away with the back of his hand, "I miss you so much." Michelle stared out the window and said nothing.

"Listen, you two. We are going to make it through this. And yes, Stephen. God can do anything."

"Then what's He waiting for?" Stephen shot back. That was just what Michael had been asking himself not so long ago. He had no easy answer for him; yet, he could not ignore his pain.

"I love you both, and I love your mother, too. There are some things that need to be worked out between us." He looked from one to the other of his children, meeting their hesitant gazes with his own. Michelle's

141

was more of a glare. He continued, "God is all-powerful, but He won't force us to do something we don't want to do. He made us with free will. I'm learning to trust Him with all of this—with you, Stephen, and you, Michelle…and your mom. He is the One protecting and loving both of you and her for me. When the time is right, I believe He will bring us all together…the right way."

Stephen squirmed around on the seat so he could face his dad. "Who's Caleb?" he demanded, changing the subject.

Wide-eyed, Michael turned to hide his shock. "He's a friend who lives out in the country." Keeping his voice even, he asked, "How did you hear about him?"

"Mom told us," piped in Michelle. Before he could think to wonder how Stephanie found out about Caleb, his daughter continued. "Stevie asked her if you got lonely all by yourself. She said you found a friend and that you and he helped fix up somebody's house." He shook his head slowly from side to side as he listened. A smile formed at the corners of his mouth, despite his surprise.

"Maybe you'll get a chance to meet my friend someday."

"Yeah," Stephen agreed.

"What about you, Michelle? Would you like to meet my friend?" No reply came. "Well, I'll see, Stephen. Maybe one weekend, when your mother says it's okay, we'll do that. Right now, it's time I got you back in the house."

Leaving the children was especially difficult this time. Michelle's growing aloofness pierced his heart. After he told them to trust God, a spotlight illuminated his own lack of trust. Even at work, whenever he was given a condescending look or a sympathetic pat on the shoulder, he wanted to declare his belief that God would restore his marriage. Though he had the desire, those faith-filled words to Michelle and Stephen were the first to pass his lips. He wondered why and determined to broach the subject with Caleb. During the rest of the ride, he listened to one of his praise tapes, hoping to lift his ebbing spirits.

TWELVE

RISKS

"MICHAEL, HAVE YOU read about Noah and the ark?" Caleb asked him that evening.

"Sure," he responded. "I read the account in the Bible and some of your notes about it in the 'Olympians of Faith.'"

"How do you think he felt, building an ark with no water in sight? People looking out of the corner of their eyes and shaking their heads... they'd never even heard of rain, and Noah was preparing for a flood! Sooner or later, all the neighbors heard. For years, day after day, board upon board, he labored to build that ark. To everyone else, he must have looked ridiculous. I've often wondered what it would feel like to have the whole world making fun of me."

"That's what I've been afraid of, Caleb." He paused, looking off in the distance at the reflection of the setting sun upon the surface of the pond. It was just visible through the open windows. Turning back, he saw Caleb, a quizzical expression on his face, watching him. "I really don't mean the whole world," spilled forth in a torrent. "No one knows this, but... it doesn't take all that much to intimidate me in that area. I can't stand for anyone to make fun of me."

"I don't like it, either. In fact," he admitted, "I don't know anybody who does." Michael nodded his agreement, but continued looking out the window. "There comes a time, though, when we have to take that chance. When God calls us to step out and trust Him and to place ourselves back on the potter's wheel for refashioning, people may laugh and point. Or criticize. Unless God has already led them through that stage, they won't understand. It's unfortunate, but most people, when they don't understand something, tend to put it down or make fun of it. At best, they avoid it. You can believe they did just that with old Noah. While speaking, he reached into his back pocket and produced his ever-present New Testament.

"But it will always be worth enduring the test." Caleb opened the little book, and as quickly as he could, found the right passage. "Listen, Michael, to what the Word says in Hebrews 11:6–7:

> And without faith it is impossible to please God, because anyone who comes to him must believe that he exists and that he rewards those who earnestly seek him. By faith Noah, when warned about things not yet seen, in holy fear built an ark to save his family. By his faith he condemned the world and became heir of the righteousness that comes by faith.

"Here's something else to think about. If you study the Genesis account of this story, you'll find the Hebrew word for the pitch, used to seal the ark and make it weatherproof, is the same word used for the atonement. Just as that pitch kept back the waters of judgment, so atonement keeps judgment out of a believer's life. What a small price to pay—simple obedience to God's Word. Noah combined faith with obedience. He built the ark. He applied the pitch. Those who believed what God had told Noah entered the ark—eight souls in all. How sad it would have been if he had not been diligent in applying pitch. No matter how meticulous the rest of the job, it would have leaked like a sieve! Not a single step could have been missed. Can you and I afford to be less diligent and obedient?"

"When you put it like that..." Michael looked at Caleb, lifted his arms slightly to either side, and shrugged. He held that position a moment, then let his arms fall back to his side. "What's the best way to handle my situation at work? Nobody is coming right out and saying it, but it's obvious that, in their minds, the divorce is already final. A few women

are making innuendoes. Even my boss acts like 'it's curtains' already."
His voice faded.

"What position have you taken with them?"

Michael thought for a moment before answering. "With most, I
haven't said anything. With Dale and Kathryn—my boss and his wife—
I've been sharing some of the highlights of our weekends here. I've
hinted that I believe my marriage will be restored."

"Hinted? Is that all?"

He cleared his throat. "Well... they seemed more interested in hearing about you and Sandy and got uncomfortable whenever I broached
the subject of my marriage." While he was talking, his face lightened.
"Speaking of marriage, the children brought up the topic again...this
time with an added flair. Stephen asked who you are, and Michelle said
their mother told them about you. Imagine that." Michael leaned back
in the chair, and a slow grin spread across his face. "It puzzled me. I
couldn't for the life of me figure out how Stephanie would have heard
of you. I sure haven't mentioned our friendship. We hardly even talk. I'd
forgotten she and Kathryn are friends."

Caleb smiled. "I can tell it gives you hope knowing that she has dis-
cussed you with Kathryn, but don't depend too much on outward signs.
They can be deceiving. Getting back to your question about how to handle people at work... do you still believe God will restore your marriage?"

"Absolutely." He hesitated before adding, "Most of the time." He
looked up sheepishly from beneath lowered brows.

"Then stand up for what you believe, but do it in love. If a situation
comes up and they start talking about the singles life after divorce, you can
be polite, yet firm. Tell them how you feel about your marriage, so life after
divorce is not a possibility. That may even open a door for you to share
about Jesus—how He is the basis for your belief. On the other hand, if you
keep still and listen to all their enticements, you put yourself in danger of
opening a door to doubt. Now, I'm not saying to argue with them or to
try to convince them. Just state your case in love and let God do the rest."

"I think I can do that, even if they do poke fun at me," he agreed.
"As long as I don't have to do what Elijah did on that mountain." Caleb
burst into hearty laughter and clapped him on the shoulder. Michael
attempted to maintain a straight face, but it was contagious. "All right,"
he managed a few minutes later, after Caleb's laughter diminished to soft

chuckles. "I guess I do want Elijah's kind of faith. Maybe not just yet."

"Michael, I doubt Elijah was born with it, either. He grew into faith as his relationship with Jehovah deepened."

"Whew! I read about him in First Kings and tried to picture myself in his place." Michael stood up and walked to the window. The sun was almost gone, with just a crescent visible over the top of the distant hills. He turned back to Caleb and continued, "Standing on top of Mt. Carmel, challenging over eight hundred false prophets before their altar—calling for the fire to fall, hour after hour, from morning to evening. Some of them even cutting themselves with knives. And Elijah's bold, 'Go on... cry a little louder. Maybe your god is asleep.' It is easy to laugh at someone else's antics. But when it came his turn to trust God...it's awesome just thinking about it." He paused, as much for emphasis as to catch his breath.

"Building the altar, stone by stone, while everyone watched and waited. Silence...but for the sounds of grating stone. Stacking wood for the animal sacrifice. Was that enough? Everything looked ready. If that had been me, Caleb, I'd have been trying to make it as easy for God to answer as I could. Not Elijah. He helped me understand what trust means. He made it as challenging for God as possible so the people would have to believe, as he soaked the altar, the offering, and even the trench around the altar with water!" Michael's eyes glistened with excitement. He grabbed his Bible, turned to 1 Kings 18:36, and stood up.

"Then, when all the preparations were finished, when every eye was fastened upon God's prophet, he raised his hands to heaven, shouting, 'LORD, God of Abraham, Isaac and Israel, let it be known today that you are God in Israel and that I am your servant and have done all these things at your command. Answer me, O LORD, answer me, so these people will know that you, O LORD, are God, and that you are turning their hearts back again.' Man, how God responded! Fire fell from heaven. It burned up the sacrifice, the wood, the stones, the dust, and even the water. Imagine having that much trust, standing in front of more than eight hundred enemies, plus all of Israel, and putting God to the test!"

He shuddered.

"That was great! I know you're not Elijah, and neither am I, but there's your answer to how to handle the people at work, Michael. Trust God to prove who He is."

"Yes, I know," he admitted.

"Whenever you begin doubting, look back to Mt. Carmel. Elijah's strength rested in God, not in himself, his surroundings, or his heritage. He lived life on the foundation of Jehovah. To him the unseen essential was the most real aspect of his life. Because you serve the same God, you can have that same trust."

"I sure need it."

"We all do. Study the lives of those men of God. There's a wealth of inspiration and encouragement waiting to be tapped. Elijah went through the process of brokenness we talked about, but in a different way. Before God used him on Mt. Carmel, He led him to the brook Cherith. There, He allowed him to realize he was an empty vessel needing to be filled. He had to depend on ravens to bring him food twice a day, and he drank water until the brook dried up...

"Then God led him to a widow in Zarephath who, at his bidding, fed him her last cake. I don't know how he felt, but I can't imagine asking Maggie Hawkins for her last bite of food, can you? Yet, at God's command, he did just that...and all were blessed. Only after such humbling did God send him to Ahab and on to the Mt. Carmel meeting that you find so exciting. Elijah's servant heart was well-developed by then. He didn't go around doing things for God, trying to help Him out. Rather, he did only what God chose to do through him. You and I can become just as in tune with God. It takes spending time with Him, loving Him, studying His Word, and then obeying it."

"Ah, Caleb. It sounds so simple and straightforward..."

"And it is. But growth may not always progress in a steady, upward line, especially after coming through a big battle. I won't tell you what happened to Elijah after his victory over the false prophets. You can read it for yourself in 1 Kings 19. All I'll say is that one woman did what over eight hundred false prophets and Baal worshipers couldn't do."

"I'll be sure to read it." They sat in silence, each thinking his own thoughts on the life of faith—Caleb looking back across the years to where he'd been; Michael thinking about the present and the future.

Michael found himself wondering why he felt such a close tie with Caleb. He could put his finger on no single fact, except that he felt appreciated—like he was of some intrinsic value to him. Somehow, he knew Caleb's interest was genuine, not for what he could get from him, but for what he could give.

Caleb spoke, his voice a welcome intrusion to his thoughts. "Have you given any consideration to how you can be a better husband to Stephanie when you two get back together?"

"If you mean, do I know what I'll do specifically, the answer is "No." I've thought plenty about it, though, and to be honest, I'm a little afraid to get my hopes up in that direction. Don't want to be disappointed."

"That's natural. It's part of the vulnerability of faith. Are you open to a suggestion…for when the time comes, that is?"

"Sure, I guess so."

"There's a Scripture verse, I can't remember exactly where it is at the moment, but it goes like this, 'Wherever your treasure is, there will your heart be.' You want to totally captivate and be captivated by Stephanie, right?"

"You know I do, Caleb."

"Then make sure you invest in her." Michael arched his eyebrows and looked at him, doubt written across his face from one side to the other. "No, I don't mean simply spend money on her. Spend yourself—a much greater treasure. Your time. Your appreciation. Your needs, desires, and fears—everything."

"That was one thing I didn't do before. No matter how good my intentions, my major investment was in me—my job, my success, me. Not too good, huh?"

"I'll leave you to answer that, my boy."

They talked long into the night, encouraging one another. During the course of their conversation, Michael reminded Caleb that never once in the time he grew up did he remember his parents hugging or kissing each other. He feared it might be hard to be open with Stephanie and the kids.

"Just out of curiosity," Caleb asked, "what kind of discipline did your parents give you?"

He thought a moment. "Not much. Far back as I can remember ,they never spanked me, though I did something one time, I forget what, and my mom bopped me good on the side of the head. My dad told her not to hit me in the ear anymore because it could hurt me. After I got older, a freshman or sophomore in high school, whenever I'd do something contrary to what he would have done, he'd make horrible faces at me. I knew right away I'd blown it again. Another failure to add to the list."

Michael sat, shaking his head from side to side. "But mostly, they alternated between yelling at me or ignoring me."

"What do you mean?"

"Listen to this. One time, as a teenager, they took me to get a haircut. My dad was so picky in that department. It had to be just the way he wanted it and not a fraction too long. Keeping this in mind, afterwards, I went to find him in the mall. Was he pleased? Hardly. You should have seen his reaction. He ranted and raved and made a scene right there in public. Talk about embarrassed! So I gave in and went back to have another quarter inch trimmed off.

"A year or two later, the same situation came up, but I didn't give in that time. He not only stopped speaking to me, he ignored me completely. For over *two months*, he acted like I didn't exist. Even during meals, he'd sit next to me at the table and not say a word to me, except through my mother. Nor I to him! Both of us, two big macho dum-dums ruled by our stubborn pride. Does that answer your question about discipline?"

"It sure does. I appreciate your trusting me with such personal things, Michael. It helps me better understand your needs today." He paused and frowned, growing more intense, shaking his head. "I'm sorry your parents understood so little about godly discipline. Very few parents are well-informed in that regard. Maybe that's why the apostle Paul wrote what he did to both the Ephesians and Colossians. In the Amplified Bible, Ephesians 6:4 says, 'Fathers, do not irritate and provoke your children to anger [do not exasperate them to resentment], but rear them [tenderly] in the training and discipline and the counsel and admonition of the Lord.' That must mean it is possible for parents to breed rebellion and anger in their children or Paul wouldn't have emphasized it. All that brings up a most important point I emphasized a while back. You've asked God to forgive you for your past failures. Have you forgiven your parents? Don't let anything in your past hamper your walk of faith. Nothing. No matter how painful." His crystal blue eyes were penetrating. "Remember, 'Forgiveness is the fragrance the violet sheds...'"

Michael broke in, "I know, I know, 'on the heel that has crushed it.'" He looked down, silent. Once again, Caleb had him. But some things seemed too difficult to tackle.

Suddenly, from around front came a sharp *tap, tap, tap*. Michael froze. It sounded like someone at the front door. Caleb got up to check,

149

patting his shoulder as he passed. He opened the door, and there stood Sandy. He had walked from home in the dark. "Mr. Caleb, I jes needed to hear a bedtime story. Will ya tell me one? Please ... then I'll go home, I promise."

"Okay, my boy, one bedtime story comin' up. Come on in and join us. Make yourself comfortable." Caleb returned to where he had been sitting by Michael and waited for him and Sandy to exchange greetings before starting his story. "Let's see, a good story." He paused a moment. "Ah yes, got one. Have you read Deuteronomy 32? The first part goes like this, 'He (the LORD) shielded him and cared for him; he guarded him as the apple of his eye, like an eagle that stirs up its nest and hovers over its young, that spreads its wings to catch them and carries them on its pinions' (Deuteronomy 32:10–11). Herein lies the Flight Training Manual for young eagles and earthbound Christians. Ready?" Sandy nodded eagerly:

> Far away on a remote and rocky mountain range, perched on the edge of a sheer cliff, is a sturdy nest—an eagle's nest. It's all thorny branches on the outside, but soft and warm on the inside, lined with feathers and fur from mama eagle's prey. Huddled inside this particular nest are two little eaglets. Twice a day, she brings them meat—worms and other eagle delicacies—and drops them into their wide-open, straining mouths. They always crave more. Come evening, she settles down on the nest to protect them from the adverse elements and night birds of prey.
>
> Now, if eagles could talk, you could hear the one baby eaglet named Erma saying to the other, named Ernie, "I don't know how we got here bro, but this is wonderful. Room service, and so soft and cozy. Ooooh ... Let's stay here forever!"
>
> Little do they suspect, mom has other plans. She knows they were never meant to be land dwellers. Their destiny is to soar through the heavens—powerful wings propelling them above the storm clouds—to rejoice in regal flight as king of the skies. But how will she lure them from their snug nest out into the rising air currents of the wide-open spaces?

Caleb paused, cocking his head toward his listeners. One eyebrow rose as he waited. Sandy picked up the cue. "How does she do it?"

Well, first, she flies figure eights for them. Then she soars to the heights, until she seems little more than a speck, and plummets to the valley floor, skimming smoothly a few feet off the ground. "Wow!" they exclaim. Ernie and Erma are quite impressed by her aerial stunts. They admire her courage and skill, but as for a desire to leave their comfy nest and follow her... forget it!

One day, quite to their dismay, mama eagle comes in and pulls the fur and feathers right out from under them. The uncovered thorns and rough sticks jab their well-fed bodies. "What'd we do to deserve this?" one asks the other.

"Nothin' that I know of." Ernie cranes his neck over the rim of the nest and peers warily down the cliff face, then snaps his beak shut and wriggles back into the nest. "But it's still better here," he advises. They stay cuddled up together until mama returns. Then, piece by piece, she breaks up the nest until they find themselves in a standing-room-only proposition.

There they totter, two stunned young birds high on that cliff. And not a ladder in sight. Even worse, mom is no longer the generous provider they've been accustomed to. All signs of friendliness gone, she moves toward them with outstretched wings. One eaglet glances at the other as she inches them closer and closer to the edge of the cliff. "Are you thinkin' what I'm thinkin'?" little Erma whines.

Ernie, the older one, answers warily, "Oh no, I'm afraid, so... H-E-L-L-L-P...!"

Caleb stopped for a moment. Sandy sat wide-eyed. Michael was unaware that his left hand was gripping the armrest as Caleb continued:

With a quick flip of mama eagle's huge wings, it's over the edge they go. Down from the heights—tumbling beak over tail feathers, wings flapping in panic—they gather speed with every inch. Their little bird hearts beat wildly from fright, pounding nearly out of their little breasts.

"E-e-e-ow!" they cry as jagged rocks, once so far below, appear ready to reach out and snatch them. Just when their last hope vanishes—Woomph! Their headlong rush stops. Instead of hard rock beneath them, why it's *soft* somehow. Feathery soft. Realization dawns. "Mom, it's you! Whew...just in the nick of time. Turning, she flies back up...up...and deposits her two badly shaken, but safe young children, onto the cliff's edge. Talk about relief! But even as Ernie and Erma are still celebrating their rescue, and in excited eagle verse, praying to never have such a dreadful, horrifying experience ever again—Whoop! It's over the edge and down again at breakneck speed.

Caleb smiled as both listeners moaned. A confused Sandy blurted out, "What's wrong with that stupid mother? Why's she scarin' 'em to death?" Caleb reached over and gave his knee a pat of encouragement and continued:

Now, some birds do get the message the third or fourth time around. Others take longer, but eventually, because they're eagles, they all begin putting two and two together. "It's Flight Training School!"

"Watch, Mom," Ernie chirps, then stands and spreads his youthful wings. "We've got the same equipment." He flaps to emphasize his words. "If we've got to go over (and it looks like we have no choice), what've we got to lose if we try?"

Mama eagle smiles to herself. Once more she swats their little fuzzy backs with her wings, but not hard enough to knock them off the cliff. She just sits and waits.

"Oh boy, let's go, Erma!" This time they stick around for a good current of air, leap into space, and start flapping in earnest.

At long last, mama eagle has company. Without knowing the exact moment it happens, Ernie and Erma are off and flying! Their figure eights look more like lopsided sevens. They bump into bushes and suffer several near misses with trees. Nevertheless, they are airborne.

In the excitement of their first solo flight, they shout to one another, "Who needs that old nest...we belong in the air!" And so in the end, Ernie and Erma realize that their greatest trial was planned by one who loved them enough to push them to their greatest triumph.

Caleb looked at his audience of two who sat speechless.

"You, Sandy, and you, too, Michael. And me. We're those young eagles. How many times are we challenged, only to cry out, 'Lord, deliver me!' He says, 'No, I'm going to develop you.' When we whimper, 'God, please take me out of this,' He replies with gentle compassion, 'No, I'll take you through.' How often do we try to twist the arm of God Almighty into blessing us by arrogantly waving our preferred choice of His promises in His face? He doesn't work that way. All He does is point to His other promises and say, 'At the moment, I'm more interested in your character than your comfort. I want you to learn faith!'"

Sandy was wide-eyed as Caleb finished. He was still thousands of feet in the air, soaring with the eagles. "Oh, Mr. Caleb, thanks! What a great bedtime story!" He dashed toward the door. "I gotta go tell Ma. It'll make 'er happy." Waving over his shoulder, he called, "See ya! G'bye, Mr. Michael." In a flash, he was out the door and down the road in the dark, arms spread out like eagles' wings. Caleb headed after him in his truck to drive him the rest of the way home, while Michael climbed the stairs to his room. *"No, I'll take you through"... that sure is the truth,* he mused, as he crawled into bed and turned out the light. He fluffed his feather pillow, snuggled deeper under the covers, and heaved a contented sigh. His last conscious thoughts followed the young eagles up and down, up and down, up...up...up...

THIRTEEN

LOSS

T HE NEXT MORNING at breakfast, Michael still had the eagle story fresh on his mind. "Caleb," he asked, "did you make up that silly story about two young eagles in Flight Training School?"

Caleb winked at him and smiled. His crystal blue eyes looked bluer than ever and full of mischief. "Well, I confess I heard or read it somewhere awhile ago, but I've embellished it quite a bit since then. It's one of those stories that gets more dramatic, though perhaps not more scientific, every time I tell it. So you liked the little eagles, huh? Now I know there's a kid at heart inside you."

Michael frowned teasingly and put his finger to his lips. "Shh... don't give away my secrets... but I loved it. Those two guys were up and down like cosmic yo-yos, without the string." He tilted his head. "Don't you think it's amazing that you would tell it to an engineer who went to the top Flight Training School in the country? I learned the world's method, and now you're teaching me God's method. Pretty interesting."

"Right you are. Say, did you notice the transition from dependence to trust in the story? That's when Ernie and Erma chose to try flying, without mom forcing them off the cliff. Trust is more challenging than dependence, I think." He paused to spoon some oatmeal and raisins into their two bowls, then gestured in the air. "Most eagles learn to fly sooner or later. That's more than I can say for too many Christians. Oh, they think they trust God. It took me a while to learn, I must say. I used to get involved in as many 'good deed projects' as possible, doing what I thought every good Sunday school boy should do." He chuckled. "Yep, I sure took to heart the verse telling me to 'work out my salvation with fear and trembling.'"

Michael sat back, breathed a heavy sigh, and ran his right hand through his still-damp hair. "Now I'm confused again. Works are important, you said before."

"They are. But my motives were all wrong. I resented the drudgery of my Christian 'duties,' so I may as well not have done them at all. Somehow I thought I must be so important to His kingdom that it wouldn't survive without my effort, no matter what my heart attitude was. Think of the young eagles flapping for all they were worth and still falling... until they learned to fly and soar. That was sort of like me. Lots of motion, but no devotion. Now, I trust the wind of the Holy Spirit to support me as I serve Him. 'Even youths grow tired and weary, and young men stumble and fall; but those who hope in the LORD will renew their strength. They will soar on wings like eagles; they will run and not grow weary, they will walk and not be faint.' That's from Isaiah 40:30–31."

Michael, his silent thoughts agreeing with his older friend's discovery, could see how dangerous such behavior could become. What a difference to serve God, soaring like an eagle! He glanced at his watch. "It's almost seven, partner. Guess I should get cleaned up a bit. Don't want to be late for my Sunday job," he said with a broad smile.

Ushering at church was a new adventure for Michael. Not only did the work lend a sense of satisfaction to his Christian walk, but it was a learning experience. Meeting and dealing with people allowed him to heal in an area of his personality in which he'd been deficient for too long. He thoroughly enjoyed the changes he saw taking place. There were always challenges of one sort or another, but he no longer feared them.

Once the service had begun, he took his place beside Caleb, Sandy, and Maggie. Pastor Fontaine was already speaking from the platform, "'Abandoned to Victory' is what I'm calling today's message. Yes, 'Abandoned to

Victory!'" the pastor exclaimed. "As I shared with you last week, people, God is calling us to a deeper walk of faith. Super cautious Christians need not apply." A few in the congregation chuckled. He paused on the edge of the first step as his gaze scanned the sanctuary. "I see those raised eyebrows. Now, trust me. No, better yet, trust God!"

"What crossed your mind when I mentioned *abandoned*?—a mother leaving her newborn infant on a stranger's doorstep? The number of incidences of that are increasing, unfortunately. Or maybe you thought of it the other way around—adult children deserting their elderly parents. That's on the rise, too, I'm sorry to say. Well, you can relax. That isn't what I mean by *abandoned*. An almost audible sigh coursed through the sanctuary, interspersed with low laughter. "Abandonment involves the ultimate kind of trust—choosing to entrust ourselves to God's plans and purposes, totally leaving behind the anxieties of the world."

The pastor fixed his eyes on Michael. "Would you like to be liberated from fear as you serve Him? You can be, but not through any merit of your own. Neither can I. Get the foundation of faith laid first, and lay it solid. Then, and only then, comes abandonment. You can't just abandon yourself to reckless trust. That leads to destruction and license, which has nothing to do with real faith. I'm talking about casting all your cares upon Him. Abandonment, born of a freed spirit, is the only possible way to live at peace with God. The only way…

"You've heard me preach on the three parts of man. You are a spirit being who has a soul and who lives in a body. Each of these three areas must be brought to the point of disciplined abandonment if you would reach the pinnacle of faith Jesus wants for you. Notice I said, disciplined abandonment. Does it seem like a contradiction? It isn't. Only those who are disciplined in the Word and prayer can afford to abandon themselves to God. Most important!" His eyes glowing with zeal, he walked the platform, went around the pulpit, and came back again to center.

"Of course, the Christian life is impossible without the Holy Spirit. But our work is often so planned that there is little need to depend on Him. He's simply crowded out. We don't trust God; we trust our own endeavors. Instead we should admit we are nothing and that the only good thing in any of us is Jesus Christ. I'm emphasizing this because there is too much work being done—fruitless work—in the name of Jesus." His voice rose. "And for His glory, we claim. Hah! It's the work of man—for his own glory. God sees right through our artificiality.

"Abandonment also means being free from the desire to prove our own righteousness. We can't do it, so we might as well give up trying. I know Scripture does tell us that faith without works is dead. Works must be there, but they are a result of...not the reason for...God's grace."

Moving toward the edge of the platform, the pastor stopped speaking. He craned his neck back and looked up toward the farthest reaches of the sanctuary. From left to right, row after row, his gaze swept the faces of his expectant flock.

"Look around you," he urged, as he extended his right arm and half-turned in a sweeping gesture of invitation. "This building is beautiful, isn't it? Not elaborate, but functional. We put in a lot of hard work, and we are grateful to have it. And we feel at home...many of you have told me so. That's wonderful but..." He walked behind the pulpit, reached down, and shook something into his right palm. Then he moved back out to the edge of the platform, under the spotlight. Holding his hand to his mouth, he blew a small mound of baby powder across his palm. In the light, the white airborne stuff billowed like a huge puff of smoke. He pointed to the cloud before him. "All of our 'churchy' activity means exactly that much to God if our motives aren't right...or if His Spirit isn't leading the activity. Have we, and I ask this of all of us, me included, abandoned our striving to the control of the Holy Spirit? If we haven't, now is the time.

"What we've done up to this point is important, but not nearly as important as what we do in the future. When we serve the Lord, are we trying to prove how great we are or are we humble? Are we propelled by a grim sense of duty or by a joyful desire to please our heavenly Father? If the latter, we can rest easy. Provision is God's portion of the covenant. Simple obedience with a pure heart on our part, the ultimate in loving provision on His. Two parts—His and ours. Let's trust God so completely that He works unhindered through us like He did in the early church."

The pastor reached toward his open Bible where it lay on the pulpit. He flipped several pages with a fervor. "Turn with me, if you would, to the book of Acts, chapter 4. Peter and John have just been released from prison where they were held for preaching in the name of Jesus Christ. They rejoined the rest of the believers, and together, they prayed. Verses

29–30 read, 'Now, Lord, consider their threats and enable your servants to speak your word with great boldness. Stretch out your hand to heal and perform miraculous signs and wonders through the name of your holy servant Jesus.'

"Look how their simple cry was honored. Scripture tells us that, 'After they prayed, the place where they were meeting was shaken. And they were all filled with the Holy Spirit and spoke the word of God boldly.' The place was shaken. Imagine! A prayer of faith that is in line with God's heart of compassion brings dramatic results."

As Michael listened, he thought to himself, *Now that's the kind of prayer I need—one that gets results.* His mental wanderings turned to Stephanie, *Oh Lord, when will this ever end?* But he knew better than to dwell on such doubts.

Drawn by a phrase the pastor was using, Michael's attention snapped back to the platform. Pastor Fontaine was bent over, as if shouldering a great weight, and plodding in a circle. One time. Twice. Three times. Then in mid-stride, he whirled around to face the people and spoke, "Processionary caterpillars are quite an interesting conformity. Round and round they crawl, following one another. Sometimes they even link up. They're like the 'blind leaders of the blind,' a phrase Jesus assigned to the religious leaders of His day. Processionary caterpillars are always on the move, but they never get anywhere." He dragged his feet around in another circle and then paused. "Too much of our activity in the church today resembles these little creatures—constant movement that fails to move anyone but ourselves.

"People, how much do we do simply because that's the way it's always been done? Are we stuck in a rut? We'd better beware of the processionary-caterpillar syndrome. It kills the productivity necessary to live a normal spiritual life. Processionary caterpillar Christians will never shake the world as the apostles did in the book of Acts. God has called us far beyond this type of mental and spiritual complacency—in fact, to the opposite end of the spectrum—to trust. Abandoned trust. Let's forget about trying to conform to an acceptable Christian role. We're more than actors playing the parts of Christians. We are Christians. Followers—not of each other, but of Jesus Christ."

Pastor Fontaine no longer paced the length of the platform, but stood behind the pulpit, gripping its outer edges with both hands. He bowed his head and prayed silently. A moment passed, then another, before he looked out at the people.

"Jesus declared, 'I am the Light of the world.' What did he mean by that? Well, light has certain inherent properties. For one, it dispels darkness. Who ever heard of the dark coming into a brightly lit room and putting out the lights?" He stopped, searching the congregation, but no one responded. "I thought as much. But walk into the most pitch black place you can imagine—an underground cave, or something of the sort—and light just one candle. What happens? It lights up the whole place. In essence, that's what Jesus did. His spotless life, His death, and His resurrection brought Light into the darkness. No blackness oozing from the pit of hell will ever extinguish the brilliance of His Light. And there's more. Jesus told His disciples, including us, 'You are the light of the world.' That's all it took." He waved both hands high in the air. "Good-bye processionary caterpillars. Good-bye careless conformity. We are the light of the world!" Both hands lowered. He looked across the faces of his congregation.

"'You are the salt of the earth,' Jesus said, as well. We can no more act the parts of Christians than salt can 'act' salty. By the way, something interesting happens when you add salt to water. It seasons it, and no matter how much you dilute the water, it stays salty. Light and salt. Both substances drastically change whatever they come in contact with. They transform.

"Brothers and sisters, we, too, become transformers the moment the Holy Spirit fills our hearts. Mere human nature is insufficient. 'Not by might nor by power, but by my Spirit,' says the LORD Almighty, in Zechariah 4:6. The lock has not been changed. The same key to Christian service still fits—abandonment to the perfect will of our Father in heaven. We have here with us today the greatest example of such trust who ever lived. Let me introduce Him to you again." The pastor swept his arm from left to right. His eyes scanned the front rows, then raised to include the entire congregation. "His name is...Jesus. Wonderful Jesus. The Lord of glory. The firstborn among many. Son of God and Son of man.

"This Jesus we follow...the very One who lives inside us...abandoned the riches of heaven and humbled Himself to come to earth as a man. He chose to trust the Father to the point of death and beyond. At His arrest in the garden of Gethsemane, He reminded an overzealous disciple that He could, at any moment, call on His Father who would immediately send a multitude of angels to deliver Him. On the cross, He had the power to save Himself. But He did not, so that the Scriptures would be fulfilled. No man took Jesus' life from Him. In love, He laid it down willingly so that man would not perish.

"If we trust His Holy Spirit, He will mold us into a people who will shake the earth." The pastor paused, then in measured steps, paced. "When we walk though this sin-darkened world, it will be lightened." He stopped, his extended right arm sweeping the sanctuary. "When He touches others through us, they will become new creations...radically changed. People, will you join me? Abandon yourselves to Jesus, and to victory in Him."

The rest of Sunday turned out to be a quiet day alone for Michael. Caleb had a planning conference at church to attend in the afternoon, so he dropped Michael off at the Country Corner, took Sandy and Maggie home, and then returned to the meeting. Later that evening, Caleb walked in the back door to the house. The lights were off. Several moments passed before he sensed that he was not alone. There, against the backdrop of the picture window, he could just make out Michael's silhouette. "Is everything all right?" Caleb asked. Silence. "Michael?"

"Huh? Oh, hi."

"Sorry I'm so late. You okay?"

"Sure. I was just thinking." He rose and walked to the front door to turn the lights on. "I guess I didn't notice it was getting dark."

"You must have been doing some powerful concentrating there, buddy," Caleb offered with a smile. His blue eyes sparkled in the reflected light.

"It's this abandonment stuff. I have a hard time with it. Seems too passive, somehow. It's the total opposite of the way I've been all my life, and it feels as unnatural as walking with my shoes on the wrong feet. I intend to abandon myself to trust God a thousand times every day, but a tough situation develops...and I do it my way again." He stood leaning against the doorway and shook his head from side to side.

He continued with a sigh, "I'm worried about Stephanie and the kids. I may not have told you that Stephen is a hemophiliac...a bleeder...so even a small cut can be serious. Then there's Sandy and his mom, my job...not much solidity in any of it. I'm feeling kind of anxious inside about going back, for some reason." He rubbed his hands on his pants. "And I guess I've been thinking about you, too. I didn't want to leave until you got home."

At this last admission, Caleb sat down on the sofa and stretched his arm across the back. "Feel like talking? I'm all ears."

Michael walked to the easy chair and sat down. "Oh, it's nothing you did wrong or anything. I just wanted to tell you how much I...I appreciate you. I really missed you today. My situation doesn't change when I'm with you, but somehow it isn't so glaringly awful. I feel stronger in my faith."

"Could it be you're avoiding things by coming out here? I sure hope not. Your trust has to be in God, not in me."

"I know, I know. Anything is possible, but I don't think I'm avoiding my problems." He paused and exhaled loudly. "This is silly. I'm trying to tell you something I can't even put into words...how important you've become to me. You don't preach like the pastor, but your whole life is one big message. You don't talk about helping people—you just do it. Jesus is so alive to you, Caleb. I wonder if I'll ever have such a strong faith."

"Now, Michael, how long have you been a Christian?" Caleb queried, his tone kidding.

"You, of all people, should know. You were with me the day I was saved a few months ago."

"Yes, a very few months, so please don't be discouraged. In a short time, the Lord has brought you a long way. If He delays His return, He'll bring you a lot further in the years ahead." He leaned forward. His voice grew intense. "Michael, faith is a lifelong, day-by-day growing process. I've been walking with my Master for several years now. You can't possibly compare the two of us in that regard. The important thing is that a genuine hunger for God burns in you. So don't get down on yourself. Every time you try to grab a situation away from the Lord's control, hand it back to Him—as many times as you have to. Abandoned trust will come. I believe you and He will be best friends one day. Just like He was with Abraham."

Each was silent for some minutes, lost in his own reverie. Michael, a little more at peace, geared himself up for the ride to town. He still had mixed emotions about leaving...more so than usual. "Guess it's time for me to be heading back. Gotta be at work early in the morning."

They both stood, and Caleb gave Michael a warm, fatherly hug as he said quietly, "Thanks for being genuine with me and for waiting to say good-bye. I appreciate you, too, more than you know." He stepped back and cleared his throat. His eyes were moist with emotion, and he looked down. "Here, I'll give you a hand getting your bags out to the car."

Together, they stowed the luggage in the trunk, and then Caleb stood by as Michael climbed slowly into the driver's seat and started the engine. Before he backed out onto the road, he pushed the button to open the window and added, "Don't forget, I'll see you in two weeks. I've got to work next weekend, remember."

"I remember. I'll miss you." He gave Michael a warm pat on the back and squeezed his shoulder. "Drive carefully, and keep meditating on all we've talked about. God bless you, son." Caleb waved as Michael drove away. He tooted his horn playfully in an effort to stifle the dull ache in his chest.

The next week and a half passed quickly with tension building to a peak on the day of the big test at Eagle Aeronautics. Pat poked his head in the lab and called, "Michael, the boss wants to see you when you get a few minutes."

"Oh, okay. Thanks, buddy," he responded, but his eyes stayed glued to the rows of gauges and dials across the panel in front of him. He was just concluding the last of a series of stress tests on his new hypersonic jet engine design. So far, everything performed above his highest expectations. The SCRAMJET prototype was lightweight and fuel efficient, yet it had a substantial increase in thrust over Eagle Aeronautics' previous supersonic ramjet engine. *Times like these make the long hours and weekends at work seem worthwhile,* he thought to himself. *Well, almost. I'd rather have spent this past weekend with Caleb, but the test had to be completed. It'll be nice to see him again,* he concluded.

"Bring the pressure on down and wrap it up," he instructed his assistant. "I'll go tell Dale the good news. That's probably what he called to find out anyway." He removed his white lab coat and hung it in the back of the storeroom before taking one last look around. *So much time in these rooms. I hope it's been for something worthwhile,* he thought. He closed the door behind him with a sense of finality.

He paused in front of the mahogany door marked, *Dale Ambrose, Chief Executive Officer,* and gave it three sharp raps with his knuckles. Then he turned the doorknob and entered the outer office. "It's me, Dale," he called softly.

"Come on in, Michael. How'd things go at the lab?"

"Better than I expected, boss. This one's a winner. Negligible pressure loss," he responded, as he sat down in one of the tufted leather and mahogany chairs opposite Dale. They were separated by an expanse of solid mahogany desktop beneath beveled glass. At one time, it totally intimidated Michael. Now, it served as a good place to rest both his tired arms. *Thank You, Father,* he prayed silently as he realized just how at ease he felt.

"I'm looking forward to hearing all the details, just as soon as you get some rest. You look beat." Dale eyed him before pushing a large, white envelope across the desk to him. "This came express mail about an hour ago. I didn't think you'd want me to interrupt the test, so I signed for it."

"That's fine, thanks," Michael assured him as he picked up the cardboard packet and removed the envelope from inside. The return address, stamped in gold-foil embossing, caught his attention: *Shelton & Parkham, Attorneys at Law.* Dread seized him. His stomach felt like it was rising to his throat. Stephanie. *Is it the divorce papers?* he wondered. With shaky fingers he opened the envelope and began reading.

Dale watched his star employee devour the letter's contents. He saw his features tense and color drain from his face. "What is it, Michael? What's wrong?"

He did not respond right away, but just sat staring at the letter he gripped with both hands. His mouth dry, he croaked, "It's Caleb. My best friend...Caleb..."

"What happened? Is he all right?"

"He's...dead." Michael's world collapsed around him. "Caleb. Dead. I can't believe it! He was healthier than I am. We were together a week and a half ago." Bitter accusations fought their way into his thoughts as he sat shaking his head. *First I lose my wife and kids, now my best friend.*

Dear God, what next? Why? he thought.

Dale, seeing how deeply the news affected Michael, didn't know what to do. He watched in silence as the man across from him fought a powerful inner battle. Slowly, muscle by resisting muscle, Michael regained his composure. "I'll need to take care of a few things. It says here I should call this attorney about Caleb's will. I'll need some time off." His words were matter-of-fact, without emotion.

"Of course. Take whatever you need. The rest of the guys can do the follow-up."

"Thanks." He shook Dale's hand, turned around, and walked down familiar corridors in a daze. If he passed anybody, he never knew it. A turmoil raged inside him, the likes of which he had never experienced.

He wanted to trust God to help him, but wanted to blame Him at the same time. His only thought for a while was, *Dear God, why? Why Caleb?* The heavens seemed like brass.

This, for Michael, was the blackest moment of his entire life. Just when he had begun to stand on his growing faith—to abandon himself to God—it appeared that God abandoned him, literally. At least, that was what Satan would have him believe. Michael almost fell into the trap, until Sandy's need snapped him out of it.

The three of them—Sandy, Maggie, and Michael—sat in the Hawkins' kitchen. Their eyes were red from crying. "Mr. Michael," Sandy sniffed, "I'm gonna miss Mr. Caleb so much..."

"Me, too, Sandy...me, too. Can you tell me exactly what happened, son?"

"Well...Mr. Caleb wuz over here this past weekend hepin' outside like he always done. He wuz high up on a ladder doin' somethin' an' then we both heared a thumpety noise. Ma, we had her on the porch gettin' some fresh air 'n stuff, an' we saw her wheelchair rollin' down the steps. She couldn't do nothin' t'hep herself, so I yelled an' took off a'runnin', an' I guess Mr. Caleb tried t'hurry 'n hep her, too. Ya know how he wuz with Ma. He wuz so worried 'bout her, he pro'bly done fergot he wuz up on the ladder, an' then he falled off it from way high, an' then he wuz layin'

on the ground, not movin' or nothin'! It wuz...terrible, Mr. Michael!"
He started sobbing.

"I didn' know what t'do firs'. I got on my knees b'side him an'...he
whispered t'me, 'Sandy,' he says, 'now you trust God. No matter what
happens. Jesus is always with you.' I...I had t'git Ma fixed back in her
chair an' put a rag aroun' the bleedin' cut on her arm where she done
banged it up, an' then I had t'run real far t'the neighbors fer hep with Mr.
Caleb...I runned as fas' as I could go, but when I brung 'em back, he was
already dead. I guess it wuz a hermerage in his brain 'er somethin'. I didn'
know how t'call ya or ya woulda knowed b'fore now. It's...all my fault
Mr. Caleb's dead, cuz I musta not locked Ma's chair right...It's all my
fault! An' he tol' me to trust God...oh, hep me trust God, Mr. Michael.
It's all my fault." He looked up, red hair for once all in place and his eyes
so tender and pleading.

Michael got up and hugged Sandy for a long while until the young
boy's wracking sobs subsided. "Sandy, Sandy, it's not your fault, son.
Please believe that. You've always been very careful with your mom's
wheelchair. I've watched you." He looked over at Maggie. She, too, had
tears streaming down her face, but was unable to brush them away. He
grabbed his hankie, dried her tears, and hugged her as best he could.
Turning back to Sandy, he added, "I'm proud of the way you handled
yourself. Things just happen sometimes. We don't understand why. If
it's anybody's fault, it's mine. Maybe it wouldn't have happened if I had
been there like I usually was on weekends, instead of at work...But
Sandy...and Maggie, Mr. Caleb died doing what he loved most—helping people. And his favorite people, at that."

Out of the depths of Michael's soul flowed gentle words of comfort as
he responded to Sandy and Maggie's despair. He knew the words were
not his own. In the past, grief had always caused him to withdraw and
feel awkward. His current willingness to reach out turned the tide of his
own sorrow. In order to encourage them, he shared about other situations where he had cried out to God in his distress. Trusting the Lord
was still the only answer.

Simple funeral arrangements were made and carried out according to Caleb's requests. Matters of probate were taken care of. Kind friends at church called to offer help. Michael was polite in his responses, but their help was not what he needed at the moment. He needed time with his Lord and Master. Throughout the ensuing days, he prayed and began studying the lives of Abraham and King David. Michael depended on his Bible for the strength Caleb had promised him was there. He read and reread the psalms and cried often. Slowly, almost imperceptibly, his grief and guilt began to fade.

In his studies, he felt a strange kinship to the man who had introduced him to the wonders of the Bible. That closeness comforted him. He read about Abraham, the friend of God who lived four centuries after Noah's flood. Faithful trust was the hallmark of Abraham's life, yet Michael noted that his ascent was not immediate, but gradual. Old Abraham did not become the friend of God overnight. Sometimes he obeyed perfectly; other times he failed miserably.

Step by step, God developed Abraham's trust in Him. First came the promise, then the fulfillment—often long afterward. He and Sarah, both way past childbearing age, received the son God had promised them. But only after they had gotten impatient enough to take things into their own human hands. Michael was amazed to learn that the "friend of God" had succumbed to his wife's prodding to "produce" a son with her maidservant, Hagar. He did, and they did. Ishmael was born.

Yes, Isaac, born of Abraham's wife, Sarah, finally did arrive. He was the apple of his father's eye and the joy of his heart. So what did God do? Asked him to give Isaac up as a sacrifice! Michael, so abruptly separated from his mentor and dearest friend, empathized with Abraham's anguish and confusion.

But God didn't fail Abraham; neither did Abraham fail God's test of trust. Even though Isaac's life was spared and Caleb's was not, Michael felt reassured somehow. He committed himself to face the future with courage.

From his reading about King David, he took heart as well, choosing to believe that if David could trust God through all his heartaches, so could he. He had always loved the story of young David and Goliath. Now, it gripped him in new and meaningful ways. He realized that when David refused to wear Saul's cumbersome suit of armor against the giant, he was choosing to place his very life in God's care. He used God's weapon to destroy Israel's enemy—the same slingshot and a few stones that he had used to protect his flocks from hungry predators. David was trusting in the foundation of past victories for the present test. Michael decided to allow the Lord to choose and develop weapons against the "giants" he faced.

David also knew intense pain and loneliness. In Scripture, he was called, "a man after God's own heart," yet he was not perfect. He committed gross sins, like having his lover's husband killed. He paid bitter consequences. The illegitimate child of his adulterous relationship with Bathsheba died. Later, his favored son, Absalom, led a rebellion against his father that led to his own death. God delivered David from guilt. He could deliver Michael from the guilt Satan threw his way. His failures were under Christ's blood—forgiven.

Yes, Michael had grown to adore Caleb. The blaze of their friendship burned brightly for a season, but Caleb was gone. And Michael was left alone.

Life had to go on.

FOURTEEN

GLIMPSES

Six months came and went. Early one Friday afternoon, the telephone rang in Michael's office at work. He picked it up. "Hello, this is Michael Nastasis."

A female voice at the other end quivered with apprehension. "Michael, this is Stephanie. I need to talk. Can we get together sometime soon?"

"Stephanie...*Stephanie?* How are you? Is everything alright?"

"Yes. Well, not completely. That's why I want to talk. Someplace where we won't be disturbed would be nice. The children are at camp for the week, but I'd rather not meet here at the house. I'm sure you understand."

"Well...yes. Let me see. Oh, I've got the perfect spot. Today is Friday. I was planning to go there anyway for my weekend retreat." He paused, held the receiver away from his mouth, and took a deep breath. "I can take off work early and pick you up at four o'clock. It's a nice drive. Then we can talk over dinner. You'll be back before too late. Sound okay?"

"That will be fine, Michael. I'll see you then," Stephanie added softly as she hung up the phone.

Her voice was a sweet symphony to his ears. His heart pounded in anticipation. Something about her sounded different from the last time he dropped off the children after visitation. The coldness in her voice was gone. *What could she want? I wonder if my prayers have been working. We'll see soon enough, I guess.* His concentration deserted him. "Father," he prayed, *"take control of my jumbled emotions and anxious thoughts. Help me keep my mind on work until it's time to go, Lord."*

The afternoon dragged until 3:30 finally came. He gathered his suit coat and briefcase, locked his office door, and headed to the parking garage. *Friday!* He heaved a sigh of relief as he got into the car. *It's Friday, and Stephanie and I are having dinner tonight! Hallelujah! Something must be up, or she wouldn't want to get together.*

He drove the familiar route to 71 Chestnut Street. A lump formed in his throat as he got closer. He struggled to keep from getting choked up. Pulling a handkerchief out of his pocket, he dabbed his eyes. It had been a long time. So much water under the bridge since that night. He shuddered. Pain still lingered deep in his memory. *But I have forgiven her for that in Jesus' name, and I know I'm forgiven for hurting her...* he reminded himself.

There it was...the old home front. He glanced in the rear view mirror to comb his hair and could not help wondering if she would ever find him attractive again. Besides a few more gray hairs, he looked about the same...in fact, in better shape from Caleb's prodding to eat right and start exercising. His heart thumped in his chest as he stepped up to the front door and tapped the brass door knocker. He felt like he was on his first date back in high school.

"I'll be right there," Stephanie called from inside. He smiled. Just like his wife...always needing a few extra minutes to get ready. Somehow the waiting did not seem nearly as annoying as it once did. Her tardiness used to be a constant source of contention. It stretched his engineering mentality to the limit.

He took a deep breath, thrust his hands into his pockets, and leaned back against the porch wall. He used the time to inspect the neighborhood, something he did not usually do on Saturday morning when he picked up the kids. The area had not changed much. *Wonder what the neighbors thought of the separation...Were they shocked? Wonder who they blame? She always was the more sociable one of the two of us,* he pondered. Suddenly, the door latch slid back and Stephanie stood in front of him with a nervous smile pasted on her lips. His eyes met hers, then looked down. *She is still beautiful, Lord. Guess I should tell her that shouldn't I?* he thought. Neither said a word, but stood staring at the porch floor.

He extended his hand instinctively to help her down the step and she received his offer. Clearing his throat and swallowing hard, he spoke, "Stephanie, you're still as beautiful as ever." Then he stopped mid-sidewalk and held her at arm's length. "No, I take that back. You're *more* beautiful than ever. Maybe it's the new eyes I have now." He smiled warmly at her.

It was Stephanie's turn to clear her throat. Eyebrows knit, she gazed straight ahead at the car door and replied quietly, "You're looking fine, too, Michael. Thinner, aren't you?"

"Yes, a little, and I feel much better. I've been running and trying to eat healthier."

"That's good. I've gained a few pounds myself, and I hate it. I forgot you'd be dressed in a suit coming from work. I didn't dress accordingly."

"Steph…Stephanie, don't worry about that. I'm going to change into more comfortable clothes as soon as we get to our destination. You look great!" He opened her car door and helped her inside.

"Thank you, Michael." There was an awkward air about her. Her eyes were sad as she looked at him, and her shoulders slumped. Something was bothering her, that much was clear. He could read her like a book.

He got into the driver's side, pushed a praise tape into the stereo, and started the car toward the Country Corner. Stephanie was quiet, so he decided to just wait until she felt ready for conversation. She did not seem any too anxious to talk; she just stared out the window. Friday afternoon interstate traffic finally thinned as they passed the outskirts of the city. He began to relax and prayed in his heart for restoration between them.

The next thing he knew, she was sound asleep with her head against the window. *That's my Steph, too,* he thought fondly as he looked at her. *She still can't stay awake in the car.* He remembered how he used to think it was so cute. Later, after they were married, he would get upset with her when she slept on a trip instead of navigating. Or when she read his carefully marked map wrong. He prayed silently, *Forgive me, Lord, for condemning her about so many little things. I just didn't know. Please give me a chance to make it all up to her.*

Stephanie whimpered as she adjusted her position. Her head slid away from the window…toward Michael. Then she lay down and curled up on the seat with her head against his side. Not knowing what to do with his arm, Michael shifted in the seat and put both hands on the steering wheel. Torn between two desires, he was uncomfortable. Finally, he gave in and caressed her hair with his right hand. She sighed in her sleep, unaware of the source of her contentment.

———

He pulled up in front of the property and turned off the engine. Stephanie did not budge, so he leaned his head back against the headrest and closed his eyes, letting out a deep sigh. *Oh, how I wish Caleb could have met her. He helped me so much to see myself clearly, and now he won't even see the fruit...I miss him so much,* he thought. His heart ached at the memory. Caleb had become such a part of him that he felt like his right arm was missing. Then he glanced down at Stephanie, stroked her hair again, and patted her hand. Her skin felt chilly. She shivered against his touch, so he shook her gently, "Stephanie, we're here. Time to wake up." She stirred and then sat bolt upright in the seat, disoriented as she squinted at him.

"Oh, excuse me," she apologized. "I'm sorry, I guess I was more exhausted than I thought. I know how you hate for me to sleep in the car." She fumbled groggily to straighten her hair and started to open her door.

"Sit tight, Steph. I'll get that for you. And don't worry about sleeping. It's okay. Honest. I'll share something with you later. Come on." He helped her out and held her arm to steady her as they walked to the front door.

She glanced around, first at the white picket fence and the flower boxes at the windows. "Michael, this house is adorable—so quaint and neat. Where are we? Caleb's Country Corner Retreat... What's that? Oh, is this the place I heard you were coming to visit on weekends? Some old man owned it or something, Kathryn said. Is that right?"

Michael chuckled. She always was so cute when she first woke up. "Yes, this is the place. I've grown attached to it these last months, and was even more so to Caleb." His voice lowered, and he stammered slightly as he mentioned his friend's name. "He passed away recently." The fresh loss grew more vivid.

"I'm sorry. I suppose you did grow fond of him, seeing him so often."

"Yes, especially during our...differences. He was like a father to me.

He was second only to God Himself in filling a void in my heart. In fact, Caleb led me to the greatest discoveries of my life. One day, when we have time, I'll share those with you." Instead of unlocking the front door, he decided to lead her around to the backyard first. They could sit in the hanging swing and talk. "Come on, I want to show you something. You'll love it," he urged, as he directed her to the path.

When she saw the view, Stephanie stood speechless. After a moment, she sighed and exclaimed over and over, "Oh, isn't this gorgeous? It's so beautiful!" On the way to the swing, she broke into a ballerina twirl—something she had not done in years. Michael smiled and thanked the Lord for her joy. *She likes the place. Maybe...Whoa, old boy,* he cautioned himself, *Not too fast.*

A little dizzy from her spin, she plopped down in the swing in a young girl's fashion and patted the seat for him to join her. She sat swaying for a moment, and then her face clouded. Joy fled at the remembrance of the purpose of their reunion.

Michael, sitting down on the other end of the swing, made it easier for her by suggesting, "So you wanted to talk to me about something important? How about getting it out now while we relax? Then, we'll enjoy our dinner more later." He looked at her encouragingly.

"Yes, I guess I should get it over with. Michael, I...I...you'll be angry when I tell you this...I'm so sorry...I..."

Apprehension gripped his heart. *Maybe it isn't good news after all. She probably wants to speed up the divorce so she can marry some guy she's been dating—nice,* he considered. He swallowed hard. "What is it, Stephanie? Please tell me what's bothering you."

Her big blue eyes filled with tears and she started to cry. She covered her face with her hands, unable to talk through choking sobs. Michael could stand it no longer. He moved toward her, reached his arm over to her shoulder, and pulled her close to his side. Surprisingly, she did not resist, but leaned into him and cried even harder.

"Michael, Michael, I did something awful. I...I paid a lot of money to that officer so he would serve you the restraining order at the hotel right after the awards banquet." The rest of the story came out in one big rush. "I wanted to see you fall hard. I was so mad at you and your job that I wanted to get back at you in a big way. Worse yet, it was me who called the reporter and tipped him off. That's why the front page story and photos came out." Sobs and wails continued. "I'm sorry, Michael. So sorry. I know you can never forgive me, but I had to tell you what I did. Guilt has been eating me up. I can't live with myself any longer."

He listened, stunned. As Stephanie poured her heart out to him, disbelief turned to searing pain, like a razor ripping across his insides. Memories of humiliation clamored for attention. The officer. The newspaper. His fits of rage. But quietly, unobtrusively, Caleb's gentle admonition crept forth: "*Michael, since you have received God's forgiveness, you must also forgive others who have hurt you, no matter how deeply ...*" *Dear Lord, this is my own wife. The mother of my children,* he bemoaned to himself. Numb, he sat and just held her for several minutes until her crying subsided somewhat. Then, as if being poured from a heavenly pitcher, the liquid warmth of compassion flooded his being. He could speak.

"Stephanie, look at me." He tilted her chin up and looked deep into her eyes. "I forgive you." He hugged her and laid his head on top of hers. Tears brimmed in his eyes. "I forgive you, honey." She sat up and looked at him incredulously as he continued. "Oh, it hurt me, yes, but not beyond repair. In fact, it helped me become a new man. So don't fret anymore about it. I'm so sorry I made you angry enough to resort to such drastic measures. You've never been a vindictive person as long as I've known you. I hurt you, too, Steph, didn't I?" She sniffed and nodded weakly.

"See, we both hurt each other. I wasn't a good husband in many ways. I should have been the leader of the family, spiritually and otherwise. I should have set the example. But I didn't. I was hardly there. I was too success-and-money motivated. They were the gods I worshiped. I acted like I didn't need another soul in the world, especially you. I was insensitive, proud, and critical. What you said to me that night was right; I did tear you and the kids down all the time. Maybe to make myself feel bigger and better. Will you forgive me, too? Please? I do love you."

She snuggled closer. Her "Yes" was a nod against his chest. Down her cheeks, tears flowed again in rivulets, soaking his shirt and tie. "I love you too, Michael. I always have. And, of course, I forgive you. I can't believe what I did to you, though...my own husband. I'll feel guilty about that for the rest of my life." She paused and looked up at him. "I never did complete the divorce proceedings. Still, I couldn't face you again, until now."

"I'm thankful you finally called, Steph, and that you had the courage to tell me the truth. But we need to clear something up right now. You don't have to carry that guilt for the rest of your life. I certainly don't want you to. Come on, let's go take a little walk. I've got something very important to talk to you about." His voice sang with a lilt of growing, childlike excitement.

He took her by the hand and led her on the path that Caleb had pointed out to him months ago. They strolled past the garden, through the grape arbors and fruit trees, past flowers galore, and down the lush green hill that sloped to the pond. Tiny birds flapped their colorful wings in the birdbath nearby, and others were nibbling from the feeders. "Stephanie," he asked with as much calm as he could muster up, "do you think you could be happy living way out here?" He let out a deep breath.

An apprehensive, yet playful smile appeared on her face and she blushed. "What do you mean, Michael?"

He faced her and gently took her chin in his hand again. "Well, first, I'm asking with all my heart if you will be my wife for the rest of our lives. I'd like to start all over together and really make our marriage work this time. I want to be the husband you deserve. And second...you won't believe it, but..." He paused for effect and then made a fast sweeping motion with his arm. "This property...is ours!" He could contain his excitement no longer. Grabbing her around the waist and picking her up in the air, he ran and whirled her around and around until they were both on the verge of collapse from laughter.

When he finally set her back on the ground, she stopped short, her eyes wide with excitement. His enthusiasm was contagious, but not completely. "Michael, you *are* kidding. Tell me the truth, now, come on. Are you sure you're not suffering from mental exhaustion, or something worse?"

"Stephanie Marie Nastasis, I'm as sane as I can be. I couldn't believe it, either. It's the most incredible thing that ever happened to me. I received a notice from the law firm acting as the executor of Caleb's estate. He had no living family left, so he willed the place to me! He felt that I would make the best use of it, in keeping with his original intent."

She stood there staring at him with her mouth open, shaking her head back and forth. Almost hysterically, she started laughing and took off running at top speed, calling back at him, "Michael James Nastasis, if I had known you'd come up with something this good while you were gone, I would have kicked you out of the house a long time ago!" He burst out laughing and chased after her.

FIFTEEN

COMPLETION

Michael awoke long before dawn. He kissed Stephanie on the forehead and tiptoed downstairs. She was sleeping peacefully, so that would give him plenty of time to be with the Lord before she got up.

In the study where he and Caleb had spent long hours together, he read his Bible and prayed, offering praise for the restoration of their marriage. He thanked God, too, for all the time he had with Caleb and for his many prayers for him and Stephanie. They were being answered... one by one. As he read the King James Version, he ran across Amos 3:3, one of the first verses Caleb had shared with him. "Can two walk together, except they be agreed?" He decided it would be perfect to read to Stephanie later.

As he glanced up from his Bible, something on top of the bookshelf caught his eye. He wondered what it was. It had been there a while, but he just now focused on it. Curiosity got the best of him. He stood up from behind the desk, walked across the room, and stretched his arm up to reach the small, flat object. He discovered a cassette tape, carefully wrapped inside a piece of light gray stationery. His eyebrows raised in surprise. Across the top of the sheet was imprinted, "*From the desk of Caleb Johannsen.*" Reawakened grief flooded over him as he began reading the note:

My dear Michael,

For a brief moment in time, you have been like a son to me. Thank you for the many wonderful memories we've shared. The trips to see me may come to an end one day, but our friendship will not. I know how much you enjoyed listening to cassettes while driving out here. Please don't wait to listen to this tape I'm leaving for you. God bless you and that beautiful family of yours. See you all in glory!

Much love,
Caleb

"See you," Michael repeated to himself, squinting to keep the tears from spilling forth, but with little success, "...see you in glory?" He licked a tear from his upper lip where it had come to rest. Its salty taste spurred him into action. With sure, determined steps, he strode to the tape player. In one swift motion he dropped in the tape and hit *Play*. He cocked his head at the soft click it made when first starting up and then crossed the room to Caleb's favorite old chair. Before he sat down, his friend's familiar voice filled the room:

How are you, Michael? Not long after you left tonight, the Lord led me into a glorious time of worship and prayer. I felt closer to Him than I ever had in my life. How awesome it was...truly beyond description! At last I understand better what the apostle Paul meant in 2 Corinthians 12 about being caught up in the third heaven. He heard "utterances beyond the power of man to put into words," the Amplified Bible says. I felt that way this evening. And to think that it was only a tiny foretaste of eternity!

I have such a longing to be with my Savior and Lord—a longing that grows more intense with each passing day. If I can in some small way influence you to follow Jesus, my life will not have been in vain. Know, my friend, that you are loved of God. He will never leave you. Give Him all your heart. You have nothing to lose and everything to gain.

The Lord strongly impressed me to make this tape for you on oneness with Him. We've talked at length about the first three steps in a life of faith, and only just touched on the fourth. Do you remember? *Agreement. Dependence. Trust.* And now last, but not least, comes *Oneness.* By the time you hear this, I believe you and Stephanie will be one again. What an exquisite reunion you will have! I'm sure this message will be more meaningful to you then—more so even than if I had shared it with you during one of our talks. Christian marriage is the nearest thing to oneness with the Lord. But even as intimate as the most perfect human love between a husband and wife may be, the Lord calls us to a relationship infinitely beyond that.

Oneness, Michael. Tender, intimate fellowship with the living God! Enthroned in all His indescribable beauty—His incomparable holy majesty declared by the heavens themselves; His compassionate heart opened wide to you. Oh, my son, do heed His call. The greatest thing in all this world is oneness with your Creator. The secret is found in bent knees, wet eyes, and a broken heart.

To experience true oneness, your relationship with Him has to be the most important thing in your life. Being "God-inside minded" might be another way to describe just such a focus. Remember my telling you way back on the day we met how we all resemble sweaters turned inside out? Society's emphasis is on the wrong side of life—the externals alone. Mine was, and yours, too. Oneness requires just the opposite. More than anything, you need an internal identification as a child of God. As spiritual "heir apparent," so to speak, you may come boldly to His throne, yet humbly into His presence by the blood of Jesus.

Intimacy with God was Enoch's trademark, and God commended him for pleasing Him. Right after this affirmation of the Old Testament saint, the Word states that without faith it is impossible to please God. Certainly then, Enoch had faith. He heard God's Words and believed them. He walked with His Lord continually and passionately, preaching for Him. Enoch enjoyed such intimate fellowship that he was translated—taken from this life without even experiencing death. Imagine that.

Walking with the Lord like Enoch requires holiness, Michael—a subject we touched on earlier. You can't be one with Him and entangled in the world at the same time. When you do pursue Him with a hungry heart…oh, the treasure houses that open up to you!

Whew! Caleb is talking heavy stuff this morning, Michael thought as he got up and pressed the *Pause* button on the tape player. He reached for his Bible, searching for the passages about Enoch. With the help of the concordance, he found them in Genesis 5:21 and Hebrews 11:5. He decided to begin reading in Genesis:

> When Enoch had lived 65 years, he became the father of Methu-selah. And after he became the father of Methuselah, Enoch walked with God 300 years and had other sons and daughters. Altogether, Enoch lived 365 years. Enoch walked with God; then he was no more, because God took him away.
> —Genesis 5:21–24

He read the passage once, then went back and reread it. One thing caught his attention. It drew his thoughts back to the reason he had begun his search—the saint's oneness with God. Enoch lived 365 years, the exact same number as the days in a year! Daily fellowship with the Lord was the key. He closed his Bible emphatically, pleased with this new insight. Then he stepped over to the cassette player and punched the *Play* button again. The realistic sound of Caleb's voice startled him:

> A close friendship with the Lord requires that you spend much time alone with Him. In some respects, it's similar to an earthly friendship—yours and mine, for example. We got to know each other so well because just the two of us were together often. If there had always been a big crowd around, we wouldn't be nearly as close, would we?
>
> You can bare your soul to a genuine friend and unload everything that's on your heart. So you can with God. There's only one thing He cannot do—share His faults in return. He doesn't have any! But He's a kind of "backdoor friend" who can see the messier parts of you and still love you. In fact, someone has said that the only way to have a relationship with the Lord is to let Him in your whole "house." Not just the living room, where you keep everything neat and tidy to make a good impression. He

wants access to the laundry room, the attic, the closets, and the junk drawers. Every nook and cranny.

If you want to get to know the Lord better, spend more time in His Word—not just daily, but hourly. As David wrote, meditate on the Word of God. Memorize it. Hide it deep in your heart. Oneness appears throughout the gospel of John as "abiding in," which means, "remaining in" Jesus: "Abide in me, and I in you," He exhorts us in John 15:4, the King James Version. In John 17:21, He prays that all of His disciples may be one with Him and each other, just as He and His Father are one. Imagine having the same closeness as the Father and His Son, Jesus! If you did, whatever you prayed for, it would be done for you. Why? Because you would be in complete agreement with His Word, which never returns without accomplishing its purpose. Whoever abides in Him doesn't continue in sin, but keeps His commandments, 1 John 3 says. It's the same principle as Galatians 5:17, that He who is filled with the Holy Spirit does not give in to the desires of his natural self.

Each of these terms, "being in Christ," "abiding in Christ," and "being filled with the Holy Spirit," represents intimacy with God. More than an intellectual recognition of Him, such oneness encompasses a radically changed life that grows with time. The filling with the Holy Spirit is an absolute necessity for Christians. Any controversy about it is a matter of interpretation and misunderstanding. Being filled with the Holy Spirit has been described in various ways, but an indication of oneness with the Holy Spirit is abundant, mature fruit—love, joy, peace, patience, kindness, goodness, faithfulness, gentleness, and self-control.

Reverend A. W. Tozer said that if the Holy Spirit were to leave many churches, nothing much would change. In fact, few would even notice He was gone. Business would proceed as usual. Don't let that be true of your life, Michael. Live like a fish swimming in the ocean of God's presence. Let his Spirit flow in and out of your heart unhindered. Unless you are walking in the Spirit, you will feel like a fish flip-flopping around in a net.

A seventeenth-century French Carmelite monk named Brother Lawrence called deep intimacy with the Lord "practicing His presence." I've read his writings extensively, and I believe he knew God very well. "Practicing His presence" means living every minute of every day, no matter what you're doing, as precious and holy to God. It means allowing the perfect Holy Spirit to live His pure life through you as you take every thought captive to the obedience of Christ. Seek to achieve the mindset that everything you do is but a part of His work to further His kingdom. Paul talked about that in 2 Corinthians 10, so be sure to read it when you get a chance.

Prayer, especially with thanks and praise, is the best way to practice His presence. You and I had some great prayer times together, didn't we? Continue to tell the Lord through your words and actions how much you love Him. You can intercede for others, too, as we often did. Here's an approach I have always enjoyed when praying for someone. I think of the person until I have a clear picture in my mind. Then, as if I were placing him in my cupped hands, I lift him up to the Lord and believe for the Holy Spirit to move as He knows best. You might try it.

Being still enough to listen to the Lord is one of the hardest yet most important tasks for Christians today, pastor and author, Jamie Buckingham, has said. I don't doubt it a bit. When I neglect my prayer and meditation, acting on my own ideas instead of listening to the Lord, things usually go haywire. Fellowship with Jesus is no mere flight of fancy. Saints of God throughout history have been willing to die rather than jeopardize their relationship with Him.

Read about Daniel during the Babylonian captivity. He agreed to be thrown into a den of hungry lions rather than give up his prayer time. Did his faithfulness go unrewarded? No, sir! Those lions didn't lay a paw on him. What's more, the heathen king sent a proclamation throughout the land declaring the God of the Jews as the one true God. Daniel's enemies suffered the same fate they had planned to heap on him.

Michael, do study the other three young Hebrews in Babylonian captivity—Shadrach, Meshech, and Abednego. Like Daniel, they valued their friendship with God beyond all the world had to offer, no matter what the consequences. The stakes mounted for them. That fiery furnace turned out to be a scorcher. But they had the privilege of marching right through the flames with Jesus at their side.

The apostle Paul knew what it was to rest contentedly in the arms of his Lord. Outward circumstances failed to sway him from his convictions. He was beaten with rods three times, stoned and left for dead, shipwrecked three times, five times whipped with forty lashes, and even spent a day and night drifting in the sea while waiting to be rescued. Did he complain? No way. Listen to his words from 2 Corinthians 4. They are the words of a man who knew the depths of oneness with Christ:

We are hard pressed on every side, but not crushed; perplexed, but not in despair; persecuted, but not abandoned; struck down, but not destroyed. We always carry around in our body the death of Jesus, so that the life of Jesus may also be revealed in our body.... It is written: "I believed therefore I have spoken." With that same spirit of faith we also believe and therefore speak, because we know that the one who raised the Lord Jesus from the dead will also raise us with Jesus and present us with you in his presence.... Therefore we do not lose heart. Though outwardly we are wasting away, yet inwardly we are being renewed day by day. For our light and momentary troubles are achieving for us an eternal glory that far outweighs them all. So we fix our eyes not on what is seen, but on what is unseen. For what is seen is temporary, but what is unseen is eternal.

—2 CORINTHIANS 4:8–11, 13–14, 16–18

Aren't those wonderful words, Michael? Only someone who had intimate fellowship with God could write them in the face of all he endured. And listen again to Paul's writing in Romans 8, one of your favorite chapters:

Who shall separate us from the love of Christ? Shall trouble or hardship or persecution or famine or nakedness or danger or sword?.... No.... For I am convinced that neither death nor life, neither angels nor demons, neither the present nor the future, nor any powers, neither height nor depth, nor anything else in all creation, will be able to separate us from the love of God that is in Christ Jesus our Lord.

—ROMANS 8:35, 37–39

Oneness with God, no matter what, son. Nothing, even imprisonment for his faith, could break Paul away from so great a love. Regardless of how often Satan tried to destroy him, he knew it all only served to draw him closer to the One he loved better than life.

The apostle John, perhaps more than anyone, enjoyed intimate fellowship with his God. He described himself as, "the apostle whom Jesus loved." On several occasions, John rested his head on Jesus' chest. What a picture of closeness! John is the one to whom the Lord unveiled His plan for the culmination of the ages. Alone, a castaway on the Isle of Patmos, John lived to receive the message of the Revelation.

Sounds great, doesn't it? It *is* great, Michael. Don't leave it there with the "sounds great," though. Make that same intimacy your goal. Fix your eyes firmly on things above. Don't let anything come between you and Him. Just say to Him, "Lord, I want You above all others. I need to be abiding in You." He'll respond. Read the psalms, starting with Psalm 18, and then write letters to Him. You will be surprised how close He'll become. He will be your very best Friend.

You've begun some good habits...like getting up early in the morning to spend time alone with Him. Read His Word and resolve every conflict by first agreeing with Him. Start your day with your own "Declaration of Dependence"—on Him and other believers. Stephanie, most of all. Your only declaration of independence should be from the snares of the devil. Whenever you need reassurance as to your place in God's eyes, study the Scriptures about being "in Him," or "in Christ." By the time you're halfway through, you'll know all over again to whom you belong.

Speaking of Stephanie and marriage...your relationship with

her parallels your walk with the Lord. You will walk through the wilderness in both. Your relationship with her can only be successful when you depend on and trust the Lord and each other completely. Especially you, Michael. It's more natural for Stephanie. You'll never be able to love her or the Lord until you break that independent spirit in you. "Drop your guard," as they say. Don't be afraid to share openly your innermost self with her, just as you did with me. Make yourself vulnerable to her, and she will to you.

The office—yes, *office*—of husband is a high privilege many regard too lightly. Don't let the world's low moral standards dilute the truth of the sanctity of marriage. You and Stephanie are an unbreakable unit...a team. Do you want your marriage to be all that God would have it become? Do you want to be the kind of husband God desires for Stephanie? Then she needs to know that you hold her best interests at heart. Jesus was willing to die for His beloved ones. He calls you to "die" to your own desires and your old nature in order to better love her. Do it, my friend...with joy set before you.

Be careful of striving to make her over into your image of what's right. Instead, through the Word, help her become all she can be in God's will. She needs you for that, like you need her. Keep in mind that you've had a big head start, so be patient. Wives love learning about how God used women in the past. Think of the many faithful women who played tremendous roles in Scripture. Rahab, the harlot, agreed to shelter the Israelite spies from the enemy and saved herself and her family, as well as paved the way for the conquest of the land of Canaan.

There's Queen Esther, who depended mightily on God. Even with the threat of her own death, she risked going before the heathen king on behalf of her kinfolk. The widow of Zarephath trusted God enough to feed the prophet Elijah from her last bit of food, and she never lacked again. Think of Ruth, who left her own people to remain loyal to her mother-in-law and trust her God.

How about Mary, the mother of Jesus, who on the simple word of an angel, believed she would bear the Son of God? How she must have feared what would become of Him, and wondered why her, of all women! Yet, she agreed with God and fulfilled her purpose. Of course, we can't forget Mary Magdalene, the former prostitute, who sat at Jesus' feet and worshiped—a true picture of oneness. She broke a bottle of expensive perfume for Him, which proved to be His anointing for burial. Not only that, Mary Magdalene was the first person to see Him resurrected from the dead! So never underestimate what the Lord may want to do with Stephanie.

Try to be less of an analytical engineer, Michael, at least where she's concerned. Let yourself love her passionately. You'll have to cultivate that union like you'd cultivate a beautiful, delicate flower. Train your feelings for her and let them grow. It may be scary at first, but you've got to take risks...with her and with life. You'll never be secure or accomplish anything if you willy-waller around. Think of a trapeze artist flying gracefully through the air. He has to release one bar before he grabs hold of the other one. Let go of the way you used to relate to your wife, and with all that's within you, reach out and grasp a new relationship with her.

Let's say you believed the two of you had good physical intimacy before. But maybe she wasn't satisfied because she knew you didn't depend on her at all. She felt left out of your life. A woman needs to know she's needed. You can't just *act* like you're depending on her, because she'll see right through it. It's a motivational factor, not an intellectual one. Be mindful of what's going on with her, even when she's quiet. A most important point. Take time to become part of her. Get involved in her life. I don't mean just interested, Michael. Involved. There's a big difference.

Belonging. Yes, that's the word that describes oneness. Recognize that, in the marital bond, you and Stephanie belong exclusively to each other. That can help you make the right choices in the future. When the bliss of your second honeymoon is past, times may come when you have to grit your teeth, cling to the commitment you've made, and trust God to carry you through.

In your Christian faith, too, belonging is important. Take joy in belonging to Christ and to the fellowship of believers. Sur-

round yourself with Christians who will strengthen you in your walk, lift you up in times of need, and encompass you in every trial. The love you have for each other and for the Lord unites you in the heart of God.

I'm talking about real belonging, not just being there—loving and not just being apathetic. It's like a child being provided food and shelter somewhere versus his being adopted into a warm family who wants and loves him. He belongs in the second home, and he can sense the vast difference. You've lived in various houses at one time or another. Some were only places of residence, but in others you felt like you belonged. You've been employed by companies where you only performed a job, while at others you really felt a part of the team. As a Christian now, you're a member of the most close-knit group on earth.

And Michael, do let loose a little and quit worrying about what everyone thinks of you. The only things you need to care about are that Jesus loves you, that you love Him with all your heart, and that you love others as He does. The rest will come and go. Whether it comes or goes doesn't make any difference in the long run. In closing, I'd like to leave one other Scripture passage with you—1 Corinthians 13. The "love chapter." I implore you to commit it to memory, lest all we have shared about the unseen essential be in vain. Listen carefully:

If I speak in the tongues of men and of angels, but have not love, I am only a resounding gong or a clanging cymbal. If I have the gift of prophecy and can fathom all mysteries and all knowledge, and if I have faith that can move mountains, but have not love, I am nothing. If I give all I possess to the poor and surrender my body to the flames, but have not love, I gain nothing.

Love is patient, love is kind. It does not envy, it does not boast, it is not proud. It is not rude, it is not self-seeking, it is not easily angered, it keeps no record of wrongs. Love does not delight in evil but rejoices with the truth. It always protects, always trusts, always hopes, always perseveres.

Love never fails. But where there are prophecies, they will cease; where there are tongues, they will be stilled; where there is knowledge, it will pass away. For we know in part and we prophecy in part, but when perfection comes, the imperfect disappears. When I was a child, I talked like a child, I thought like a child, I reasoned like a child. When I became a man, I put childish ways behind me. Now we see but a poor reflection as in a mirror; then we shall see face to face. Now I know in part; then I shall know fully, even as I am fully known.

And now these three remain faith, hope and love. But the greatest of these is love.

—1 CORINTHIANS 13:1–13

My dear Michael, love is greater than faith. Please remember that always. I want you to know I've been enriched by our time together. God bless you ever so abundantly. See you and yours on that great day!

The whir of the tape player was all that could be heard for the next few minutes...then the soft click of the mechanism shutting off. Still, Michael sat, thinking of Caleb. He could almost see those crystal blue eyes twinkling as Caleb walked off into the waiting arms of his precious Lord. And then his turning around with a wink and waving as he said, "So long, buddy—for now..."

Michael stayed a long time in the semi-darkness, his thoughts filled with happy memories of their time together. He missed him, but the deep ache was fading and being replaced with a heightened sense of expectancy. The future looked bright. He had Stephanie back, bless God. "And you knew!" he whispered, as if to Caleb. "You knew even then when you made the tape that she and I'd be back together. I wonder...did you know you were going? That you'd be moving on to higher ground? Yes, it seems you did."

He shivered, got up, and began pacing the length of the floor. Louder, he asked, "Is that what comes from walking in oneness with You, Jesus?" His pacing ceased. A gentle touch settled his restless heart. He sensed

God was speaking, reminding him how Joseph made plans for his bones to be taken to the Promised Land. *That was no more miraculous than my finding the tape this morning,* he thought. Misty-eyed, he shook his head in awe.

I have not changed, the Spirit spoke deep in his heart. *I am the same yesterday, today, and forever.*

Michael waited for more, but that was all there was, except for the blossoming joy in his spirit. He felt new, washed, clean, and ready to get on with the day. "Thank You, Lord," was all he could say over and over. He thought of Stephanie, still sleeping upstairs, and sighed audibly. A contented smile lit up his face. "Thank... You... Lord."

"That's it!" Michael exclaimed suddenly. "I'll serve her breakfast in bed. Knowing Caleb, I just bet he stocked the freezer. We'll have the same thing he first served me—homemade granola with blueberries, a honey-raisin bran muffin, and hot spiced herb tea." He could not wait to see her face. His heart fluttered with the excitement of a newlywed on his honeymoon. On his way to the kitchen, he did a little shuffle.

Sure enough, Caleb had made plenty and stored it away. Carefully, he scooped the granola into two ample bowls. He defrosted some plump blueberries and bran muffins in the microwave and poured milk for the cereal into two creamers. Then he set the trays—placemats, a plate for the muffins, fruit spread on the side, big mugs for the herb drink, cloth napkins with napkin rings, and silverware.

Oops...there was one thing missing—a fresh flower in a bud vase. He stepped outside in the grass, still damp with morning dew, and clipped the prettiest red rose he could find. Red roses were her favorite. When all was in place, he leaned back to survey his work. He grinned. "Thanks, Lord, for the idea. Hope the shock isn't too much for her!" One more thing. A love note to tuck inside her napkin. On it he wrote with care, "My dearest Stephanie, my wife...welcome home. You are the joy of my life. I love you. Your devoted husband, Michael." Finally, he tiptoed upstairs with a tray in each hand.

He found her propped up in bed reading. The book was one he had left on the nightstand, *No Wonder They Call Him the Savior,* by Max Lucado.

She looked up as he inched into the room. He was trying to balance both trays. "How sweet of you! This is better than a honeymoon...I can't get over the changes in you. And this book is great. I can hardly put it down. I never thought of Jesus in this way."

"Well, good morning, my love. I didn't think you'd be awake yet, and here you are reading." He leaned down to kiss her. "Max Lucado is one of my favorite authors. Glad you like him." He tilted his head. "Did you sleep okay?"

"Mm-hmm." She sighed and smiled, her eyes shining. "How about you?"

He grinned and nodded. "I've missed you so much."

She lowered her gaze. "Not as much as I've missed you. Are you sure you can forgive me?"

"Oh, sweetheart...I've already forgotten it, so you'll never have to ask again. Here, let me get this set up for you." She inhaled deeply of the red rose and smiled. When she unrolled her napkin to put it on her lap, the note he had tucked inside fell out. She read it, then closed her eyes and lifted up the rose to smell its fragrance again. Her smile was radiant.

They ate, sitting side by side, in bed. Stephanie raved about the breakfast, and Michael raved about her. Once finished, he read her the Bible verse that spoke of walking together. She hugged his neck in response. They had not been as happy since they were first married. Reveling in their newfound closeness, they spent the rest of the morning getting reacquainted. To Michael's supreme delight, he even received the honor of leading her to Jesus the way Caleb had done with him. Her childlike trust made it so much easier. Eventually, they decided to head back to the city to start sorting and packing. It would be a long process, so they figured they may as well tackle the job head-on.

During the drive, Michael shared some things he had learned from Caleb, as well as a few new discoveries he had made about himself. Stephanie listened and even asked questions. For the first time since he had known her, she stayed awake in the car!

He told her, too, about Jed, the gas station attendant he met on his first drive. He shared how Jed and his wife had lost their son in a farming accident, and because they were so poor, they never had a moment to get away and recuperate. Struck with sudden inspiration, he asked, "Say, Steph, would you mind if we gave Jed our tickets to the Bahamas? You know, the ones the company gave me along with the *Golden Eagle Award*. They're in my briefcase in the trunk. I had the date extended, hoping you and I would be able to go together one day. Jed and his wife have probably never been anywhere like that...and they would need spending money, too, I guess. We can send a money order later."

She stared at him in amazement and teased, "Are you sure I'm sitting next to Michael James Nastasis—the one I married? You're a totally different person. I've never seen anything like it!"

They laughed with glee as Stephanie tucked a small note inside the envelope with the tickets. It read, "Dear Jed, Jesus wants you to know that He loves you and your family." Soon they arrived at the gas station where Jed worked. He wasn't on duty, so they left the sealed envelope with the manager.

"Now, Steph, remind me to notify the airline of the reservation name change," Michael remarked as he pulled onto the interstate ramp.

When they returned home, they began sorting in the family room. Together, they threw things into three boxes labeled "To take," "To give away," and "For yard sale." Overcome with joy, they giggled like two teenagers as they looked through old picture albums—from dating days, wedding, honeymoon, and baby pictures. Nostalgia filled them with sweet peace.

R-r-ring! R-r-ring! The phone. Stephanie jumped up to answer it. "Hello? Yes, this is Mrs. Nastasis." She hesitated. "Excuse me? Something...something wrong with Stephen? Well, what is it...one of his bleeds? No, not an accident...oh, I see...of course. We'll be there to pick him up right away. Have Michelle ready, too, please. Good-bye."

Michael, having come to her side at the sound of "something wrong," encircled her shoulder with his right arm. "What's the matter with Stephen?" Fear tinged his voice.

She was trembling. "I...I don't know exactly, honey. The lady said he's okay right now, but he must be sent home from camp for medical reasons. She wouldn't tell me what it was. She said it wasn't an accident or one of his bleeds and that she would discuss the details when I got there. Whatever could it be that he'd be sent home early? He hasn't acted sick at all…that I've noticed. Maybe I've just been too preoccupied with everything else going on. I probably should have let you talk to her. Sometimes I don't listen well when I get upset. Oh, Michael, I'm frightened. But I'm so thankful you're here."

"There, there, honey," he soothed, hugging her tight. "God is with us; we have nothing to be afraid of. Why don't we change clothes and get on our way?" He looked around at the family pictures strewn on the floor. The mess would have to wait. "I'm really glad I'm home, too. I'd hate for you to have to take care of this all by yourself, whatever it is."

SIXTEEN

FRONTIER

MICHAEL DROVE TO the camp as fast as the speed limit would allow. Neither said much as they squeezed one another's hands. A sign reading *Camp Whitewater* appeared and Michael followed the winding dirt road to the entrance. As soon as he pulled up onto the cinder parking lot, he jumped out and opened Stephanie's door. Arm in arm, they raced toward the office.

He stopped short. "Wait, Steph. We should have prayed. I didn't even think of it." He paused a minute, then took a deep breath. "Father, forgive us for not coming to You first. Thank You for Your promise that You will never leave us or forsake us. Thank You for lifting us out of this miry clay of fear and setting our feet on the solid rock of faith. We come before You on behalf of our son. Lord, You know what's wrong, and You hold our future in Your hands. We trust You completely. Thank You for the peace that passes all understanding, as we keep our minds stayed on You. In the name of Jesus, amen."

"That was beautiful, hon," Stephanie said as they hurried on together. "I've never heard you pray before."

"I know. You don't know how sorry I am for that. We should have been praying as a family all these years. But we're starting over, right?" His eyebrows rose questioningly.

She nodded as they pulled open the door marked *Camp Whitewater Administrative Office*. A secretary glanced up from her typing and removed her glasses. "May I help you?" she asked in a weary tone.

Michael spoke first. "Yes, ma'am. The camp director called a little while ago about our son, Stephen Nastasis. She said something about sending him home for medical reasons. We'd like to talk to her."

The secretary frowned. "Do you have an appointment, Mr. Nastasis?"

"Well, no, but she said to come right away to pick him up and that she would discuss the details with us then."

"I see. Just one moment." She straightened her shoulders with an air of importance and disappeared. Returning momentarily, she said, "Miss Knox will see you now. Follow me, please."

"Thank you," Michael and Stephanie spoke in unison. She led them into the director's office and closed the door behind them.

"Good afternoon. Come in." Miss Knox remained seated behind her desk. She paused and looked at Stephanie. "I was expecting just you, Mrs. Nastasis. Your name is the only one on Stephen's Emergency Notification Card." She leaned forward in her chair and looked down at the pen she was twisting between her fingers. "I'm sorry to have to be the bearer of bad news." Michael and Stephanie stiffened at her words and waited. "As a precautionary measure, our camp has started screening all the children for certain high-risk, communicable diseases. Your son tested positive for HIV antibodies."

Michael shifted in his chair. Stephanie clutched his arm. He cleared his throat. "Excuse my ignorance, ma'am, but what are HIV antibodies?"

"Sir, the common name for the disease from the HIV virus," she stopped and took a deep breath, "is AIDS—Acquired Immune Deficiency Syndrome." Her words were clipped, delivered in a precise and professional manner. "Stephen shows HIV antibodies, which means the virus itself is present in his blood."

"AIDS! Dear Lord, no," Michael breathed. "Where in the world could he have...?"

Stephanie gasped, frozen in her chair. "Miss Knox, there must be some mistake. Our son can't possibly have AIDS. He's in perfect health."

The camp director frowned and continued cooly, "Our screening test indicates that he does, indeed, have the virus. I would recommend that you get a confirmatory test, of course, but in the meantime, I must request that Stephen be removed from camp. If the other children and parents find out, they will be alarmed."

Visibly numbed, Michael and Stephanie stared blankly at each other, at Miss Knox, and then down at the floor. They both shook their heads back and forth. Finally, Michael spoke again. "AIDS—that's...serious, isn't it? The only thing I know is that many people die." His voice broke mid-sentence, and he reached for Stephanie's hand. It was clammy. Her face was white.

"Mr. and Mrs. Nastasis, I'm really not in a position to answer that for you." She reached in a nearby file drawer, pulled out a large envelope, and handed it to Michael. "Here is a packet of information about the disease. Take it with you. The brochures by the federal government and several private health organizations contain up-to-date facts. I'm sure they will answer your questions. You will find phone numbers of helpful agencies, among other things." She rose behind her desk and cleared her throat. "If you'll excuse me, I'll get Stephen and Michelle for you." She vanished before the sound of her voice faded.

They sat in stony silence for quite some time. Then Stephanie leaned over and whispered hoarsely, "Michael, will Stephen really...die...from AIDS? I mean, does everybody die?" Tears filled her eyes. "I can't imagine how he could have gotten it. I've heard people say that only homosexuals and drug addicts get AIDS." She shuddered. "Stephen is just a child. He's only six." Her voice dwindled.

Michael shook his head back and forth, still in shock. "I don't have any idea how, Steph. One thing I do know, though—we will get a second opinion," he stated with authority. "This could all be a mistake from some small-time lab. We'll have the university hospital at home check him out thoroughly. I've got an old buddy who heads up the lab there. We'll get the best care money can buy." He leaned back in his chair, somewhat relieved.

Just then, with Miss Knox standing behind them, Stephen and Michelle appeared in the doorway. Michelle's face was expressionless, almost hard, when she saw her father. Stephen's eyes widened like two saucers. He let out a yelp as he ran over and threw himself in Michael's arms. "Dad! Boy, oh boy...you're with Mom. Wow! When did you get home?" He clung to his father and buried his face in his jacket.

"Stephen..." Michael squeezed him tighter. He realized Miss Knox was staring at them, and he reddened. Michelle would not meet his eyes. He grabbed Stephanie's hand and urged, "Come on, everybody, let's head home. We've got lots of catching up to do." He stopped and reached around Stephen's legs to shake Miss Knox's hand. "Thank you, ma'am, for the information. We'll read it carefully," he added as they walked away.

"You're welcome. Good luck to you."

He looked back at her. "Luck is one thing that won't help us a bit. Thank God, we have more than luck to depend on. We have Jesus Christ."

Her lips parted in a cynical smirk. "Whatever you say, sir." With a shake of her head, she dismissed them and closed the door.

Michelle, shuffling along behind them, was the first to speak on the way to the car. Bitterness dripped from her voice. "I don't understand why we have to leave camp before everybody else. It's not fair. I just made new friends. Just because you're home now doesn't mean you can run our lives. We've managed fine without you—"

"Michelle Renee Nastasis!" Stephanie interrupted. "Hold your tongue, young lady!"

His daughter's words cut Michael like a knife. He wanted to retaliate, but something held him back. Standing next to the car, he turned around, knelt down, and took Michelle's hands in his. He spoke with the gentlest of tones, "Michelle, I know none of this has been easy. You and I need some time together, just us two, for a heart-to-heart talk. You deserve that. I'll tell you this much now. The reason you're leaving camp early is...Stephen isn't feeling well, and we need to get him to the hospital for some tests." She looked into his eyes. He saw some of the hardness melt. "Come on, hop in the car."

Stephen broke in, "No, Dad, I'm not sick...I promise. I feel great. An' I never told anybody I felt sick. Why do we have to go?" He tugged open the door and started to cry, thinking about Michelle being mad at him for having to leave.

Michelle added, "Yeah, and it's Saturday. I bet they won't do the tests today, anyway."

Michael looked up at Stephanie. "Listen to your father, kids. Let's get in the car. We'll be home soon, and you can play for a while before bedtime."

Pouting again, Michelle yanked her door open. "So what's the big deal with you, anyhow? For months you didn't even want Dad in the house.

Now you want us to listen to him. I'm so glad you guys are lovey-dovey again. That's just far-out!" She slammed the door and folded her arms angrily across her chest. Her brown eyes were fierce.

Michael and Stephanie decided to withhold harsh words. She would need time to adjust to their reconciliation. Stephen, on the other hand, laid his head back and began singing camp songs, complete with hand choreography. He chattered a while about the latest happenings until he fell sound asleep with his head on Michelle's shoulder. Soon, she fell asleep, too.

As Michael drove, he adjusted his rear view mirror so he could see the children. His heart swelled with love. Michelle's long, straight, dark hair and smooth olive skin formed a striking contrast to Stephen's wavy blond hair and caramel-colored tan, dotted with freckles. He thought in wonder, *They sure are beautiful kids.* It was clear that Michelle was the moody one, with his own fiery temper. Stephen resembled Stephanie, in coloring and personality. Everyone loved him. Michael felt a lump rising in his throat as he remembered their conversation with Miss Knox. *AIDS. Dear Lord, what if Stephen really does have it?* He glanced over at Stephanie and pulled her closer to him. She looked into his eyes and whispered, "Michael, I'm so scared." Her hands clutched the large envelope she had not dared to open.

"I know, Steph. I'm scared, too." He squeezed her shoulder and kissed the top of her head. "Thank God we're together, hon'. Just thank God." She nodded and snuggled closer to him.

Doctors confirmed their worst fears a few days later—Stephen was HIV positive. They narrowed the cause to blood transfusions he had received quite some time earlier, during one of his severe hemophilic bleeds. Michael and Stephanie passed through the consultations in a daze, trying not to let their son see their panic and grief. They learned that HIV patients often remain totally symptom-free for a long period of time, even years, after infection. That explained why Stephen said he was not sick. He tired easily, but that was nothing unusual, given the hemophilia he'd had since birth. To their amazement, they found out that many hemophilic children were already "sero-positive." Rigid blood donor screening laws had not gone into effect until 1985.

The more they learned about the dreaded disease, the more despondent they became. "Incurable." "The Black Plague of the twentieth century." "Experimental drugs offer little hope at this point." "Make the most of every moment. He'll go downhill fast once he starts developing symptoms."

Not a single report was very encouraging. Michael and Stephanie agreed to wait until Michelle was with them to break the news and settled on a picnic at the Country Corner.

Armed with materials, precautionary instructions, and a schedule of appointments for periodic exams, they left the hospital and drove to a neighbor's house to pick up Michelle. The next errand was going home to get their pet black labrador, Ebony, from his pen behind the house. Then they stopped at the store to pick up the children's favorite picnic foods and headed for the highway. Stephen sensed something was wrong. He did not let out a peep the whole way. Nor did Michelle.

Soon, they arrived. Stephen squealed with delight when he saw the pond behind the Country Corner and discovered he could go fishing with Dad. Michelle was entranced with the birds and flowers, as well as the sheltered pathway through the grape arbors. Michael and Stephanie sat in the swing, talking and praying, while the children played for a while. Then they spread a blanket on the grass and fixed the picnic supper. When all was ready, Michael called, "Michelle, Stephen…come and get it!" The two came running and plopped down, out of breath.

Michael motioned for everyone to join hands. He led them in prayer, "Father, we thank You for this time together at last. We ask You to bless our food and our fellowship. Mend all that has been broken in each of us, I pray, and help us to make the most of every moment. In Jesus name, amen." When he finished, Michelle looked at him quizzically, but Stephen was beaming. Stephanie wiped a tear from the corner of her eye.

"Dad, Mom, Michelle," Stephen bubbled, "I've just got to tell you somethin'." He looked like he would burst with a secret. "While you were gone, Dad, one day when I was pretty sad, my friend Joshua told me all about Jesus. How much He loves me…and how I could even have Him living in my heart." He patted his chest vigorously with his little hands. "So I believed that Jesus is my Savior…and He came to live inside me. He did! That means someday I'm going to heaven to be with Him forever." Stephen was grinning from ear to ear. "And then I didn't get as lonely missin' you, Dad, 'cause I'd just pray to Jesus and tell Him how I felt…

"And d'you know what else? Every day, I asked Him if we could be a fam'bly again real soon and that you would all have Him in your hearts, too. I 'member one time when I was home from school 'cause I had a cold. I was by myself in my room talkin' to Jesus 'bout how bad I wished you and Mom wouldn't hate each other anymore. It started rainin' outside and then I really felt sad. So I got outta bed and kneeled down…," he ducked his head and glanced up, a sheepish grin on his face, "in case He might hear me better." He paused and took a deep breath.

"When I was done, I looked out my window at the sky, and guess what! There was the bestest rainbow I ever saw. And see, Jesus did answer my prayers, 'cause here we all are, and we just prayed to Him…like a real fam'bly!" Stephen jumped up from the blanket and ran huge figure eights in the grass, clapping his hands, whistling and yelling at the top of his lungs, "Ya-a-y! Hurray for Jesus! Ya-a-y Jee-sus!"

Ebony chased along beside him, barking and leaping and rubbing against his leg. They were a sight. Even Michelle giggled. Finally, boy and dog came running back and collapsed together, panting, on the edge of the blanket.

Michael and Stephanie could not believe what they had just witnessed. Joy and sorrow welled up inside them.

When Stephen saw his parents' wet eyes, he sat up, shocked, and wriggled over to them, almost knocking over the thermos of iced tea. Michelle went around behind them and kneeled. Wrapping her arms around both their shoulders, she burst out crying. Stephen pleaded, "Hey, you guys, that was supposed to make you laugh. What's wrong? Aren't you glad we're a fam'bly?" The next moment, he was sobbing, not knowing why.

Michael spoke quietly, "Kids, your mom and I couldn't be happier to be together again…it's all just too much…" He choked back the tears. Stephanie squeezed his hand and wiped away a lone tear from his cheek.

"That's right, kids," Stephanie added as she hugged them both.

Michael continued, "Thank you for praying for us, Stephen. God did hear your prayers." The tears would be denied no longer. He sobbed, "I'm so sorry for all the time we've lost…and for all the hurt I caused you. Dear God, I'm so sorry…"

"Me, too," Stephanie sniffed loudly. "We love you."

Stephen climbed in his dad's lap and hugged his neck, then tried to reach over and grab his mom at the same time.

"Dad, Mom…please don't cry. Dad, you've never cried before. I can't stand it." He sniffed and rubbed the back of his hand on his nose. "We're not mad at you, honest. We forgive you…don't we, Michelle?" Stephen nodded at her urgently, coughing on his tears. His sky-blue eyes were getting bloodshot behind the long, curly eyelashes. He knelt in his dad's lap and tilted his face up under his dad's lowered head to look him in the eyes. Then he did the same to his mom.

Stephanie rested her head on Michael's shoulder, and Michelle hung on to them both. Michael stroked Stephen's hair and held him tight. Long spans of silence passed. Slowly and carefully he began, "Stephen, Michelle, we have something to tell you that is very difficult for your mom and me. I guess that's why we're pretty emotional." Stephanie patted his arm. He took a deep breath and exhaled. "The tests you had, Stephen…well…they showed positive for a very serious illness. It's …it's…AIDS. The doctors think you got it from some infected blood you were given when you had one of your bleeds." As if to stave off the reality of what he was saying, he hugged Stephen even tighter. "That's why you had to leave camp early, son, because the AIDS virus is not understood by everyone. People panic when they hear someone has it, even though you don't have any symptoms."

Michelle broke in, "Oh no, Dad, not AIDS. They've been teaching a lot in school about how bad it is. The library has posters up and everything." Her voice rose. "Stephen has it? My own brother? Hasn't he had enough sickness already?" She flopped back in the grass, grabbed a handful, and threw it forcefully. "Boy, life just isn't fair. I mean, Stephen bugs me sometimes, but I sure don't want him to…"

"Die. Right, Michelle?" Stephen completed her sentence with caution.

She sat up, looked at him, and then scooted over beside him. "Don't say that awful word, Stephen. You're not going to…die." She whispered the last word and added emphatically, "I won't let you!"

"Michelle, I don't think you have any say-so if I do or not. But dyin' wouldn't be so bad. If I had to, I mean. I'd miss you and Mom and Dad...and Ebony, too, but from what Joshua showed me in the Bible, heaven is going to be super. I'd be with Jesus, 'cause He's my Savior...in my heart." He rubbed his chest. His parents looked at him, astonished at his insight.

"But hey, guys," Michael offered, "we may all be forgetting something." He paused to collect his thoughts. "Caleb—the special friend of mine who owned this property—spent a lot of time teaching me about an important ingredient in life. Stephen, you've touched on it. He called this ingredient 'the unseen essential,' because no one can see it. But it's very important. That unseen essential is faith. With faith in Jesus Christ and His Word, Caleb said we can face anything. Guess that means even AIDS, as scary as it is...And remember that Jesus does still heal people miraculously today, just as He did when He walked this earth two thousand years ago. Sometimes He heals them only through death. I don't know what He has in mind for you, Stephen, but I sure wish I did. Our job is to study the Bible together until His Word becomes a real part of us, pray, and get as close to the Lord as we can. The rest is up to Him. He's God."

He stopped and pointed his index finger in front of him. "That reminds me. Just this morning, your mom and I were reading a Bible passage in Luke 18 where Jesus was telling a story, as He often did. He wanted to show the people they should pray and never give up. This story was about a city judge who could not have cared less about God or man. He wasn't a very good guy, but he had authority...

"Then there was this widow. She kept going to the judge to try to get legal protection from someone who was taking advantage of her. She stayed after him until he finally threw up his hands in frustration and helped her. He did it, not because he cared about a poor widow or because of what was right, but just so she'd quit bothering him. After Jesus told that story, He asked His listeners if an ungodly ruler acted on a widow's persistent request, won't a righteous God respond to His own people who pray to Him day and night?"

They all listened with rapt attention and nodded. Michelle was the first to speak. "I think I see what the story could be saying to us. It isn't fair that Stephen got the AIDS virus from a blood transfusion, because he's a hemophiliac. But instead of us trying, like the old lady in the story, to get some man to help (who probably doesn't even care anyway!), God wants us to pray all the time to Him that Stephen will get well. Is that right?"

"Yes, very good, Michelle. Instead of panicking, He wants us to depend on Him and follow His guidance as to what to do. It's easy to get on the wrong track, thinking He's leading one way, when He's not. Let me give you a 'for instance.' Mr. Caleb left me this property in his will." He paused to let that news soak in. Their eyes grew wide at his words. "That's right. It's all ours.

"Well...I'm embarrassed to say that, without talking to God about it, I went right back to some of my old ways of doing things. I tried real hard to start a business out here—a bed and breakfast hotel. But from the beginning, it was a total disaster. Nothing worked right. A couple of investors cheated me. I almost got ulcers over the deal. Now that doesn't mean *every* business is wrong, but it simply wasn't the right thing for Caleb's Country Corner Retreat at that time. I don't know yet what God has in mind for us to do with this property in the future." He looked around at all of them.

"With Stephen's illness, it's just as important that we depend on Jesus for guidance. He might want to use medical science right in town to help him. Or maybe a specialist far away. Then again, He might not want to use much medicine. But in the end, if God still allows AIDS to claim Stephen's life, we must trust completely that He knows what He's doing." He swallowed hard at the thought. "And we've got to remember that He loves Stephen a whole lot more than we do."

Stephanie had been quiet for a long time. "You know, Michael, I've been hearing a lot about Jesus' sudden return to take His people with Him. The "rapture," I think they call it. We don't know when that will be, but the world is sure in a mess. Maybe before Stephen's illness even runs its course, we'll all be gone anyway..." She paused in concentration and her brow furrowed. "That parable you were just talking about...didn't we read this morning where, right after Jesus told it, He asked His disciples, 'When the Son of Man comes, will He find faith in the earth?'"

"That's right, Steph. Jesus did ask that." He stopped short. There was a faraway look in his eyes as he gazed at the horizon. "And that means He's still asking us...the Nastasis family."

Stephen's blond head bobbed up and down. His blue eyes opened wide. "I don't know if Jesus'll find faith in the earth or not. I just hope He finds it in me." Then, pointing to Michael, Stephanie, and Michelle, he added, "and you...and you...and you!" They stared at him in wonder.

Stephanie jumped up. "Hey, guys, I think I felt some raindrops. Anybody else?" They looked at the sky. None of them had noticed the dark clouds forming overhead. Before they knew it, they were caught in a downpour. They hurried to gather up their picnic lunch, but it was too late to save more than a remnant.

"Run!" Michael shouted. "Under the porch! Hurry!"

Together, they bolted, squealing and giggling and squishing in the grass. Once under the porch roof, they huddled close and peered out at their soggy picnic, then at one another. They looked like drowned rats. Safe under the shelter, they laughed at the whole mess.

Suddenly, Stephen gasped. "Wow! Hey, everybody, look. Look over there!" He was pointing and jumping up and down. "A rainbow, a rainbow, a rainbow! Maybe Jesus painted it just for us!"

Michael hugged him from behind. "Yes, son," he replied softly, "He very well may have." Then he stopped short. He couldn't believe his eyes. He squinted to be sure. In the distance beyond the dark cloud, he spotted a bird soaring high in the sky. *Flight Training School!* He pointed. "Look, you guys. See the eagle way up there? Oooh, boy, that reminds me—have I got a g-o-o-d story for you! Mr. Caleb told it to a special young boy named Sandy and me not so very long ago. I'll take you to meet him and his mom real soon."

EPILOGUE

As I TURN the last page of *The Unseen Essential,* my own dog, Luke, is still snoozing at my feet. I do not think he's budged an inch.

Part of me wants our story to continue. In spite of myself (the often detached, scientific type with an insatiable thirst for facts and figures), I have grown fond of Michael and Stephanie, Michelle and Stephen, Sandy and his mom, and of course, Caleb. More prayer and thought have gone into the preparation of this book than any other we have written. Certainly, no subject matter has so deeply burrowed its way into my heart of hearts. Now that the writing is finished, as always I wonder...*Did we convey the intensity of the message?* I hope so. It has been said that all creative ventures spawn such plaguing questions near the finish line.

Michael's struggle to "walk by faith and not by sight" reflects my own to a great extent. Only his specific circumstances do not. By

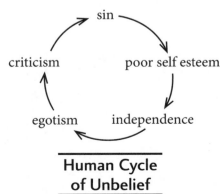

Human Cycle of Unbelief

the grace of God, I was blessed with a more nurturing childhood than he. His inner insecurities, though carefully hidden from view for many years, left deep scars. Michael is an engineer; I am a cataract surgeon. He has young children; Shea and Pit were both in college during the writing of this book. Michael's marriage neared the brink of disaster; my marriage to Heather weathered a few rough spots years ago, but we have never split in bitter divorce, nor even separation. Now, we are growing deeper in love with each passing day. And the days do fly by.

Thank God, we have beaten the odds. But many dear friends in Christ have not. In a Bible study group that Heather and I once participated in with about sixteen other people, three of the main leaders opted to change marriage partners. Tragic. Divorce claimed three casualties in one tiny Christian circle, bruising us and many others.

Well then, how am I like Michael? We both have highly independent, hard-driving natures that, without the Holy Spirit, find it nearly impossible to be otherwise. Our impatience and insensitivity to others along the way

Divine Cycle of Faith

crop up now and again. Our inborn need to be self-reliant and success-ful—the best in our field—is something we have in common, as is the belief that nothing less than perfection will do. Maybe Michael's and my strivings stem from different emotional deficiencies, but the results are the same. That chronic independent streak runs deep in both of us. I feel certain we have plenty of company in the body of Christ.

Moment by moment, day in and day out, I face the choice of having to decide between God's perfect will or my own stubborn one, between His unfailing promise or my own means. Whether it be for the skill to perform so many delicate surgeries, stamina to complete another race, wisdom for ongoing investment enterprises, or love for my fellow man, the decision is mine. Looking at it logically—God Almighty vs. me. I should not hesitate. Why do I, then? Why do we?

God promises victory through faith. Scripture also reminds us, however, in Isaiah 54:16, that God created the destroyer to wreak havoc. Satan, who delights in our entrapment in unbelief, is still allowed by divine ordinance to roam about. He is looking for those he can draw away from a life of faith. To a great extent, Satan is enjoying success in the earth today. But he does not have to.

Michael, unknowingly, was stuck for years in what I have called the "human cycle of unbelief." That is: sin (his father's as well as his own) produced poor self-esteem; poor self-esteem bred independence, which led to egotism and criticism. These developed into strongholds in his life and increased the tendency toward further isolation from God.

How many of us have the same problem? The entire cycle repeats itself, digging deeper with each pass. Jesus breaks those shackles and pulls us off the futile merry-go-round. Much of the power of the "human cycle of unbelief" stems from a misconception of a father's love. Michael's sufferings are typical of far too many, I fear.

Through God's grace, they may find healing of their character flaws. Jesus reveals a Father's love big enough to start the process, as the contrasting "divine cycle of faith" suggests.

In many respects, Caleb could have been my mentor. He was the kind of guy I would like to be when I am his age—healthy, vital, involved, wise, and full of love for others. Most of all, he had a close relationship with the Lord. I have long felt that age need be no barrier to godly participation in life. At fifty-five, I pray to never stop enjoying God and His creation. One of my favorite heroes, the biblical Caleb, conquered his mountain (still inhabited with a gruesome giant or two) at the age of eighty-plus years. Too many of our elderly saints are either choosing or being pushed into the spectator's role when they should be discipling the next generation. What a loss to the kingdom!

In closing, I would like to leave Caleb's own four "steps" of faith fresh in your mind. **Agreement** with God and His Word in its entirety is the first step. An all-or-nothing decision is required here (quite like signing a contract), but you work it out over a lifetime of getting to know God. As a symbol, Caleb used Jesus' parable about buying a field containing buried treasure. Each of us is a treasure in God's eyes—so valuable that He gave His all to buy our salvation. Yet, He is the treasure to us, as well. Our response should be like the man plowing the field in His parable. He quickly sold everything he valued to make the treasure his own.

Dependence is the second step, symbolized by Jesus' parable of the vine. Cut off from Him, we can do nothing of value. Remember that a grapevine is not allowed to produce a harvest for the first three years of its existence. It grows strong during that time by having its branches radically pruned, while those remaining are trained to develop properly. Self-sufficient Michael had to come to the end of himself before he could ever learn to rely on God. You may have heard of the saying, "God helps those who help themselves." Maybe you have always assumed it came from the Bible. Well it didn't! The truth is, God helps those who realize they cannot help themselves.

True dependence involves joyfully enduring those maturing years and clinging to Jesus for all we are worth. When the time is right and all the unnecessary sidetrack-prone branches have been clipped away, the Holy Spirit, through us, brings life to whomever He touches. Then we cannot lay claim to any fruit of dependence. You and I are mere branches who stayed attached to the Vine. We should not lose sight of one other important fact, though. God has so ordained it that without branches there can be no fruit.

Abandoned **trust**, the third step, poses a difficult challenge for most of us—choosing to surrender to God's perfecting process when we do not have to. Caleb used two illustrations to help Michael remember trust. The first was a potter and his clay. Do you remember how the potter's wheel troubled Michael? As long as he only saw clay being shattered and reworked by a cold and uncaring potter, he would not surrender himself as clay in the Master Potter's hands. Gradually, though, he trusted enough to see through painful circumstances to Jesus, whose love was shaping a beautiful vessel out of his life.

Second, like the young eagles—the illustration of the transition from dependence to trust—we are easily confused by unexpected tribulations. We get so miffed with our Provider for pushing us out of our comfort zone and then for giving us the option to step out in faith. Today's infamous "couch potatoes" relish the feeling of lounging in safety at home, watching the world pass by. And waiting to be fed, of course. You and I were never meant to be "couch potato Christians," any more than eagles were meant to stay in the nest.

Soaring in the heavenlies—that is our calling. Eagles are not grounded because of a measly storm. No way! They simply set their sights on high, thrust with their wings, and rise above it. We will, too, when we trust Him implicitly to be "the wind beneath our wings," as the song goes. We are to be transformers, aren't we? But first we have to be transformed.

Intimate **oneness** with God culminates the fourth step of faith. Caleb chose marriage to best portray such closeness. As Michael and Stephanie were restored to each other, so the unseen essential restores us to our Lord. Walking daily with Jesus—agreeing, depending, and trusting—is the most blessed friendship anyone can ever have. For that purpose, God created man.

Michael's story, unique as it is, could be anybody's. Mine or yours. It demonstrates a few key principles of the kind of faith I have learned to embrace. In other words, how does the unseen essential translate into the daily grind of living? Rather than focus on any specific number of "steps," I pray you will be inspired to seek God—to look beyond your own circumstances, trials, and temptations, or even blessings, to Jesus. Nothing is too difficult for the Author and Finisher of your faith.

Let me exhort you. Whatever your situation, whatever dilemma lies unsolved, earth does not hold the answer. I know from experience. Joy comes not from a successful career alone. Neither does it come from sports, friends, or even a great marriage. By comparison, these things are temporal, and they will all pass away one day. With or without your consent. My friend, I give you the eternal, unchanging Jesus. Fall in love with Him over and over again.

———

I find myself letting out a sigh of relief. "Well Luke, another book is finished. Come on, boy, let's go for a run together—just you 'n me. And yes, Jesus, too." He barks and bounds around to show his approval of the idea. You know, I never have to ask Luke twice. It is humbling to realize how much our dog wants to be close to me. Quite unlike me with the Lord sometimes. Oh, the Master of the universe deserves far more.

ABOUT THE AUTHOR

JAMES P. GILLS, M.D., received his medical degree from Duke University Medical Center in 1959. He served his ophthalmology residency at Wilmer Ophthalmological Institute of Johns Hopkins University from 1962–1965. Dr. Gills founded the St. Luke's Cataract and Laser Institute in Tarpon Springs, Florida, and has performed more cataract and lens implant surgeries than any other eye surgeon in the world. Since establishing his Florida practice in 1968, he has been firmly committed to embracing new technology and perfecting the latest cataract surgery techniques. In 1974, he became the first eye surgeon in the U.S. to dedicate his practice to cataract treatment through the use of intraocular lenses. Dr. Gills has been recognized in Florida and throughout the world for his professional accomplishments and personal commitment to helping others. He has been recognized by the readers of Cataract & Refractive Surgery Today as one of the top 50 cataract and refractive opinion leaders.

As a world-renowned ophthalmologist, Dr. Gills has received innumerable medical and educational awards. In 2005, he was especially honored to receive the Duke Medical Alumni Association's Humanitarian Award. In 2007, he was blessed with a particularly treasured double honor. Dr. Gills was elected to the Johns Hopkins Society of Scholars and was also selected to receive the Distinguished Medical Alumnus Award, the highest honor bestowed by Johns Hopkins School of Medicine. Dr. Gills thereby became the first physician in the country to receive high honors twice in two weeks from the prestigious Johns Hopkins University in Baltimore.

In the years 1994 through 2004, Dr. Gills was listed in The Best Doctors in America. As a clinical professor of ophthalmology at the University of South Florida, he was named one of the best Ophthalmologists in America in 1996 by ophthalmic academic leaders nationwide. He has served on the Board of Directors of the American College of Eye Surgeons, the Board of Visitors at Duke University Medical Center, and the Advisory Board of Wilmer Ophthalmological Institute at Johns Hopkins University. Listed in Marquis' Who's Who in America, Dr. Gills was Entrepreneur of the Year 1990 for the State of Florida, received the Tampa Bay Business Hall of Fame Award in 1993, and was given the Tampa Bay Ethics Award from the University of Tampa in 1995. In 1996, he was awarded the prestigious Innovators Award by his colleagues in the American Society of Cataract and Refractive Surgeons. In 2000, he was named Philanthropist of the Year by the National Society of Fundraising Executives, was presented with the Florida Enterprise Medal by the Merchants Association of Florida, was named Humanitarian of the Year by the Golda Meir/Kent Jewish Center in Clearwater, and was honored as Free Enterpriser of the Year by the Florida Council on Economic Education. In 2001, The Salvation Army presented Dr. Gills their prestigious "Others Award" in honor of his lifelong commitment to service and caring.

Virginia Polytechnic Institute, Dr. Gills' alma mater, presented their University Distinguished Achievement Award to him in 2003. In that same year, Dr. Gills was appointed by Governor Jeb Bush to the Board of Directors of the Florida Sports Foundation. In 2004, Dr. Gills was invited to join the prestigious Florida Council of 100, an advisory committee reporting directly to the governor on various aspects of Florida's public policy affecting the quality of life and the economic well-being of all Floridians.

While Dr. Gills has many accomplishments and varied interests, his primary focus is to restore physical vision to patients and to bring spiritual enlightenment through his life. Guided by his strong and enduring faith in Jesus Christ, he seeks to encourage and comfort the patients who come to St. Luke's and to share his faith whenever possible. It was through sharing his insights with patients that he initially began writing on Christian topics. An avid student of the Bible for many years, he now has authored nineteen books on Christian living, with over nine million copies in print. With the exception of the Bible, Dr. Gills' books are the most widely requested books in the U.S. prison system. They have been supplied to over two thousand prisons and jails, including every death row facility in the nation. In addition, Dr. Gills has published more than 195 medical articles and has authored or coauthored ten medical reference textbooks. Six of those books were bestsellers at the American Academy of Ophthalmology annual meetings.

As an ultra-distance athlete, Dr. Gills participated in forty-six marathons, including eighteen Boston marathons and fourteen 100-mile mountain runs. In addition, he completed five Ironman Triathlons in Hawaii and a total of six Double Ironman Triathlons, each within the thirty-six hour maximum time frame. Dr. Gills has served on the National Board of Directors of the Fellowship of Christian Athletes and, in 1991, was the first recipient of their Tom Landry Award. A passionate athlete, surgeon, and scientist, Dr. Gills is also a member of the Explorers Club, a prestigious, multi-disciplinary society dedicated to advancing field research, scientific exploration, and the ideal that it is vital to preserve the instinct to explore.

Married in 1962, Dr. Gills and his wife, Heather, have raised two children, Shea and Pit. Shea Gills Grundy, a former attorney and now full-time mom, is a graduate of Vanderbilt University and Emory Law School. She and her husband, Shane Grundy, M.D., have four children: twins Maggie and Braddock, Jimmy, and Lily Grace. The Gills' son, J. Pit Gills, M.D., ophthalmologist, received his medical degree from Duke University Medical Center and, in 2001, joined the St. Luke's practice. "Dr. Pit" and his wife, Joy, have three children: Pitzer, Parker, and Stokes.

THE WRITINGS OF JAMES P. GILLS, M.D.

A BIBLICAL ECONOMICS MANIFESTO (WITH RON H. NASH, PH.D.)
The best understanding of economics aligns with what the Bible teaches on the subject.
ISBN: 978-0-88419-871-0
E-book ISBN: 978-1-59979-925-4

BELIEVE AND REJOICE: CHANGED BY FAITH, FILLED WITH JOY
Observe how faith in God can let us see His heart of joy
ISBN: 978-1-59979-169-2
E-book ISBN: 978-1-61638-727-3

COME UNTO ME: GOD'S CALL TO INTIMACY
Inspired by Dr. Gills' trip to Mt. Sinai, this book explores God's eternal desire for mankind to know Him intimately.
ISBN: 978-1-59185-214-8
E-book ISBN: 978-1-61638-728-0

DARWINISM UNDER THE MICROSCOPE: HOW RECENT SCIENTIFIC EVIDENCE POINTS TO DIVINE DESIGN (WITH TOM WOODWARD, PH.D.)
Behold the wonder of it all! The facts glorify our Intelligent Creator!
ISBN: 978-0-88419-925-0
E-book ISBN: 978-1-59979-882-0

THE DYNAMICS OF WORSHIP
Designed to rekindle a passionate love for God, this book gives the *who, what, where, when, why*, and *how* of worship.
ISBN: 978-1-59185-657-3
E-book ISBN: 978-1-61638-725-9

EXCEEDING GRATITUDE FOR THE CREATOR'S PLAN: DISCOVER THE LIFE-CHANGING DYNAMIC OF APPRECIATION
Standing in awe of the creation and being secure in the knowledge of our heavenly hope, the thankful believer abounds in appreciation for the Creator's wondrous plan.
ISBN: 978-1-59979-155-5
E-book ISBN: 978-1-61638-729-7

GOD'S PRESCRIPTION FOR HEALING: FIVE DIVINE GIFTS OF HEALING
Explore the wonders of healing by design, now and forevermore.
ISBN: 978-1-59185-286-5
E-book ISBN: 978-1-61638-730-3

Imaginations: More Than You Think
Focusing our thoughts will help us grow closer to God.
ISBN: 978-1-59185-609-2
E-book ISBN: 978-1-59979-883-7

Love: Fulfilling the Ultimate Quest
Enjoy a quick refresher course on the meaning and method of God's great gift.
ISBN: 978-1-59979-235-4
E-book ISBN: 978-1-61638-731-7

Overcoming Spiritual Blindness
Jesus + anything = nothing. Jesus + nothing = everything. Here is a book that will help you recognize the many facets of spiritual blindness as you seek to fulfill the Lord's plan for your life.
ISBN: 978-1-59185-607-8
E-book ISBN: 978-1-59979-884-4

Resting In His Redemption
We were created for communion with God. Discover how to rest in His redemption and enjoy a life of divine peace.
ISBN: 978-1-61638-349-7
E-book ISBN: 978-1-61638-425-8

Rx for Worry: A Thankful Heart
Trust your future to the God who is in eternal control.
ISBN: 978-1-59979-090-9
E-book ISBN: 978-1-55979-926-1

The Prayerful Spirit: Passion for God, Compassion for People
Dr. Gills tells how prayer has changed his life as well as the lives of patients and other doctors. It will change your life also!
ISBN: 978-1-59185-215-5
E-book ISBN: 978-1-61638-732-7

The Unseen Essential: A Story for Our Troubled Times... Part One
This compelling, contemporary novel portrays one man's transformation through the power of God's love.
ISBN: 978-1-59185-810-2
E-book ISBN: 978-1-59979-513-3

Tender Journey: A Story for Our Troubled Times... Part Two
Be enriched by the popular sequel to *The Unseen Essential*.
ISBN: 978-1-59185-809-6
E-book ISBN: 978-1-59979-509-6

DID YOU ENJOY
THIS BOOK?

We at Love Press would be pleased to hear from you if

The Unseen Essential, a story for our troubled times...Part One

has had an effect on your life or the lives of your loved ones.

Send your letters to:

Love Press
P.O. Box 1608
Tarpon Springs, FL   34688-1608

A Note From the Publisher

We hope that you will also enjoy *Tender Journey*, the sequel to *The Unseen Essential*. You will share more of Michael and Stephanie's new life together, Stephen's battle with AIDS, and Michelle's trying teenage years. Sandy will play a continuing important role in the story. You will also meet new characters that you will be sure to love.